		DATE DUE	

"We've spent the last 20 years building management into a science. In this book, David Siegel asks us to turn it into a bridge. Nothing more, nothing less. It's a 'must read' for both the entrepreneur and venture capitalist."

"David Siegel curates the web in a way that helps both newcomers and pros really understand what's happening on the Web today and how it will affect all of us in the future. Audiences will be challenged, informed, and entertained."

"David Siegel's vision of the future is stunning. And accurate. The free agent of the future will have as much power and greater agility than large corporations do today. I recommend this book for anyone who is ready to dive into the new Internet economy."

"This is the most rational approach to understanding customers since *Crossing the Chasm*. Everyone needs to take the Internet this seriously! Even a division of a large company can hold Siegel's six meetings and start acting more like a start-up in the new connected business world."

"David Siegel may well be the Peter Senge of the Internet. If you appreciated the insights of *The Fifth Discipline*, you'll applaud the common sense, people-centered approach Siegel takes to the Web."

FUTURIZE
YOUR ENTERPRISE

Business Strategy
in the Age of the E-Customer

by David Siegel

John Wiley & Sons, Inc.
New York • Chichester • Weinheim • Brisbane • Singapore • Toronto

OUACHITA TECHNICAL COLLEGE

ISBN 0471-35763-4

Printed in the United States of America.

10 9 8 7 6 5 4 3 2

CONTENTS

Acknowledgments

Futurize Your Enterprise was shaped as much by its project team and reviewers as by its author. Peer reviewers from around the world critiqued early manuscripts. Beth VanStory, Ken Morris, Judy MacDonald, and Nick Willson provided constructive comments. Tom Troland; Stephen Mendel; Donald Kennedy, PhD; Evelio Perez-Albuerne, MD; and John C Spinosa, MD, PhD, contributed to specific chapters. Heidi Danglemier, Barbara Meyer, Scott Davidoff, and Steve Thomas came through with many helpful suggestions. Coleen Corbett at Toysrus.com graciously supplied the detailed information for Chapter 1.

Publisher Henning Gutmann, one of our earliest supporters, kept the faith throughout. Editor Renana Meyers kept us on course with her relentless focus on *our* customers. In the trenches, she wielded her red pen with surgical skill. The Wiley production team, led by Elizabeth Doble, Susan Olinsky, and Sasha Kintzler, and the marketing team, led by Ann McCarthy, kept us on a straight path without losing sight of the big picture. For their dedication and high level of professionalism, I am grateful.

The online photo collection campaign that yielded 171 of the faces you see in this book is the result of an extraordinary effort by Glen Sheehan, Jay Bain, and David Thibodeau at McCann-Erickson/A&L. Jennifer Buckendorff at Amazon.com and Emme Levine at Fatbrain.com directed many web surfers to our photo site, and Michael Kaminer and Patrick Kowalczyk of Michael Kaminer Public Relations lent us their promotion expertise. Thanks to all of our readers who came to the site and contributed photos.

Our partners at Equilibrium Software, Steve Denebeim and David Gartner, helped us process all the photos for publication. Many thanks to Instinctive Technology's Francois Gossieaux and Kevin Roy for providing the eRoom service that enable us to communicate, share files and track changes during the book's development.

The Siegel Vision team was the first group of people on the project and the last to leave. Jason Chan applied his numerous talents to virtually every aspect of this book, from critiquing the cover designs to producing the Futurizenow.com web site. He rose to every technical challenge that faced the team and still managed to create the lucid illustrations gracing the book's interior. Project manager Mike Pederson thrusted and parried his way through the logistical challenges of producing the book in three locations at once. He kept both his cool and his head in countless emergencies. Lead editors Kendra Kurosawa and Cathy Johnson dug out valuable ideas from under thickets of rough prose. They remained steadfast even as the thickets got thicker and the hyphens flew. Tiffany Knoeck and Krista Jensen, our valiant proofers, dodged hyphens and bullets to write the wrongs. Researcher Evantheia Schibstead pulled rabbits out of hats to get us needed information. Tamara Vining provided support. Robert Stankus, our volunteer proofer, saved us from ourselves. All these people checked facts, inserted commas, took them out, and put them back in again – all while looking at thousands of photos of penguins. Indexer B. Radley shaved two days off the project at a time when two days really counted.

Joe Silva, the John Henry of Quark XPress, flew to Seattle to create the visual experience you have before you. From producing the cover mechanicals to designing and producing the book's interior, Joe's focus on quality and detail has led to yet another Siegel/Silva production. Our thanks to Seattle's Macrina bakery for their coffee and potato bread, which sustained us during the final weeks of production.

Special thanks go to Don Peppers and Bruce Kasanoff at the Peppers and Rogers Group for their support; to the people at Studio Verso for their friendship; and to my father, whose insistence on clear communication and common sense has had a profound effect on my career.

IF YOU HAD VISITED MADAGASCAR IN 1850, you might have run into
Charles Darwin, who was there studying orchids. One day he found
an unusual orchid with a 15-inch tube, at the bottom of which a sweet
nectar emerged every night. Darwin hypothesized the existence of a
hawk moth with a 15-inch tongue to pollinate the plant. People laughed
at him – no one had ever heard of a moth with a tongue that long. In
1903 – 21 years after Darwin's death – biologists in Madagascar discovered the elusive nocturnal moth.

In nature, the food shapes the organism. If the environment changes,
the food usually changes, and all the species that have coevolved in that
environment must respond or die.

In business, the customer shapes the corporation. People's needs,
tastes, and desires shape what a company can offer. Very few companies
today sell the same products or services they sold just ten years ago. Yet
almost all companies are still organized the same way.

Over the next ten years, the Internet will drive changes in consumer
behavior that will lay waste to all the corporate re-engineering and cost-
reduction programs that have kept so many MBAs and programmers
burning the midnight oil. These changes will be so profound that companies will have to realign themselves with an even sharper focus on the
customer than they have now. Even the emphasis on quality – espoused
by such experts as W Edwards Deming, Malcolm Baldridge, and Jim
Collins – will be less important in the face of new and rapidly changing
demands.

The Internet is behind this change in the business landscape. It is either your worst nightmare or your next big opportunity. The question is: How will you respond? You could leap headlong into e-commerce with an arsenal of tactical tools for online sales and marketing. Or you could take a more holistic approach, one that starts by changing the way you view the Internet itself. Which do you think will benefit your company more in the long run?

In consulting with Fortune 500 companies and start-ups, conducting seminars for business audiences around the world, and writing two books that influenced the first generation of web designers, I have learned a lot about what works and what doesn't work online. In my collaboration with many companies on web strategy, I've found that 90 percent of the problems companies have online are caused by management, not technology.

In this book, I'll present a comprehensive strategy that asks you to rethink your corporate structure and your relationship with your customers. The concepts are unorthodox. No company currently embraces all the principles and processes I describe. But by 2005, I believe they will be commonplace. My goal in this book is to give you a clear understanding of what it will take for your business not only to survive, but to succeed in the coming decade.

Read This Book in the Way That Works Best for You

In Parts 1 and 2, I describe the tools and methodologies you'll need to transform your management-led organization into what I call a customer-led company. Real-world examples illustrate the principles I present. In Part 3, I use fictional case studies to show those principles at work. The case studies are stories of people solving problems and shedding their Old World mindset. Feel free to skim through those chapters first, to get a feel for the total approach, before embarking on Parts 1 and 2.

Part 4 is a trip to the future, in which the Internet is no longer a tool but a platform for work, community-building, and individual empowerment. These futuristic scenarios may seem radically different from the practical approach of the first three parts, but by 2002, their relevance will become clear. Part 4 is an early glimpse of the drastic changes we'll face in the next decade.

About the Web Site

Futurize Your Enterprise actually has seven parts. Four of them are in your hand. The other three are online at Futurizenow.com. The book and the web site are meant to go together! While I've specified a small number of web addresses in the text, Futurizenow.com has all the updated links and ongoing discussion that make the book complete. Every major point in this book has something worth investigating on the site. It is an important part of the experience I've prepared for you.

www.futurizenow.com

This book is dedicated to you, the reader.

PART 1

Principles

I am pessimistic about systems and optimistic about individuals.

— James Cameron

The Toast Is Burning

CHAPTER 1

IN 1996, RETAILING GIANT TOYS "R" US, the nation's largest toy retailer, with $11 billion in sales and more than 1,400 stores, launched its first web site. Initially run and maintained by two marketing people under a miniscule budget, the site was little more than an online brochure. Visitors saw information about the company, a store locator, and a few games for kids, but they couldn't buy a single Barbie online.

In June 1998, the company launched its e-commerce catalog. They moved the team out of marketing and started a new division, called Toys "R" Us Direct. With five full-time staff and many contractors, a budget of $2 million, and several online partners, the catalog was more than just an electronic shopping cart. It also had a gift registry, in-store promotions, product-recall information, e-mail notification, and other services.

By April 1999, Toys "R" Us had lost the first round of e-commerce to eToys, a three-year-old start-up with $30 million in sales. Its market capitalization was almost equal to that of the veteran company, whose first store opened in 1948. What to do? The executives at Toys "R" Us finally decided to get serious about selling online. They broke the web team off from the corporate headquarters in New Jersey and partnered it with a high-profile venture capital firm to set up a separate subsidiary in California's Silicon Valley. With a new staff, a state-of-the-art distribution center, and a $50 million war chest, Toys "R" Us returned to the fray.

Online, where the credit card meets the browser, the people at eToys have the advantage: They know the Web better, they have more experience with the online customer, they don't have to charge sales tax, and they don't have to worry about taking sales away from existing stores. In this territory, *they* are the real veterans.

Now that Toysrus.com has enough money and enough distance from the parent corporation, what should its strategy be? How will it measure success? What secret weapon can the new division build to defend its supremacy in the industry? Or is it a case of too much, too late? If you were advising the CEO of the new subsidiary, what would you reommend?

If Toys "R" Us succeeds online, its secret weapon won't be cash. It won't be technology. It will be a compelling customer experience and the partnerships that provide lasting value. The company's only hope rests not in its cash capital but in its intellectual capital. All the money in the world won't help if the new division manager doesn't ask the right questions.

What is Toys "R" Us really up against? A start-up? No. In reality, the company's biggest adversary is its Old World mindset. Externally, Toys "R" Us must learn to provide e-customers with a satisfying experience, both pre- and post-sale. Internally, the new subsidiary's management must avoid replicating the parent company's brick-and-mortar culture. As more companies wake up to the reality of the Internet, they will ask not how to build a web site but how to build a web business.

1990 ——— **Old World** ——[**2000**]——— **New World** ——— 2010
Supply-Driven   Customer-Led

A one-time event: The transition from the Old World of business management to the New World of e-customers is unique. Before 2000, companies pushed products through the channel to waiting customers. After 2000, customers pull products and services through on demand. By 2010, most buyers will be connected, completing the Customer-Led Revolution.

Here at the turn of the century, many companies are beginning to smell the toast burning. Americans have been putting up with Detroit's cars, Hollywood's movies, Nashville's songs, Silicon Valley's computers, and New York's financial products the way they put up with encyclopedias. In the Old World, the customer had little choice. In the New World, customers will have all the power. Just as a tsunami sweeps the landscape, the Customer-Led Revolution will sweep away businesses that still cling to Old World strategies.

The Customer-Led Revolution is just beginning. People still want transportation, entertainment, tools, and security, but they are about to ask for them in ways we can barely imagine today.

Which Way to the Beach?

I once heard a division president give a speech to the group of people responsible for the company's first efforts online. It was a big company – the initial "assault team" was about 100 people. The president encouraged this group to "take the beach" so that the rest of the company could follow. It was clear to everyone he didn't know where the beach was. He was sending them into unknown territory and expected them to conquer it. He wanted them to do what he and others in the company weren't willing to do: surf on in and figure it out for themselves.

That president is living proof that we fear what we don't know. Most executives don't know the territory. They don't realize there is no beach. They don't know there is no vantage point, no high ground, no point of control. The Internet is an ocean of people swimming alone and in groups. Their demands are new and challenging, and they are not going back to the old ways of doing business.

What's your vision of the future? Can you even see two years ahead? What good is corporate vision if your customers aren't going to cooperate? How many landing parties will you lose before you realize they're not properly equipped or headed in the right direction?

In the last few years, I've had the opportunity to watch hundreds of companies, large and small, walk to the edge of the sand and resolutely dip their toes in the water. My goal in this book is to encourage companies to jump in and learn to swim. I'll show you how to harness the power of your customers to make and sell your product or service – not just buy it. I'll show you how your customers can make all the strategic decisions you thought you needed to make. And I'll show how your customers will reshape your web site and your organization if you'll just let them.

To futurize means to prepare your business for the New World of e-customers. As the Customer-Led Revolution sweeps across your industry, your company will have to change. In this book, you'll learn to futurize your enterprise both externally and internally.

To futurize your company externally, you'll learn to take the customer's view of your web site. You'll see that most companies don't ask the right questions when they're preparing to go online and that what they offer is not really what the customers want. You'll learn how to turn any web site into the strategic tool it should be – not the marketing mouthpiece it has become. Most important, you'll see that new thinking at the top is the only way to begin the journey to a customer-led future.

To futurize your company internally, you'll learn to let your customers lead the way. You will let *them* have the vision. You will conduct what I hope is the last major reorganization in your company's history. Together, we will organize your company completely around customers and let your customers pull you where you need to go.

We all read the same headlines every day. The Internet has taken off, and so far, it's only taken a few companies with it. No one wants to be left behind. Jack Welch, CEO of General Electric, says it's time to stop waiting for the revolution to come to us. He says that, for all companies, the Internet is now priority "Number 1, 2, 3, and 4." Great concept, but where do we start?

THE CEO'S CRYSTAL BALL

A 1999 survey of 600 top-ranking executives found that:

92% said the Internet will reshape the world marketplace by 2001

37% expected serious competition from start-ups

16% expected competition from their own customers

86% said the Internet would force significant changes in organizational structures

Survey by Booz • Allen & Hamilton/Economist Intelligence Unit

---

Letting Customers Lead

In March 1999, Steve Ballmer, president of Microsoft Corporation, said, "Software is going to play a far broader role in our lives than we can even imagine today. When we took stock of our ability to meet these future opportunities, it became clear that we were organized to meet today's needs, but not those of the next decade."

With that self-appraisal, Microsoft announced a complete restructuring of the company, away from products and toward customers. To serve its e-customers, Microsoft executives realized the company had to, in Ballmer's words, "move away from the alignment by products and technologies that had served the company since its inception."

Microsoft realigned itself to parallel its four main customer groups: 1) information technology managers, 2) knowledge workers, 3) software developers, and 4) consumers. Each division is empowered to bring out the best in Microsoft's core technology for the benefit of its customers.

This choice is not an obvious one. It takes insight and research to find your top customer groups. Microsoft executives learned that knowledge workers, whether they're in a small consulting firm in Bombay or at General Motors' corporate headquarters, are much more alike than they are different.

E-customers aren't loyal to a brand. They are loyal to other customers and the employees with whom they have established a relationship. They may be attracted to a specific business proposition, but their memories are very short. Solve one problem for them, and they have another. Companies must earn their networked customers' loyalty with *every* new deal.

Take a look at the customer-led manifesto at Cluetrain.com. It contains 95 theses about the emerging networked market. The first five theses are the most important:

1. Markets are conversations.
2. Markets consist of human beings, not demographic sectors.
3. Conversations among human beings *sound* human. They are conducted in a human voice.
4. Whether delivering information, opinions, perspectives, dissenting arguments or humorous asides, the human voice is typically open, natural, uncontrived.
5. People recognize each other as such from the sound of this voice.

One goal of this book is to make it clear that markets really *are* conversations. I hope this statement will become your new mantra. It isn't an analogy or a helpful learning device – it's the new reality.

A customer-led company aligns with its customers inside and out. In a customer-led company, everyone contributes to the customer's experience. The company provides ways for the customer to talk not only with the employees but with other customers as well. The web team facilitates those conversations.

Should everyone in the company contribute to the web site? Yes. Should everyone in the company be talking to customers in chat rooms and online discussion groups? Yes. Should executives take time out of their busy days to answer e-mail from ordinary customers? What do *you* think? Hewlett-Packard has a system for answering every e-mail message it receives. The company tracks and follows up on any outstanding inquiries, even a request for parts for an audio oscillator made in 1939.

> **FUTURIZING THE WEB TEAM**
>
> The Web is not a marketing thing. CEOs who like their sites remove the Web as a marketing function and make it a core business function.
>
> – Michael Fischler, founder, The Pubs Group

The customer experience and the employee experience are the two halves of the new conversation. That conversation will be your guide. Listening and following are the hallmarks of the winners in the New World.

Diary of a Car Buyer

Today, no car manufacturer has a web site that listens. All the manufacturers' sites are essentially online brochures. Most car manufacturers actually discourage customer communication! California's "Lemon Law" requires them to respond or to replace a car if a customer files a complaint. The companies fear they'll be bombarded with e-mail messages and saddled with the responsibility of answering every message they get.

What does the customer see on the site? Sections for minivans, sedans, convertibles, and sport-utility vehicles. Information about financing. And, of course, a nifty color selector. This product-driven, keeping-up-with-the-Joneses approach leads to a very boring customer experience.

A customer-led approach would be very different. As Microsoft did, the company would first take a hard look at who its online customers are. A customer-led auto manufacturer site would provide areas for commuters, families, students, sport-driving enthusiasts, businesses, and so on. Car owners from each group could share their experiences online. People looking for new cars are much more likely to believe actual owners than pages of standardized marketing jargon. Once prospective buyers see how satisfied these customers are with their cars, they'll take the next step: the test drive.

Is it possible to test-drive a car online? Absolutely. Suppose you're looking for a sporty, yet sophisticated, convertible. You go to an auto magazine's web site, where you find several articles written by professional drivers. Then, you get "in the driver's seat." From Java-based simulations of the Corvette, the BMW convertible, the Mercedes SL, the Porsche 911, and the Jaguar XK8, you choose the Porsche. After a quick tour of the cockpit, you choose one of four famous test tracks. A brisk one-megabyte download, the light turns green, and you're on your way – behind the wheel of a Porsche 911.

Yuck. I can't imagine a worse way to test-drive a car. Yet some car companies would love to build such a simulation, and they would spend plenty of money doing it. The futurize way is to put people ahead of technology. Let's try again.

Suppose the magazine holds an event where real people shopping for convertibles get to test-drive the five cars. A group of tire-kicking shoppers spends the day driving the cars. They describe their experiences – unedited – on the magazine's web site. When you visit the site, you decide to follow the story of the 40-year-old consultant from San Francisco. He has a sport-utility vehicle and is looking for a weekend getaway car. You read about his day on the track. You learn with him what torque means to the average driver, what causes the rear wheels to drift, and how each car handles a panic stop on wet pavement.

Because you identify with the consultant, you get a lot out of reading what he has to say. You appreciate it when he says the Porsche is the most fun, but also the most – in his opinion – unsafe. Ruling out the BMW (wrong attitude), the Corvette (no finesse), and the Jaguar (wrong image), he decides on the Mercedes. After reading the unedited comments of three to four of the drivers, you have an excellent idea of how each car drives.

But wait. It gets better. You can read about how the consultant shopped for and bought his Mercedes. And he's kept a diary of his new-car experience for the last eight months, so you can see how he's enjoying the SL. You can even send him questions by e-mail – he answers in a day or two – and read his FAQ, the questions he gets most frequently. Why does he do it? Because he loves the attention, and he loves his car. He also loves the free gasoline he gets, compliments of the magazine, as long as he keeps up his web diary.

Magazines can hold this kind of event. Car manufacturers can't. But they can *sponsor* events like the shoppers' test drive on a magazine's site. Company employees can participate in the online dialogues, as long as they do so earnestly. If employees are really excited about their company, its philosophy, and its products, customers will want to meet them and ask them questions. Once a customer establishes a relationship with an employee, the employee can invite the customer to the company's own site to continue the discussion.

Misalignment in Hollywood

All film studios create web sites for their films. It's another cost of launching a movie. All studios put up the same content: the cast, the storyline, behind-the-scenes anecdotes, awards, clips and images, and an occasional screensaver or mystery game.

Have they left anything out? Bios of the studio heads? The studio's stock price? The movie's mission statement?

Wait a minute! Where are the customers? Everyone enjoys movies, and everyone enjoys giving opinions about movies. Why don't studios let the film-viewing public create the sites' content? People are aching for a chance to express themselves, but the studio lawyers have convinced the executives that the risks outweigh the benefits. What are the liabilities? Someone might criticize the film. Someone might criticize the person who criticized the film. And the studio could get bad press as a result. Who cares what people say, as long as they spell the name of the film correctly?

People are discussing the films online already – in newsgroups, on America Online, in communities like Hsx.com and Film.com. The studios could harness all that energy. Given the chance, viewers would love to express themselves and be recognized for their abilities as critics.

To encourage positive debate, a studio might give visitors the ability to vote on the reviews and then feature the most popular reviews at the top of the film's home page. How much does that cost? Nothing! Yet the challenge and opportunity for recognition would get people writing their most witty, insightful reviews.

Reviewers might find themselves with growing online audiences eager for their next reviews. Now here's the beauty part: This gives the studio a chance to listen more closely to its customers than it ever has before. Popular reviewers might qualify to become part of the studio's special advisory board, brought in to help shape a film during development. Members of the audience could start to give studio heads a better idea what will play in Peoria.

The more tools and opportunities a company gives its customers to express themselves, the more they will participate. The rules don't need to be very strict. The watchers don't need to be very watchful. As we'll see in later chapters, customer-led communities are self-policing. Companies that don't understand that principle will fail to make the transition to the customer-led future.

The successful movie studio of the future will facilitate the conversation between those making the films and those consuming them – from the initial pitch to the final cut.

The Customer-Led Model

A management-led company relies on management's vision to set the course. A customer-led company is completely aligned with customer groups, both internally and externally. A customer-led company encourages conversation between customers and employees, and among customers. Rather than shying away from personal contact, a customer-led company actually encourages contact with the employees and facilitates customers meeting each other. This new emphasis on listening creates the conversations that move the company forward.

Many companies listen to their customers, but only tactically. Car companies listen to customers to see how many of which model to make or which colors are popular. Golf club manufacturers try to understand the customer's perception of various high-tech features. Hotels listen to complaints and try to fix the problems. A tactical emphasis on customers is a way of validating and refining management's vision.

A customer-led company listens to its customers *strategically*. It asks big questions: What business should we be in? Who are our core customers? Should we build products or services? Can we reorganize internally to serve the new, more demanding customer? Customer-led companies bring their customers into the long-range planning process.

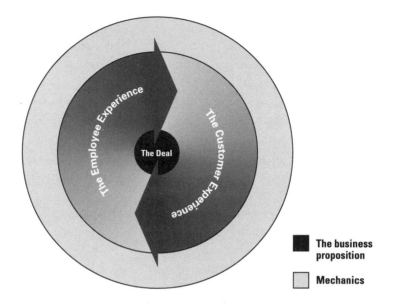

The business proposition

Mechanics

The customer-led company has a porous interface between customers and employees. This represents a dialogue around "the deal," which represents a particular business proposition. As customers pull the company from one business proposition to the next, customers and employees blur into one, like tigers chasing each other around a tree. Everything else is just mechanics.

A customer-led company fosters loyalty through relationships. *Everyone* in the company is responsible for the customer's experience. The boundary between customer and employee becomes more porous. Customers and employees get to know each other, rely on each other. The conversation gets more interesting. Transactions are simply part of the conversation, just as they are at the corner grocery store or café.

The transition from a management-led to a customer-led company removes the old distribution-driven bottleneck that forces customers to talk to the company through special representatives. When customers can send e-mail directly to almost anyone in the company, those bottle-necks disappear. The old official branding mechanisms no longer

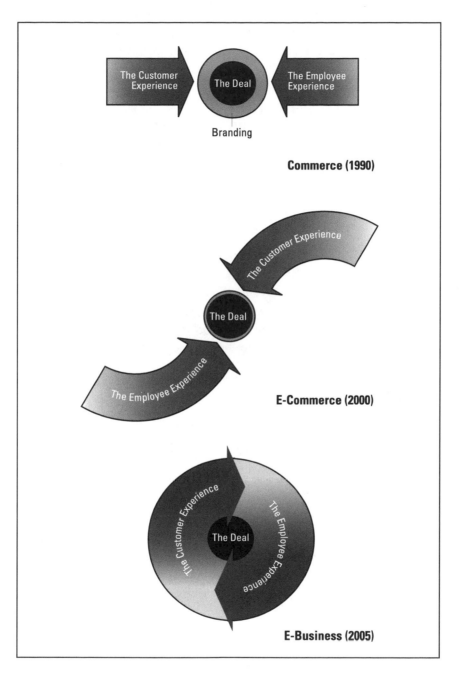

Commerce (1990)

E-Commerce (2000)

E-Business (2005)

The transition from a management-led to a customer-led structure eliminates the communication bottleneck between employees and customers.

contribute to customer loyalty. The e-commerce site opens up to become more of a communication tool. Rather than measuring brand penetration or web-site sales, the company starts to measure the quality of the employee experience and the customer experience around each new business proposition.

Today, there aren't many customer-led companies in the world. The Internet will change that. Perhaps the biggest difference between the way we do business today and the way we will do business tomorrow is that we will all become better listeners. And that may change more than just our companies.

Futurizing

Companies that are serious about doing business online will have to learn how to swim in the turbulent sea of customer demands and changing business rules. They will need a completely new approach to their online customers, an approach I outline in this book. Whether you have $50,000 or $50 million to build your online business, your first step should be to transform the way you perceive the challenges that lay ahead. If you can't do that, no amount of money in the world will help you against the companies that can.

Global interconnectivity is a tsunami event, a tidal wave of cataclysmic change sweeping the world. From 2000 to 2010, perhaps two billion people will go online. These people will change the business landscape more than any group or event in the last century. Are you ready? If you're not, that's okay. By the time you finish this book, you will be.

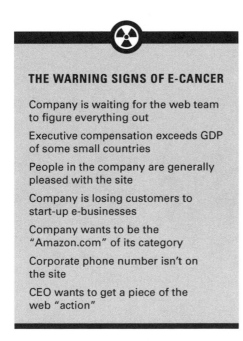

THE WARNING SIGNS OF E-CANCER

Company is waiting for the web team to figure everything out

Executive compensation exceeds GDP of some small countries

People in the company are generally pleased with the site

Company is losing customers to start-up e-businesses

Company wants to be the "Amazon.com" of its category

Corporate phone number isn't on the site

CEO wants to get a piece of the web "action"

Why Most Web Strategies Fail

CHAPTER 2

FROM MY OFFICE IN SEATTLE, I can get most anywhere in 24 hours. When a patient calls, I grab my little black bag (which contains my little black notebook computer) and head to the airport. One Monday morning, I find myself walking into the headquarters of a Fortune 500 firm, black bag firmly in hand.

The company has more than 50,000 employees and a 12-person web team. The web team has been on a roller-coaster ride for two years. Every day it's something new. These are the only people in the company capable of getting something onto the web site. A constant stream of requests pours into their office, everyone needing something up on the site yesterday. They are in the crossfire of marketing, human resources, support, investor relations, and every other department in the company. They get 700 e-mail messages a day. They are always behind schedule. Are they the proud representatives of their company online? No. They're tired, overworked, and jumpy.

When I arrive, they're glad to see me. I'm someone they can relate to. They've just had a meeting with the CEO, and he doesn't like the new site design. "I'll know it when I see it," he told them. Apparently, he hadn't seen it. Now they're frustrated. They're not mind readers. They hope I can break the cycle and come up with a brilliant solution that satisfies everyone.

In that environment, the solution the web team wants doesn't exist. This is a turf war. The team has brought me in as ammunition, hoping to use me tactically. If I don't say what they hope to hear, they'll look for an expert who'll support their side of the argument. These maneuvers are just symptoms of a disease I call misalignment. I ask them, "Why do you care what the CEO thinks? Your CEO doesn't have the authority to say what should go on your web site or how it's presented. The people who have that authority aren't about to give it up. Who are they?" The web team is puzzled. They've been yelled at by too many internal groups to come up with an answer. "Your customers!" I say. "If you don't listen to them, they'll find someone who will."

If the CEO thinks he has the authority to say what the web site should look like, I would suggest asking the board of directors what they think. I would ask what the customers' role is in creating their online experience. Authority isn't control – it's responsibility. The number one problem with most web strategies is that decision makers exercise too much control and not enough responsibility.

In this chapter, I identify the six most common mistakes companies make online. These six traps are so prevalent it's hard to find a company that isn't in at least two. Even successful web companies fall into these traps, limiting their ability to gain their customers' loyalty.

Trap 1: Not Taking the Medium Seriously

In 1997, two established chain-store competitors decided to get into e-commerce. Company A hired an experienced, enthusiastic person to find new office space, hire a staff, and build the system from scratch. The company budgeted $3 million for the first year. Company B insisted on watching costs, going for short-term profitability and some proof that the Internet was a viable business space. Company B's management took a few company engineers and a marketing person and started building an online system in-house.

A year later, Company A's e-commerce group had grown to 80 employees. They had brisk sales and an energized team atmosphere. The group went back to headquarters for more money and got it. Company B's project wasn't working. They had underestimated what it took to build a system on the Internet. They brought in consultants. They hired experts. They started to panic. Company A was eating their lunch. In the end, Company B was throwing more and more resources at an already sunk investment.

After two years, both companies had spent almost the same amount of money, but Company A was already profitable. Its autonomous Internet team had a very successful initial public offering. Company B managed to launch its site, but it still didn't have a fully functioning system.

What was the difference? Company A treated its web effort not as a new business opportunity, but as a completely new business. Company B focused on money rather than customers.

Every day another company treats the Web as a trade show or an extension of its catalog. And every day, a company wakes up to the fact that its original plans for the Web aren't adequate. Companies make their online plans simply by looking at what other companies have done, setting up a vicious cycle of useless features and meaningless messages.

I have had the opportunity to talk with a lot of companies about what they want to achieve online. Reading between the lines of most companies' proposals and efforts reveals one unstated goal: *to look like they know what they're doing online.* That accounts for all the cool features and spinning logos on web sites today. Companies that admit they don't know where to start often achieve more online than companies that *think* they know where to start.

Trap 2: Trying to Do Everything for Everyone

Almost every company, whether start-up or multinational, tries too hard to please every visitor who comes to its web site. Not surprisingly, no one is really satisfied. Many e-commerce companies take a department-store approach to visitors and merchandising, hoping to put enough on each web page that every visitor finds something to like.

You can see this approach on the home page of most large companies. The top screen of the site's home page is called the area "above the fold." This prime real estate becomes the battleground for all the company's divisions. It's often packed so densely with features that no visitor could possibly feel welcome. By trying to do everything for everyone, the company does nothing for anyone.

Now go to a site like Timezone.com. This site for high-end watch enthusiasts is not professionally designed. It is, however, extremely popular among watch collectors. Their enthusiasm for the site overflows on every page – some collectors practically live there. Visitors can spend hours learning about watches and the people who make them. It's a very lively community, with a high degree of trust among its members. They think nothing of helping each other out or sending a check for a purchase, though they may never have met offline. People offer at least 100 new watches a day, some for more than the price of a new Mercedes.

Take Timezone.com down, and there would be some very unhappy people. For many of them, the site is a place where they're always among friends. If you haven't spent much time at a site with that degree of community, you should. Sites like Timezone.com and Chessclub.com, which hosts more than 70,000 games per day, are on fire.

Trap 3: Technology for Technology's Sake

The technology trap is a bottomless pit, and many, many companies have fallen into it. A company's web site is often born in the technical support group. The fall starts when a company's information technology (IT) group puts a web front-end on various internal applications and gets caught up in the thrill of creating new user interfaces.

It doesn't take long for the IT group to wrest the site from tech support. The group manager simply convinces the CEO that it's time to "do things right." Soon the site starts to look "cool," in the same way that racing-car graphics look cool. The IT people don't know when to stop – they've got big plans. They have feature lists as long as your arm. A monster database system. A Java interface (if you see a Java program used for marketing purposes, you know the tail is wagging the dog). Quality content and customer feedback are usually not high priorities.

Examples of technology traps are everywhere: scrolling stock tickers, spinning logos, blinking buttons, background images that make the text hard to read, animations, virtual passageways, roll-overs (areas that change as the mouse moves over them), and VCR-like interfaces. The insidious part of the trap is the white-lab-coat effect. When the vice-president of technology tells upper management he needs millions of dollars for the next state-of-the-art system, complete with "secure sockets," "fuzzy logic," and an "unspoofable DNS protocol," executives – fearful that the worst could happen – tend to sign on the dotted line. Technology people often command more authority than others because no one else understands what they're talking about. When they get their way, it just reinforces their worldview.

You can tell how far your company has fallen into the technology trap by how long it takes to make a change on the site. If it takes seven days to correct a spelling error (a common delay time at many sites), your company is in trouble. If it's easy to make a change to the home page – for example, if a special intranet lets one person easily manage the page content without IT assistance – then you know the technology serves the purpose.

At Yahoo!, a company with some of the most sophisticated technology on the planet, the IT group plays a subservient role. Founder Jerry Yang insists that the site reflect the needs of its customers, and Yahoo!'s customers' top three concerns are 1) speed, 2) speed, and 3) speed. The company shows its dedication to customers by continually beating every other large site in page-response time. Keeping a very complicated site simple is one of Yahoo!'s biggest accomplishments.

Trap 4: Brochureware

Another bottomless pit is the marketing trap. The marketing and communications (marcom) group – which just took the company's site away from the IT group – has a big agenda: the HTML-ization of every marketing document it can find. A company in the marketing trap often has a site with an elaborate menu structure, long documents, sanitized case studies, and plenty of press releases – all in a color scheme lifted from its current brochures.

The site may balloon to thousands of pages. Every division of the company has its own guidelines for putting up content – not because it has its own customers, but because it has its own marketing group. Bombarded by several different branding efforts, site visitors often can't tell, from one page to another, whether they're still on the same site.

Marcom takeovers usually result in brochureware – sites sucked dry of interesting content. These sites are safe. They're also rarely visited. In the Old World, the term "communications" meant broadcasting messages to audiences. Today, it means talking with and listening to people.

The group that controls the company web site has a lot of power inside the company. When the marketing group gets its hands on a site, it has to keep showing how web-savvy it is. The result: virtual worlds – online theme parks, universities, expos, villages, malls, and other architectural masterpieces. Once these construction projects get going, they are hard to stop.

The way out of the marketing trap is to let the customers do most of the work. For example, most online bookstores use customer reviews to give the shopping experience a more human voice. Customer book reviews strongly influence other customers' book purchases. A single comment may convince a particular visitor to buy a book, and the books with the most comments – not necessarily the highest rankings – sell best. The fact that the company welcomes customer reviews on its site gives customers a good feeling about doing business there.

Trap 5: The Introverted Web Site

A company's web site is a remarkable mirror of the company's organization and philosophy. If the company doesn't know what it's doing internally, that eventually shows itself on the site. If the web team's charter is based on internal, rather than external, goals, the web site will naturally reflect the company's organizational chart. I call this an introverted web site – a site organized by internal issues rather than customer needs.

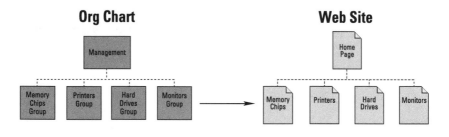

The introverted web site: Most companies' web teams put up information about or for each division in the company. The web site, consequently, mirrors the company's org chart.

An introverted web site is usually organized around content, mirroring its physical counterpart (i.e., a store, a magazine, or a newspaper). The company looks at its products and services and simply puts them on the site, reinforcing its brick-and-mortar approach to the Web. These sites don't scale well – they tend to get less organized and more confusing as the company adds more content and receives more visitors. They don't promote loyalty, and they don't make anyone feel at home on the site. No one bookmarks any second-level pages. The home page continues to attract everyone and spirals out of control, forcing the company to try to put everything on the front page to accommodate the wishes of all its customer groups simultaneously.

It's rare to find a company whose web site *doesn't* mirror its org chart. That's fine if the organization is divided along customer lines. For example, recruiting companies are usually structured around corporate clients and job seekers. Consequently, their web sites have two sections: one for corporations offering jobs, posting job listings, and looking through the résumé database; the other for job seekers wanting to post résumés and search job listings. These companies divide their audience upon entry, sending each visitor to the appropriate home page. These sites are naturally extraverted. They are in alignment with customers as a natural result of their internal structure.

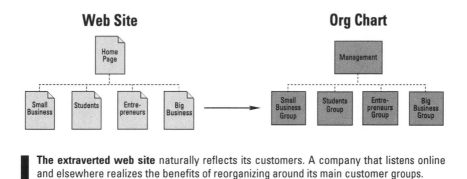

The extraverted web site naturally reflects its customers. A company that listens online and elsewhere realizes the benefits of reorganizing around its main customer groups.

An extraverted web site scales naturally to accommodate more customers. Rather than trying to do everything for everyone, the extraverted web site entices different kinds of customers to their own second-level pages (also known as neighborhoods) within the site. Stores, newspapers, and magazines all address different audiences with one product, but online it's possible to address each audience separately.

Once on her neighborhood page, a particular customer sees relevant information, meets people like herself, and gets the clear impression that the company understands her needs. By talking with her in a voice she can relate to and listening to her needs, the manager for that group of customers continues to modify that neighborhood to more appropriately serve her demanding audience.

The extraverted site invites visitors to bookmark the neighborhoods for the group they most identify with, taking the pressure off the home page. The company encourages people to come back to their favorite neighborhood for all the news, information, dialogue, and features they want. Extraverted sites scale naturally, adding new neighborhoods and further refining their customer models as more people come to the site.

Trap 6: Taking Yourself Too Seriously

I once consulted for a company that makes a specialized product (for the purposes of this discussion, let's say they make in-line skates). The company didn't have a web site. Management wanted to do it right the first time around, so they hired an experienced web site manager to put it all together. This person was very enthusiastic about her new job, but she wasn't very interested in strategy. She decided the site would be aimed at skateboarders who were curious about in-line skating and skaters who wanted to upgrade to a better pair of skates. She didn't see any need to waste time asking these potential customers what they wanted. Her first question for me was whether to host the site on Windows NT or Unix.

The company had brought me in to help get things started. My first question of the web site manager was, "Who's your target audience?" She said it was obvious: the company's employees. They were skateboarding or in-line skating all the time. Most of them had joined the company because they wanted to be part of the industry behind the sport they loved. In short, they were the perfect people to critique their own site.

Then I asked, "How many people here have computers on their desks?" Only a few. "How many have computers at home?" A couple of people did. "How many of the employees surf the Web more than an hour a week?" One person did. "How many have e-mail?" Three people did. "How many have ever bought anything online?" Only she had. "So," I said, "if the employees are the perfect audience, then you can save a lot of money by not building a site at all. Nobody here surfs the Web! If you don't know who your online customers are, how can you possibly build a site to accommodate them?"

We parted ways shortly thereafter. The site manager developed the site she had envisioned. She wanted the site to be the authoritative source of information about in-line skates: online factory tours, information about new wheels, braking systems, and the exciting features of the new skates. To this company, it was a matter of getting a designer who could make the site cool enough to attract the skating crowd. Without asking the right questions up front, it doesn't really matter which designer they hire – they will blame the designer when the site doesn't live up to their expectations.

Futurizing

Most web strategies fail because they start with the company's mission statement and end with a call to action. If the web team gets bounced between the marketing and IT departments, or if the budget for the site comes from one of these departments, your company is already in trouble. The more these groups own the site, the more lifeless it will be. If your customer-support people are in charge of the site, you might have a chance. If your customers are in charge, you're futurizing.

As we'll see in the next chapter, customer-led companies naturally have extraverted web sites. Rather than doing everything for everyone, a customer led company aligns divisions within the company with important customer groups.

In the process of building an extraverted, customer-led web site, some groups will be left out. That's a good sign. No one can please all of the people all of the time. In this book, I'll show many examples of extraverted web sites and customer-led companies focusing on customers and reaping the rewards.

I said there were six traps, but I lied. There are really seven. In the next chapter, we'll see how many companies are stuck in the biggest trap of all: e-commerce.

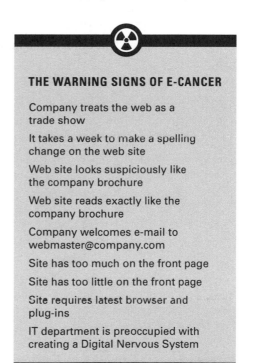

THE WARNING SIGNS OF E-CANCER

Company treats the web as a trade show

It takes a week to make a spelling change on the web site

Web site looks suspiciously like the company brochure

Web site reads exactly like the company brochure

Company welcomes e-mail to webmaster@company.com

Site has too much on the front page

Site has too little on the front page

Site requires latest browser and plug-ins

IT department is preoccupied with creating a Digital Nervous System

E-Business

THE FIRST PRINTED BOOKS imitated handwritten manuscripts. The first photographs were portraits. Many early motion pictures captured theatrical plays on screen. So it's not surprising that in the late 1990s, companies tried hard to re-create their familiar business environments online. They thought the World Wide Web would provide the new "front-end" to their existing business practices.

Re-creating the physical world online is a temporary, transitional, and often unnecessary strategy. If your company's online strategy still relies on mirroring the company's physical processes, if your digital nervous system is about to automate all your paperwork, you've gotten this book just in time. In this chapter, I define e-commerce and e-business and map out a strategy for moving from management-led e-commerce to customer-led e-business.

E-Commerce

Business web sites have followed a fairly natural evolution. At first, companies put up sites with marketing jargon and stock photography. I call these sites brochureware. That's where more than 90 percent of all sites are today. The sites don't do anything for anyone except the marketing manager. Brochureware is really an exercise in moving the brand online – it simply automates the delivery of a marketing message.

The next stage after brochureware is electronic commerce. Many companies are now building e-commerce sites, which usually means putting their catalogs on their sites and taking orders online. A basic application of e-commerce involves a transaction and a virtual shopping cart. Service forms of e-commerce provide customers with access to reports, data, advice, and other information on a paid subscription basis or in exchange for viewers looking at ads. Good e-commerce companies automate their best salespeople. Mediocre e-commerce companies do a mediocre job of automating their best salespeople.

It's easy to see why brochureware isn't winning online. It's harder to understand why e-commerce isn't a recipe for long-term success. The answer is that in most e-commerce models the web team is the only group in the company that communicates with the online customers, reinforcing the bottleneck between customers and company representatives. That model doesn't foster the employee-customer conversations that deepen the relationship and encourage loyalty. Instead, there is a better, more appropriate way to grow a business online.

E-COMMERCE FOUNDATIONS

Internal web groups struggle to learn what they need to learn while fending off the competition. Companies with large catalog operations, like REI.com and Sharperimage.com, have managed to hire good people and capture market share. But most companies haven't been able to capitalize on the e-commerce opportunity simply by putting up a catalog and buying banner ads.

An autonomous online division or subsidiary is the best way for established companies to engage in e-commerce. Companies like Office Depot, Barnes & Noble, and Charles Schwab have managed to do quite well with this approach. Their goal should be to become number one in their respective categories without regard to whether they are hurting the offline business.

A pure play is a company whose sole income comes from its web site. Pure plays – like Golf.com, Listen.com, Yucky.com, and Webvan.com – are lean, mean e-commerce machines. They are usually venture-backed, web savvy, and very aggressive. In e-commerce, a pure play has a huge advantage: It doesn't have to charge sales tax and doesn't have any average or bad salespeople dragging down profits.

E-Business

Dell Computer Corporation is one of the computer industry's most progressive companies. Michael Dell built an e-business before anyone coined the term.

Dell knew his customers. He gave them a way around the usual routes to procurement. He let them order computers one at a time, while still giving them the contract discount. He let them order by phone, with a credit card, even on weekends. Rather than building new products in long planning cycles and having the products sit on the shelf, he started building customers' products as soon as they ordered them.

When the Web came along, Dell.com was a natural extension of the offline business. It's impossible to tell the company from its web site. The site is simply another aspect of doing business with Dell. The entire site is aligned by customer categories, not hardware model lines. The site directs each type of customer to a special second-level page, where the entire line of Dell products is presented and explained in a way that is relevant to each customer's needs.

Dell truly partners with its business customers online. More than 15,000 customers now have Premier Pages – an extranet that ties Dell's order-entry system right into the customer's procurement software to make ordering and tracking easy.

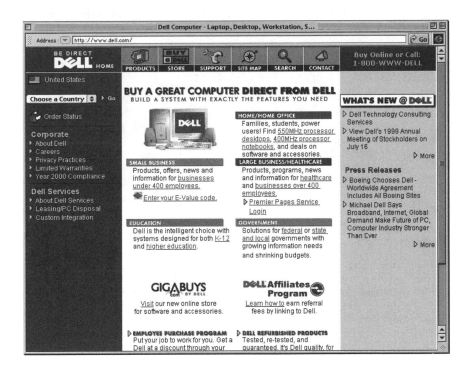

Dell.com is not only an e-business, it's one of the few models of a *customer-led* e-business. On this extraverted site, the company does not list its product models on its home page. Instead, Dell provides second-level neighborhood sites for enterprises, small businesses, educators, home consumers, and government. This intense focus on the customer is a natural outgrowth of Dell's philosophy.

Dell brings customers into the product-planning and manufacturing processes, not just the sales process, and management encourages everyone in the company to have contact with customers. That broad employee-customer interface prevents the communication bottleneck that occurs if only the web team is in touch with e-customers. These employee-customer relationships not only foster loyalty to Dell but will help the company adapt in the future.

In e-business, everyone in the company uses the Internet to deliver a complete range of ever-changing goods and services. In e-business, the web site is not a communication bottleneck but becomes a medium for communication, like the phone. E-business doesn't require that a company do everything for customers online, only that everyone in the company use Internet tools to the extent they serve the customer best.

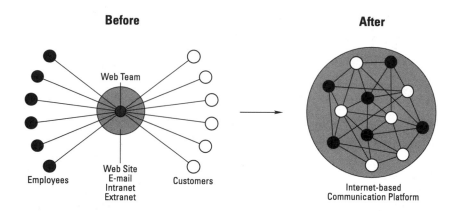

The communication bottleneck in the Old World occurred when customers had to deal directly with sales personnel to get questions answered. That mentality migrates to the web site, forcing all e-mail messages to go through a company's webmaster. Once everyone in the company is online and doing e-business, the bottleneck opens, allowing everyone to communicate.

Many e-businesses have sprung up without going through the e-commerce phase. Most are services, and their online business models make their predecessors look primitive. A good example is Connected Online Backup. Connected automatically backs up a customer's computer files via the Internet at night and stores them on a server. If a customer inadvertently leaves her laptop at a hotel during a business trip, she can still get to and use all her files. If a customer's computers are damaged or stolen, all the information is still safe, organized, and ready to download. Pricing is hundreds of times cheaper than back-ups done with tape drives and system administrators. The manuscript for this book was written in San Francisco and Seattle, but the files were backed up nightly and stored at Connected's East Coast office for just pennies a day. That's e-business.

In 1999, Marriott International booked more than $100 million in hotel rooms through its web site, Marriott.com. But Marriott isn't stopping there. Soon, most of the company's hotels will have high-bandwidth access in every room, increasing contact between the company and its customers. Guests will be able to use e-mail, order room service, send each other messages, receive faxes, and book tickets to local performances and events – all from their rooms. Their travel preferences will automatically go with them from one Marriott hotel to another. *That's* e-business!

E-business is both a more focused and a more comprehensive approach than e-commerce. Its goal is to give specific audiences a complete and personalized experience. E-business may contain e-commerce as simply one element of a larger strategy. An e-commerce platform consists of hardware and software. An e-business platform is an attitude shift – it gives customers the ability to get what they want, when they want it, the way they want it. A company on an e-business platform responds more appropriately to new customer demands.

Transitioning to E-Business

Most online stores are virtual re-creations of their physical counterparts; the site section names corresponding exactly to the signs hung in the various departments of a physical store. In 1997, this was an accomplishment. As we'll see, that approach may make a little money, but it doesn't take your company into the future. The new e-customer demands more than shopping carts and virtual aisles.

Because e-business can include e-commerce, most companies can evolve from e-commerce to e-business simply by getting everyone involved in the effort. As Marriott International knows, once you have customers paying for rooms online, you can extend that relationship to include many other aspects of their travel experience.

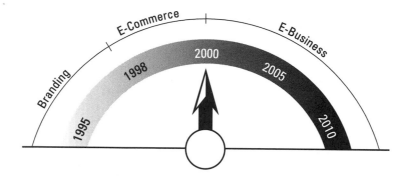

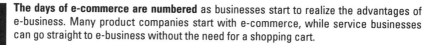

The days of e-commerce are numbered as businesses start to realize the advantages of e-business. Many product companies start with e-commerce, while service businesses can go straight to e-business without the need for a shopping cart.

The Discovery Channel, National Geographic, and start-up Quokka Sports have all been doing e-business for years. All three companies created new divisions and new content for their sites. Discovery.com sends teams around the world to bring back sounds and images of animals. Nationalgeographic.com encourages adventure teams to submit proposals and chooses several each year to fund. Quokka.com follows extreme sports participants as they test the limits of human endurance in such events as the Whitbread solo sailing race around the world. On all three sites, adventure participants send daily reports from far-flung places and respond to customer questions. These sites report that their audiences prefer to follow people in the field as the expedition unfolds, rather than reading a summary after it's over. By connecting the journalists and adventurers with their audiences, these sites have redefined adventure journalism and have found the advertiser response very rewarding.

In e-business, the communication bottleneck widens, then disappears, allowing more and more of your employees to interact directly with customers. Eventually, your initial web team spreads its know-how to the entire company, enabling everyone to communicate with e-customers.

In e-commerce, the web team goes fishing every day and brings back the catch. In e-business, the web team teaches everyone in the company to fish. Ideally, your web team should disappear in a few years. Does your company have a phone team? Or a chief refrigeration officer? As your company moves from e-commerce to e-business, the web team will plant the seeds that eventually lead to its own destruction. That evolution will happen only if management intends it to happen.

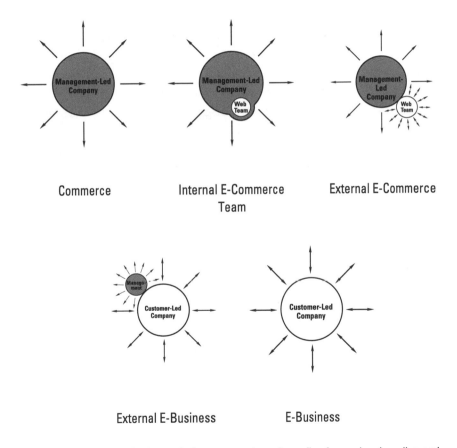

Commerce   Internal E-Commerce   External E-Commerce
                        Team

External E-Business   E-Business

From commerce to e-business: At first, companies going online focused on branding and technical support. Then the companies added e-commerce web teams to automate existing processes. Now management realizes that everyone in the company needs to communicate with the new e-customer.

Ernie

Ernst & Young helps its clients make financial and management decisions. Since 1996, the company has offered an online service called Ernie (ernie.ey.com). For a relatively low subscription fee, clients can e-mail Ernie, a fictional character who replies within two days. The messages are routed to people inside the company who answer the questions and send them back to the Ernie desk, where a staff of ten people replies officially in Ernie's "voice." Another part of Ernie lets clients explore the previously asked questions and the data behind them.

Ernie was designed as a low-cost entry point for growing companies who wanted access to Ernst & Young's analysts but couldn't afford a substantial engagement. It is so popular, thousands of small companies have signed up for the service. Some have since become consulting clients. Ernie set the standard for online delivery of consulting services by focusing on a simple, consistent experience for the customer.

Ernie is a new way of communicating with the company. It's a new way of listening. Ernie is a success because clients want the company to listen to them 24 hours a day, seven days a week. You can think of Ernie as a service form of e-commerce – Ernie automates the company's best customer representatives. It's a great start, but there is much more to do.

Most of Ernst & Young's clients want Ernie in addition to their regular consulting services. Most people using Ernie would rather have answers sooner than later. The real-time demands of e-customers will force consulting companies to offer a consistent online customer experience as a foundation for all their communications. The company should begin to position Ernie as the standard gateway for interaction.

Imagine that a client ends up asking a certain analyst a lot of questions. Why should the answers continually go through the Ernie team to be put in Ernie's voice? Because many analysts have no idea of the context for these questions, and because many analysts have a hard time expressing themselves in ways clients can understand, the Ernie people help make the client's experience more meaningful. But the real value of Ernie is in the internal training and the mind-set it brings to the company. If every analyst could speak directly to clients in an appropriate way, there would be no need for Ernie as a separate service. Ernie would eventually be part of the company's culture. And that's the value of e-business.

If Ernie remains a separate offering, the company will take an à la carte approach to communication tools. Instead, they should build on Ernie's success by giving it to all their clients and working to reduce the turn-around time. This is a good example of how a first effort can be an enabler or a bottleneck, depending on how the rest of the company adopts it.

Loyalty

Few companies can afford to stay in e-commerce for very long, even if they would like to. New business propositions lure customers away every minute. Customer turnover, or churn, is expensive – only companies that take a brute-force approach to the Web can handle very much of it. In making the transition to e-business, a company must do everything it can to increase loyalty and decrease customer churn.

Some companies rely heavily on branding as a loyalty tool. But in Internet time, brands are less sticky than you might think. It takes more effort to maintain an online brand than an offline brand. The noise factor is high. Customers can't have 50 relationships with 50 companies. They seek simplicity, not complications.

Some companies talk about stickiness – the ability of a site to attract visitors and hold their attention online. But stickiness by itself may not be worth much. If thousands of teenagers are chatting in your company's chat room, but you can't sell them anything, it doesn't matter how "stuck" they are. If your company's Super Bowl ad drives millions of people to your company's web site, make sure you don't have to wait a year before they all come back.

Online, customers are more interested in a company's business propositions than its brand. Suppose you offer products at a 40 percent discount off the suggested retail

> **BRANDING**
>
> In the customer-led future, company brands will weaken significantly. Because companies will be pulled apart by their customer divisions, they should plan on restructuring and promoting product or even division brands.
>
> For example, Hertz Rental Cars has three customer groups: purchasers, business accounts, and vacationers. Now that the company has had a site for several years and established itself online, the company would do well to create a separate site and brand for each group.

price. Online customers know that suggested retail price doesn't mean much anymore. They'll buy your product or use your service until they find a company offering a 50 percent discount. If that happens, your company brand won't save you. When all factors are equal, customers will flow quickly toward a better business proposition.

Many online purchasers now use a comparison engine to find the best deal on a given item. Companies increasingly use real-time pricing and auctions to get a competitive advantage. As we'll see in later chapters, customers can now auction demand as easily as suppliers can auction goods and services.

Customers are starting to use agents (software that acts on their behalf) and wallets (web software that keeps track of credit cards, passwords, account information, and the like) to help shield them from the mechanics of a transaction at your site. All of which means customers may not even see your company's web site when they do business with your company online – or decide not to.

Fortunately, there is something customers are more loyal to than your brand or your business proposition – people. More specifically, people they can relate to. So if you sell mountain bikes, invite mountain bike fanatics to your site to talk about the latest models and accessories. Engaged customers will be less susceptible to offers from competitors because they'll call your site home. We'll see many more examples in coming chapters.

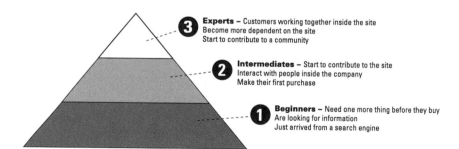

The customer-loyalty pyramid is deceptively simple. Few online companies expend the effort to guide customers on the path from beginners (not loyal) to experts (very loyal). As your company starts to relate to its customers as individuals, it draws them to the top of the customer-loyalty pyramid.

Loyalty isn't customer traffic. Loyalty is customer retention. You can't force customer loyalty by shoving more customers onto your site. You must pull them through your site by giving them a chance to get what they want most. If the business proposition is attractive and new customers feel at home on your site, you'll find the intermediates and experts will turn into your sales force. They will become walking billboards for your business. As customers work their way up the loyalty pyramid, your company must reward them at each step.

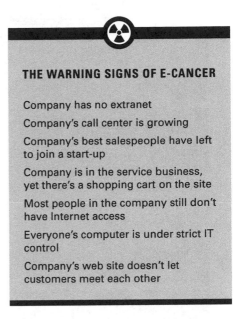

Eventually, they will bond with each other and your employees, giving you the stickiness you're really looking for. (In the next chapter, we'll look at each of the three customer tiers in detail.)

From Management-Led to Customer-Led

Recall that a management-led company has mechanisms for listening to customers yet still has divisions based on products and service offerings. On the other hand, a customer-led company focuses on groups of people, rather than types of products or services.

So far, I've focused on a shift in operations: expanding your company's e-commerce effort so that it is more inclusive. If your company is management-led – and almost all companies today are – you have a choice. You can expand your business operationally toward e-business, or you can change your company culturally to one that is customer-led. In the following table, a shift down the columns is cultural, while a shift across to the right is operational.

Many successful Internet start-ups are in the upper-right corner. Like their offline counterparts, they often have a management-led culture. If your company is management-led, a shift to the right – from commerce

		Commerce	E-Commerce	E-Business
MANAGEMENT-LED COMPANY	**Customer Experience**	Brochures, brochureware web sites, marketing campaigns, dealers, intermediaries	Automated sales and transactions, automated customer service, affiliate programs, banners	Great content, customer service, and resources online; Editors and content-providers work tirelessly
	Employee Experience	Tools and techniques for predicting what people will want. Call center. Cashiers, clerks, and tellers	Slaves to the machine: e-commerce tools rule	Intranet, employee university, extranet, knowledge management system
CUSTOMER-LED COMPANY	**Customer Experience**	Outbound research, 800 number for feedback, going where customers are, listening, engaging customers on their turf	Customers contribute most of content on site. Customers are rewarded for bringing in their friends	Customers provide most of the content, customer service, and resources to each other; Facilitators help customers help themselves
	Employee Experience	Focus groups, customer advisors, customer owners	Chief Net Officer and e-commerce group rely on customer-group hosts to help customers – track down e-mails, answer requests, etc.	All employees touch customers, build their own intranet, train each other, share knowledge willingly

to e-commerce to e-business – is tempting because it's easier to expand a business operationally than to change its culture. But I ask you to postpone that decision until you've finished reading this book.

Changing from a management-led company to a customer-led company – realigning internally and externally the way Microsoft has – is more difficult but much more important to your company's long-term success. It's a cultural shift that naturally flows toward e-business. (In Part 4, you'll see several examples of companies in the lower-right corner of this chart.)

Futurizing

Misguided assumptions about e-customers have been the demise of many commercial web efforts. In a *Business Week* interview, Microsoft president Steve Ballmer said, "Whenever you feel lost, ask your customers." In e-business, the customers are in charge, whether you think they are or not. Fail to make the decisions I describe and they will be made for you.

There is only one way to do e-business: fully committed. Everyone in the company must be dedicated to the effort. You can't have ten people for every thousand working on it. You can't delegate it. You have to encourage everyone to jump into the water and support them in teaching each other to swim. I'm asking you to make the biggest cultural change in your company's history. Fortunately, the next chapter will show that you don't have to do it alone. Your customers will be more than happy to do more than their share of the work.

The E-Customer

CHAPTER 4

IN 1858, HERBERT COLERIDGE asked the English populace to help him assemble the material for a new dictionary. He ran newspaper ads asking for words and their first uses in print. He expected to receive 100,000 slips of paper and estimated he would complete the project in two years. Sixty years later, after more than *6 million* slips of paper had been submitted, the first edition of the *Oxford English Dictionary* was published. Coleridge didn't live long enough to see the masterwork, but most of the slips of paper came from unpaid volunteers, as he had envisioned.

Were Coleridge alive today, he could have compiled his dictionary in months, not years, with the help of e-customers. As I'll show in this chapter, e-customers are an exponential source of energy without equal in the offline world.

People Like to Participate

When I was designing the cover for this book, I put several designs on my server. I sent e-mail messages to my business friends and asked them to visit a secret web page and vote for their favorite candidate. These are busy people. I expected about 20 percent of them to respond. To my great surprise, within two days I'd heard from at least 60 percent of them, some of them several times. One person even wrote to say he'd slept on it and had changed his mind! I heard strong opinions – often backed up by a paragraph of reasoning or a complete commentary on each design. Over the next three weeks, apologetic e-mail continued to trickle in from people who had been out of town. In the end, the response rate was better than 90 percent.

Everyone loves to express his opinion. Aint-it-cool-news.com is a Hollywood scoop site run by Harry Jay Knowles, a film buff who operates out of his bedroom in an Austin, Texas, suburb. Every day, he infuriates studio executives by publishing rumors, gossip, and early movie reviews on his for-profit site. He gets tips, scripts, and inside information from more than 1,700 volunteers, most of whom live and work in Los Angeles.

The Globe, a public-private partnership funded by the u.s. government, brings scientists and students together to study the environment. Through a web site, a database, and a teacher-training program, more than 50,000 students and teachers from over 6,500 schools in more than 80 countries now collect millions of measurements every year on water, soil, atmosphere, and climate. Earth scientists mine these data to study environmental trends.

At Cornell University's Laboratory of Ornithology, more than 13,000 people participate in the annual Feederwatch program. Anyone with a bird feeder can sign up, purchase an inexpensive information kit, and submit bird counts via the Feederwatch web page. Researchers use the data to study long-term migration trends of various species.

When iVillage, Inc. began in the summer of 1995, the founders relied on a handful of volunteers to start the discussions around issues of interest to women. Today, The Women's Network calls on about 1,300 volunteers nationwide to serve as moderators for online discussions.

People Like to See Themselves

When you see a group portrait, whose face do you look for first? When you scan a page of stock prices, which stocks do you look for first? On the Web, people's desire to see themselves is more than just vanity. People naturally prefer to place themselves as anchors in their own frame of reference.

Cyndi Howells, working out of her home outside Seattle, runs CyndisList.com. It's arguably the largest directory of genealogy links online, with more than 41,000 sites linked, categorized, and cross-referenced, in more than 100 categories. Perhaps the largest such site is Familysearch.org, the official genealogy site of the Mormon Church.

When the site opened in May 1999, it received more than 600,000 visitors on the first day and 1 million on the second. These people were eager to use the database, not because they wanted to learn about their relatives per se, but because they wanted to learn what their relatives could teach them about themselves.

At About.com, more than 600 semiprofessional "guides" work out of their homes and offices in 20 countries, forming a people-based directory. Guides, who have their names and photos posted at the top of their chosen categories, write editorials, maintain links, and respond to customer feedback. Most guides put in 10 to 20 hours per week and receive a 30 percent share of the ad revenue sold on their site sections. Many who operate areas with heavy traffic have converted their hobbies into full-time jobs. When About.com went public, the company set aside a large amount of stock for guides. Yet for most guides, being recognized as an expert is the main compensation.

People also see themselves in others. On a site that focuses on prenatal care, whom do you think visitors would rather see on the first few pages: pregnant women or expert doctors? Wouldn't it be better to have actual patients tell people about the doctors than to have the doctors appraising themselves? Wouldn't it be better to let visitors contact people who have been through what they are about to go through? That relationship is the catalyst that starts the conversation that turns into the next market opportunity.

Where does all that energy come from? It's natural. Rare in Old World business, personal energy is one of the biggest power sources on the Web. More than 10 million people have personal home pages online, each of which takes time and money to build and maintain. People devote resources to their personal home pages because 1) they want to express themselves and 2) they want to meet other kindred spirits. With the principles of self-expression, participation, and identification in mind, let's look at the three stages of customer participation to learn how to harness that energy.

Beginners, Intermediates, and Experts

Every business has new, existing, and preferred customers. For some reason, many companies fail to grasp the importance of addressing those groups differently online. Remember the customer loyalty pyramid in Chapter 3? Beginner, intermediate, and expert customers correspond exactly to the tiers of the loyalty pyramid.

Beginners are not necessarily new online customers, but they're new to your site. For example, although I'm a seasoned investor, the first time I logged on to Schwab.com I was a beginner. The first time I made an error trying to execute a trade, I realized the site is set up for experts, not beginners. The second time I made an error executing a trade, I realized this company has a hard time putting itself in the customer's shoes.

Beginners always start by browsing. Remember your first visit to Yahoo!? Rather than using a search feature, you browsed the categories, right? That's what a newcomer to a town, school, gym, or job would do, wander around to get a feel for the place. A beginner is tentative, wondering if he should click the back button just one more time to try another link in the category. A beginner's allegiance is likely to be with the directory that brought him to your web site, not to your company.

Most beginners don't give a company much time to make an impression. In a split second, they decide whether the site has something to offer them or not. If they decide to stay, they need some direction. Contrary to popular belief, security is not their number-one concern. Comfort is. As we'll see in later chapters, making a beginner's first experience engaging and comfortable is harder and more important than it seems.

Intermediates are online customers who've crossed a certain psychological threshold. They've done business with a company once and have decided to return. At that point, the intermediate customer expects the site to reveal more than she saw on her first visit, and she may want to participate more as well. She might want to contribute a product review or join a discussion group. Although submitting a review may be routine for an expert customer, the first time an intermediate customer reviews a product, she will probably feel a sense of accomplishment and even empowerment. How many sites make a customer's first online contribution a special experience?

If markets are conversations, who is going to start the conversation? A company can try to engage an intermediate customer one-on-one, but it might not get very far. Intermediates are often shy at first. But give an intermediate a chance to listen to an ongoing dialogue, and eventually he'll be drawn in by something he cares about and start to contribute. When intermediates explore your company site, will they be able to find people they can relate to – both customers and employees – and have the opportunity to join a discussion?

Intermediates want a site to adapt to *them*. They want it to respond to their preferences and still give them the opportunity to explore new areas. They may want to be notified of any changes by e-mail, rather than having to return to the site. They are willing to invest the time it takes to understand everything a site has to offer, especially if they have some idea that the rewards are worth the effort. As an intermediate becomes more advanced, she starts throwing more switches, looks for places to contribute, and begins to integrate the site into her daily or weekly routine.

Experts come in three flavors: junkies, residents, and guides. Although they behave differently, they are your most important customers. They have more leverage and expect more attention than those below them.

A junkie prefers searching to browsing. He knows what he wants, and he counts the seconds until he gets it. He likes to come in, buy a sledgehammer or order a cake, and get out. He wants to check his stocks, the weather, or the traffic. He's often an information or gadget addict. He wants his virtual "dashboard" set up just the way he likes it.

A resident, on the other hand, is just the opposite. She can spend hours at a site. A resident spends most of her time in conversations or activities with other residents. She is more likely to be an introvert than an extravert. She gravitates toward others with common interests. Perhaps shy at first, she becomes bolder – even outspoken – once she has found a place she can relax and feel at home. Residents respond to humor. They support others. They empathize, send birthday greetings, write haikus, and answer questions. They love to answer questions. They love to be recognized. They are usually eager to log on and can often be found online on a Friday night. Residents usually give to a community what they themselves want most in return.

A guide (volunteer, community leader, monitor) is usually a resident who has taken on a degree of responsibility within an online community.

She provides the adult supervision for the community, carrying on in the same helpful ways she did as a resident but in a more formal capacity. A newcomer to the site can always ask a guide for help.

Guides may put in as much as 50 hours a week. They're almost uniformly not interested in being paid for their work. They may not mind an honorarium or a gift but would be suspicious of any site that paid its guides well. Guides owe their allegiance to their flocks, not to the barons or lords who own the pastures. They enjoy certain benefits, but they find their highest reward in the simple act of helping others. They love being recognized. A good guide is always willing to take on an apprentice and share responsibility.

A guide who accepts an offer to work full-time becomes a host. A host is generally still more loyal to her flock than to the company that hired her. A host may become a customer champion within the company, deepening the customer-employee relationship and increasing customer loyalty. Or she may rebel against company policies and fight politics all the way out the door. Everything hinges on the host's employment contract (both written and verbal) and the company's ability to keep that contract.

These visitor categories are not a measure of familiarity but of participation. Beginners may come to a company's site repeatedly and remain beginners. Beginners become intermediates when they accomplish

AOL – A CASE STUDY

By 1997, America Online, the world's largest Internet service provider, had more than 10,000 community leaders and other volunteers helping keep its 10 million customers happy. The company paid these volunteers, some of whom worked up to 40 hours a week, by giving them free memberships.

Not surprisingly, some volunteers performed better than others. When the company had problems with a few of them, it circulated a set of guidelines for interacting with customers. Many guides, who had a stronger allegiance to the customers than to the company, felt the new rules were vague and inappropriate. When AOL tried to enforce the rules, a firestorm erupted. Several guides were "fired," and several more left.

In 1998, the disgruntled volunteers set up several web sites describing their censorship by AOL. They submitted documents to the Department of Labor claiming that AOL had treated them as employees yet hadn't paid them. The former community leaders have raised their voices in the press as well. These people, who helped build AOL into the largest online community, have enough resources and clout with the membership to cause the company a great deal of pain.

something on the site. Companies also mistakenly believe that visitors who use a site's power tools must be experts. True experts emerge from the ranks only on the merits of their contributions.

E-Communities

At every level of participation – beginner, intermediate, and expert – visitors to your site may want to form communities. Online communities form both horizontally and vertically.

A horizontal community is made up of site visitors who share a common circumstance or attribute (demographic). All people named Bob are potential members of a Bob community. Teens, families, seniors, teachers, parents, people with Crohn's disease, and Californians are all candidates for membership in horizontal communities.

Most horizontal communities are not very strong. It's hard to relate to others solely on the basis of demographics. If you have a site for families, don't expect the community phenomenon to take off like a rocket. A person who is grieving doesn't necessarily want to join a group of others who are grieving.

A vertical community brings people together through a common interest (orchids, history), a shared activity (ballooning, swing dancing), issues or shared values (gun control, saving old-growth forests). These are psychographics. Clubs and professional societies are good examples of vertical communities. Mothers Against Drunk Driving (MADD) and Planned Parenthood are large vertical communities containing many active subcommunities.

Vertical communities tend to be smaller, more concentrated, and more likely to generate solid bonds among members. A site for archery enthusiasts will tap into a source of energy hard to turn off. Quilters will find each other and a way to share their work. And orchid fanciers will link to each other's sites.

You can see the difference between horizontal and vertical communities by comparing a gym and a country club. The people who frequent a particular gym probably wouldn't care to be stuck on a deserted island together for a month. Why? Because, although the gym members share a common interest in fitness, they probably chose their gym on the basis of location or cost. On the other hand, the people who belong to a country club like to use the facilities, of course, but they also subscribe to the values of the club. They are willing to travel across town to be in the right one. Those shared values give the club members a good chance of getting along on a deserted island.

Vertical communities often form web rings – sets of successive links that point to other sites with similar interests or values. Rings are an informal way of creating communities and subcommunities. Vertical communities are almost always willing and eager to build their own community centers online from scratch.

Members of vertical communities demonstrate much more loyalty toward each other and their respective communities than members of horizontal communities do. As people work their way into a vertical community, they form tight bonds with the existing members. At the core of the community are the elders. Tremendously influential, the elders guide and make key decisions for the community.

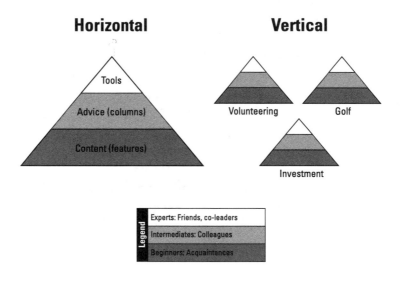

Each customer group and level of participation within that group has unique needs and attributes. Visitors to horizontal sites usually have tangible needs. Visitors to vertical sites seek community.

For tighter bonds to form within horizontal communities, visitors must have the opportunity to break into smaller subgroups. Rather than breaking up a community of teenagers into demographic subcategories such as age or hometown (further horizontal categorization), it's best to encourage them to form vertical communities around interests such as music and sports.

You can't turn a gym into a country club. You can't force communities to appear on your company's site. You can only provide a friendly environment and the conditions for them to sprout.

Owning Our Words

There is no need to censor expression in an online community. Given the appropriate tools, communities are self-policing. Let's look more closely at the movie studio site example from Chapter 1. Suppose a studio builds a site around several of its movies, and the company wants to be sensitive to people who are offended by certain kinds of language. Rather than dictating what's appropriate and what isn't, the studio should set up different discussion areas, based on a rating system that informs people of what to expect. The system has categories from one to five, with one being "appropriate for young children" and five being "anything goes, you're on your own here." Visitors to the site will be able to choose the discussion area where they feel most at home. The studio can also start a beginner forum, where newcomers can learn the conventions and ask questions before venturing into the discussion groups on their own.

Every community has troublemakers. It's easier for people to cause trouble online than in person, because they don't have to say things to people's faces. Most communities have a message posted on the welcome screen that reads, "YOU OWN YOUR OWN WORDS." That means visitors and members of the communities are responsible for what they say and should think twice before saying anything negative.

Troublemakers, who make up only a tiny percentage of most communities, are usually quite vocal. If a troublemaker doesn't get the attention he seeks, he usually storms off to another group. Experienced elders send e-mail to the community members privately, asking them to refrain from taking the troublemaker's bait and simply wait for him to leave.

The Open Source Movement

It might seem foolish to suggest that your customers would actually build the products you sell them, but e-customers are often more than happy to do just that. E-customers are even willing to help contribute to the services they pay for! The Open Source movement deserves special mention as an example of self-governing communities that have been tremendously successful. The Web itself is the product of people pitching in to write public-domain software.

Open Source is the name for software that anyone can freely use, alter, and distribute. Hundreds of people – e-customers! – often contribute to a single program, testing it, fixing problems, and returning it for others to improve. Volunteer programmers sometimes earn compensation through the sale of related books and programming contracts.

Most of the world's e-mail relies on a program called Sendmail, written by Eric Allman in the 1970s and maintained by a small group of volunteers. The Apache web server, which began as a volunteer project in the early 1990s and is still maintained by a core group of programmers, continues to dominate the server market. Commercial competitors like Netscape and IBM have failed to topple this volunteer category killer. In 1998, IBM conceded defeat. The computing giant now offers and supports Apache as part of its product line.

The Linux operating system, the current poster child of the Open Source movement, is the first large-scale operating system built and maintained by volunteers. It is freely available, with over 8 million installations worldwide. Several companies have sprung up to help people modify, install, test, troubleshoot, upgrade the source code, and add new functionality.

Most people involved in the Open Source movement participate for philosophical reasons. They don't think anyone should profit from the infrastructure of the Internet. They want the Web to remain democratic and affordable for all. They vow to keep dominant companies from imposing their standards on the Internet as a whole.

In 1998, Netscape purchased a user-contributed set of links called Newhoo. Now dubbed Netscape Open Directory, this site has more than 10,000 contributing "editors." The site is similar in structure to Yahoo!, but at any time, anyone can sign up to extend a category. If you are an expert at something, you can start a new subcategory and maintain all your links under that subject, including annotations. Category editors are welcome to help each other and to combine their categories or grow new ones. This network grows organically rather than in the hands of program and product managers. Useful links stay in; unused links tend to be removed. As with Netscape's browser, which now has hundreds of volunteers working to add features, anyone can add or build on Netscape Open Directory.

Many companies, realizing that customers are often willing to modify products to suit their own needs, are joining the Open Source movement. Customers who don't want to wait for a company to release new features simply develop the features on their own. Hundreds of previously proprietary products are being exposed to the unknown adventure of community modification. You might think product stability, reliability, and support would be impossible in such an environment, but that isn't so. Like any common resource, Open Source software evolves according to the needs of its users, who have a vested interest in maintaining its quality, security, and continuity.

A NOTE TO AD AGENCIES

Most companies that hire ad agencies to build web sites don't make that mistake a second time. Customers aren't interested in sending e-mail to a company's ad agency. The ad agency business model, based on repeated placement of mass-market ads, doesn't let the agencies "get" the Web. Their culture doesn't let them get it. And their executives don't let them get it. Ad agencies are used to creating pitches, campaigns, closed messages, lifestyle imagery, scripted dialogues, and the hard sell. They can do image work, build brands, and measure recall, but they have no idea how to confront a medium in which the product or service can be customized, priced, and delivered on demand.

I encourage traditional ad agencies to learn what the online agencies have learned – that it takes relearning, commitment, and partner- ship to be successful in the New World. There aren't any big awards in cyberspace, only the sound of customers paying for goods and services. Imagine what would happen if people could vote with their TV remotes, saying "I never want to see that ad again" or "Do you realize I'm not in the market for feminine protection?" or "Yes, my dog is in his senior years, tell me more."

Ad agencies must learn how to listen to and address individuals. Everyone in an ad agency should spend more time in e-communities listening, participating, and learning. The more time they can spend with – and as – e-customers, the better they will understand how to serve their clients.

Futurizing

McCann-Erickson/A&L, an ad agency in San Francisco that understands e-customers, talks about the difference between "leaning back" and "leaning forward." Watching TV, we're relaxed, passive. Surfing the Web, we're active and involved – going places, meeting people, and doing things.

Perhaps the most important lesson to learn is that the e-customer can't be pushed. You can't push people up to the top of your loyalty pyramid. You can only give them the means to get there themselves. You must be willing to open the doors and see what happens. Only by letting go of old ways can you and your company participate in the discussion.

We've seen the seven major traps companies fall into when they go online. Now that you understand the value of talking to your customers and listening to them even more, the next chapter will focus on the quality of that dialogue.

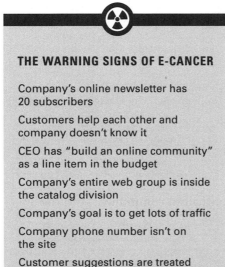

THE WARNING SIGNS OF E-CANCER

Company's online newsletter has 20 subscribers

Customers help each other and company doesn't know it

CEO has "build an online community" as a line item in the budget

Company's entire web group is inside the catalog division

Company's goal is to get lots of traffic

Company phone number isn't on the site

Customer suggestions are treated as complaints

The Truth Economy

CHAPTER 5

ON JANUARY 17, 1998, MATT DRUDGE, a former CBS gift shop clerk, reported in his Internet newsletter, the Drudge Report, that *Newsweek* had decided not to publish a well-researched story on an alleged affair between President Clinton and a White House intern. Just 24 hours later, Clinton learned that his life was about to change. On December 19, 1998, he became the second president in U.S. history to be impeached by Congress.

A lot changed that day in January. Matt Drudge, whose daily online readership soon exceeded the weekly readership of *Time* magazine, became a force of change within the journalism community. And the Internet took its place as a powerful new tool for journalists across the world. As Drudge put it:

> We have entered an era vibrating with the din of small voices. Every citizen can be a reporter, can take on the powers that be. The difference between the Internet, television and radio, magazines, newspapers is the two-way communication. The Net gives as much voice to a 13-year-old computer geek – as to a CEO or Speaker of the House. We all become equal.

Why did *Newsweek* hesitate to publish the story? Because the editors and publisher had a lot to lose if they were wrong. Drudge, who prior to the event had been publishing his report to a very limited audience, had nothing to lose. For the first time in history, individuals have access to what has become a mainstream distribution mechanism, and they are starting to distribute the truth in ways that bring new meaning to the word "underdog."

Truth Is the Great Equalizer

Go to your favorite online directory and try to find a cigarette company marketing to customers online. You won't find one. Why? Because for companies with something to hide, a web site is a liability. Online, consumers take on a different personality: Given the opportunity to be in touch with a company, they ask hard questions; they expect answers.

Now go to Dawn-dish.com, the web site for Procter & Gamble's Dawn dishwashing liquid. In addition to giving tips on using the product, the site includes a list of frequently asked questions (FAQ). One question is whether suds (soap bubbles) help clean dishes. The answer:

> The main reason we make sudsing liquids is that people expect sudsy dish water. Suds also help keep the water temperature warm. (And, they do a great job of hiding the dirty dish water!)

This candid admission is a small step, but a brave one. This web team is trying hard to break the grip of a corporate culture that insists on putting a sparkling clean shine on every message it sends. Just to show you how progressive and honest the team is, the Dawn-dish FAQ ends with the following message:

> If you are under 13, please do not send us an e-mail because our lawyers tell us we cannot answer your message.

Although corporate lawyers will try almost anything to prevent lawsuits, 12-year-olds with questions about dishwashing liquid know how to get around this kind of hurdle. Rather than dealing with issues of privacy and parental concern, lawyers make rules that no sane person would follow or enforce. This is not an isolated case – at the Häagen-Dazs site the minimum allowable age for an e-mail is 16.

Go online and visit some consumer product sites. Many companies – especially large ones – are afraid to get too deep into issues that make them uncomfortable. No one in the company wants to be responsible for attracting any media attention. Most of their sites are hermetically sealed – they don't link to any sites on the Web outside their own domains. They have recipes, games, prizes, experts – everything but discussion. Unfortunately, many executives are satisfied with that approach. They think customers are buying it, but they are wrong.

All service companies feature case studies on their web sites. Yet nothing ever goes wrong in those scenarios! Do companies think customers believe that? Prospective customers know there may be problems. If they're smart, they will have called the company's references and discussed actual and potential problems. Everyone knows projects don't go perfectly. The critical question is: How does the company deal with problems? To publish a series of perfect case studies is to tell prospective customers to go somewhere else if they want to be treated as grown-ups.

> **MURPHY'S WEB LAWS**
>
> 1 If you're not willing to talk about an issue, your customers will take it on as a crusade
>
> 2 The more you ignore them, the stronger they get
>
> 3 If there is one person on earth from whom you want to hide a certain web page, that person will see the page within 24 hours of your putting it online
>
> 4 If you have something to hide, you are in trouble whether you put it online or not

Online, you have no choice but to tell the truth about your product or service. This is the basis of what I call the truth economy. People get suspicious when they see a hermetically sealed site. Your company's site is only one click of the back button away from a well-filtered list of competitors who will be happy to welcome your customers. In the truth economy, honest, open companies prosper; companies with something to hide don't.

Truth Is a Double-Edged Sword

In the truth economy, you must track your most disenchanted customers as closely as you track your most loyal ones. Yahoo! has a list of links to what it calls consumer-opinion sites. These independent sites are the handiwork of everyone from boycott organizers to consumer watchdogs to unhappy customers. Most major corporations, and many small ones, must now deal with one or more of these sites. They often contain detailed accounts of customers who feel mistreated and unheard. Many consumer-opinion sites are little more than amateur rants, put up in a huff and then abandoned. But others are more organized. There are boycott sites and anti-boycott sites. Some sites publish internal company memos and e-mail, hoping to shame the companies into changing their ways.

Consumer advocacy has much more leverage online than it does in the world of traditional mass media. At Untied.com, Jeremy Cooperstock runs a web site for customers and employees who wish to air their grievances against the airline. Cooperstock collects hundreds of complaints, tracks their progress, and displays the number of responses from United (as of August 11th, 1999, he had recieved 8 responses to 732 complaints). He publishes the stories of employees who have been fired or have quit, and he gives the company every chance to explain itself or make things right.

Then there's McSpotlight.org. This vast online anti-McDonald's campaign contains thousands of searchable documents, printable leaflets, a detailed account of a famous lawsuit in England, links to all kinds of anti-McDonald's resources, and even a guided tour of the McDonald's site, explaining where the company gets its "facts" and publicizing complaints of employees. McSpotlight.org is maintained by the McInformation Network, an independent group of volunteers from 22 countries.

Less credible sites, from Aspartamekills.com to Starbucked.com, may not be balanced, fair, or particularly professional, but they do get visitors. If people are willing to put that much energy into their anti-corporation sites, you know those companies could put more effort into prevention.

Recall the customer-loyalty pyramid from Chapter 3. Although most people will have neutral or positive experiences with your company, it's important to recognize that the pyramid has two negative levels as well. At the first negative level are customers who have experienced correctable problems. Because no company is perfect, your company will always have some customers at that level. Once they are there, however, they need special attention. The company should develop tools to track those individuals and keep them from turning into nightmares. Every company has a few nightmares. Some are worse than others. But if they make national news and could have been prevented, chances are the company hasn't spent enough time listening.

You can spend an entire day browsing Yahoo!'s consumer-opinion section, and you should. Some of the stories will amaze you. Because customers can find each other easily on the Web, they can quickly reinforce each other's opinions. Your company may already be the subject of

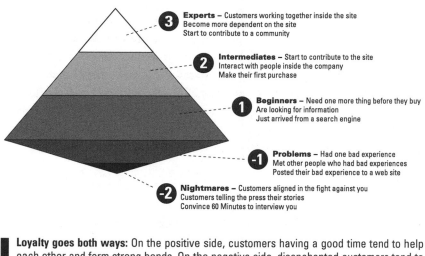

Experts – Customers working together inside the site
Become more dependent on the site
Start to contribute to a community

Intermediates – Start to contribute to the site
Interact with people inside the company
Make their first purchase

Beginners – Need one more thing before they buy
Are looking for information
Just arrived from a search engine

Problems – Had one bad experience
Met other people who had bad experiences
Posted their bad experience to a web site

Nightmares – Customers aligned in the fight against you
Customers telling the press their stories
Convince 60 Minutes to interview you

Loyalty goes both ways: On the positive side, customers having a good time tend to help each other and form strong bonds. On the negative side, disenchanted customers tend to help each other and form strong bonds.

discussion boards at several sites. Find out. If it isn't, that doesn't mean you don't have any worries – tomorrow could be the day a dissatisfied customer lets the world know.

Are your disgruntled employees talking with each other online? With people dedicating themselves to exposing employee abuse at companies large and small, it's quite possible that someone you interview in the near future could ask you some pretty sticky questions.

Truth Flattens Hierarchies

For the last 20 years, management books have told managers that companies must become flat – reduce layers of management – and support active teams. All that is merely practice for making the jump to the New World. The World Wide Web is a democracy with no constitution. No one's in charge. It's bigger than any corporation or government. And it works.

Vestiges of planned economies reside in our companies and institutions. Customers and employees in the New World will dismantle those structures the way East and West Germans tore down the Berlin Wall – they will use the truth as their sledgehammer.

Meritocracies will replace hierarchies. An internal labor market in your company will run without any authoritarian control. People will assign themselves to projects. People will collaborate naturally, the way they do on the Web: messily, organically, sometimes inscrutably.

In the New World, hierarchies are death traps. As the Cluetrain.com Manifesto says: "Hyperlinks subvert hierarchy." In the coming chapters, you'll see that when people – customers, employees, any group – can easily hook up with each other, authority shifts to the individual. It won't matter how long you've been with the company or what your position is. What will matter is whether you can solve your customer's problem.

Truth Empowers Individuals

Online, size is not an advantage. Truth is. People tend to root for the little guy – and for the truth. Those who try to cover up the facts just manage to draw more attention. E-customers ask difficult questions, and they expect honest answers. Every issue has many facets. Online, customers are just two clicks away from all the facets companies don't want them to see.

In fact, visitors to your company's site may be asking those questions and seeing those facets on your site right now. A free online service at Thirdvoice.com is the Web's answer to introverted, controlled web sites. With Third Voice software installed on their browsers, visitors to your site can say whatever they like. People can gather around your site and hold a freewheeling discussion, leaving your webmaster out of the loop.

The Third Voice software acts as an overlay to any site. Comments stay on the Third Voice server, and people can contribute anonymously. You can use the technology to go to the Third Voice site itself and leave any message you like. Now, anyone who's fed up and doesn't want to take it anymore has a powerful new tool for self-expression.

You realize what this means, don't you? Now that anyone can use such tools to leave comments on your site, you *must* get those tools yourself and monitor the activity. It's an option for surfers, but not for you. Enter carefully – anything you say on the overlay to your own site can and will be used against you.

Individuals – both inside and outside your company – will become more powerful. As you zoom in from markets to groups to individuals, you'll be forced to deal with people on a more personal level. Managers who empower individuals will become more powerful themselves.

In March 1997, Pierre Salinger, former press secretary for President John F. Kennedy and a long-time reporter for ABC NEWS, presented what he called definitive proof that a U.S. Navy missile caused the 1996 crash of TWA flight 800. "The truth must come out," he said. In a 60-plus-page report, Salinger presented documents he had found on the Internet, documents that had convinced him that the missile theory was, in fact, true.

Because Salinger was such a credible source, many people in the traditional news media covered his story. Residents of many online discussion groups, however, had seen the documents and knew they were a hoax. Within 24 hours, Salinger's claims were shot down like a Scud missile in broad daylight.

The Internet is not a collection of documents. It's a network of people. Individuals have power to the extent that they can learn whom to trust. Anyone who mistakes this living, global village for a filing cabinet will find the evidence puzzling indeed.

Truth Is Bigger Than Individuals

The World Wide Web is the tangible, evolving evidence of human expression. It is not too different from a human brain: a messy collection of facts, partial facts, inferences, dreams, connections, relationships, interpretations, misinterpretations, static, and incoherent messages.

Out of this brain grows a sort of collective mind. This e-mind has a collective will and a collective power. It is complex, yet it reveals patterns. It is both out of control and in control. It is made of people, not software. And it is growing stronger every day.

The world's newspapers, taken together, are a primitive expression of the collective mind. When the people elect a president, they are expressing a collective desire. When children choose a particular purple dinosaur toy from among thousands of other toys, they express a common desire. The Internet, as a repository for all the world's information and misinformation, is a billion-way conversation. It is the collective mind of all the people who touch it.

You can't steer the collective mind; you can only follow it. Any company that thinks it can create markets for its products is living in a fantasy world. The Internet works through billions of interconnections that together create a whole bigger than the parts. Think of a school of fish.

When the school swims in one direction, certain fish are in front. When the school turns, other fish become leaders. Yet the group acts as one. How do the fish know what to do? They watch their neighbors and respond quickly. The entire school searches for food, splits up, regroups, responds to threats, corrects course, and arrives at its goal thousands of miles away – all without a designated leader or pre-set chain of command.

The truth economy is a direct result of this higher level of connected consciousness. Before the Internet, it was easier for institutions to keep secrets and control the main channels of information. Technology and demand have combined to split those channels into thousands of smaller streams. People determined to find the truth get their cues from others in seconds.

The truth doesn't cause scandals. People who think they can cover up the truth cause their own scandals. The Internet helps keep honest people honest and makes dishonest people think twice before doing something they'll need to hide.

Futurizing

The truth economy gives Old World companies the opportunity to switch from scripted monologue to open, honest dialogue with their customers. In the New World, companies will admit their faults, listen to their customers, and put their messages in the customer's context. Even if your company doesn't have a web site, the truth economy will find you. Better to embrace it than to hope it goes away.

The Internet isn't all things to all people. It's individual things to individual people. It throws companies and individuals into the same water, where individuals float and companies often don't. Part 1 has been an exploration of the new landscape. The principles you've learned are the tools you will need to breathe, swim, and thrive in the New World. In Part 2, I'll show you how to apply those tools to crafting a New World web strategy.

THE WARNING SIGNS OF E-CANCER

There is a minimum age for sending an e-mail message to the company

Consumer-opinion site aimed against the company makes national news

All site content must go through marketing and legal

CEO wants to buy a web company to raise stock price

Executives all say they "get" the Web

Management thinks employees don't tell each other what their salaries are

People download Thirdvoice just to see what others have to say about the company

PART 2

Practice

*There never was a demand for [corporate] messages, and now it shows, big time.
Because the Internet is a meteor that is smacking the world of business with more
force than the rock that offed the dinosaurs, and it is pushing out a tsunami of demand
like nothing supply has ever seen. Businesses that welcome the swell are in for some
fun surfing. Businesses that don't are going to drown in it.*

– Doc Searls, Cluetrain.com

Introduction

In Part 2, we'll put the New World principles I've introduced to work. This is where the rubber meets the mouse pad and ideas turn into actions. Because almost no companies today are truly customer-led, I'll describe the process of reaching that goal one step at a time.

In Chapter 6, I'll present the digest version of my online boot camp for beginners, intermediates, and experts that will help everyone get up to speed. In the next chapter, I'll take you through six crucial meetings that will help you reorganize your web site. Then we'll turn your company inside out to realign it with its top customer groups. After that, you'll spend some time in the rain forest familiarizing yourself with online ecosystems. And to wrap it up, I'll address the kinds of questions you and your company are bound to have as you make the journey to the New World.

I recommend you skim these chapters first to get a sense of the outcome. Then go back and read the parts you feel are most applicable to your company's transition.

Futurizenow.com, the companion web site, provides more resources and a full Internet boot camp experience. Take advantage of all the tools online, and revisit these chapters often as your company embarks on its customer-led journey.

Management by Surfing Around

CHAPTER 6

DR C. EVERETT KOOP, former surgeon general of the United States, is chairman of Drkoop.com, an e-business that helps people get information on a wide range of health issues. The company went public in 1999. The 82-year-old doctor has three offices, puts in up to 80 hours a week, and manages to find time to answer 10 to 20 e-mail messages a day from people who have submitted questions via the web site.

Dr Koop is a web-savvy executive. He surfs the web, communicates by e-mail, teaches courses using online reference materials, and writes many of the articles for his web site on his personal computer at home. He also conducts live online chat sessions with e-patients around the world. But most important, he understands the value of connecting people with information.

Interviewed for this chapter, Dr Koop told me that a man had come up to him in a restaurant just a few days before and thanked him for saving his mother's life. The man's mother had been in the intensive care unit, where she was being given eight different medications. He wrote down the names of all the medicines, went home, turned on his computer, and went to Drkoop.com. Dr Koop explains, "On the site, we have a Java applet we call the Drug Checker. Did you know that over 100,000 Americans die every year from adverse reactions to drugs or drug combinations? This man entered the names of all these drugs into our Drug Checker and learned that several of them conflicted with each other. He printed the results and showed the page to his mother's doctor, who immediately stopped four of the medications."

Dr Koop noted, "About a third of all Americans take alternative medicines of one kind or another yet don't tell their doctors. Some of these medicines can interfere with their prescription drugs, causing problems doctors can't understand. For that reason, we're going to share our Drug Checker with any other health site on the Web – it's too important to consider a proprietary advantage. I want people to be able to play a much more active role in their health-care decisions. We're going to give people the tools to do that. There's no prescription better than knowledge."

I asked Dr Koop what he thought a web-savvy executive should know. He told me, "Executives should answer e-mail messages from customers who come to their web sites. They should develop a culture around using computers and e-mail to communicate with both customers and employees. For example, if doctors followed up with their patients by e-mail, they could add tremendously to the quality of patient care with only a small investment of time. Executives don't have to know how to use all the available technology, but they must understand what it can do for them. They must be aware of the possibilities and hire people who can help them better understand how to use the Web for the benefit of their customers."

Dr Koop is a firm believer in patients' rights. His dream is to put a medical school for patients online so they can better understand their choices and participate in their health-care decisions. He has a group of people working on electronic patient charts that will give individuals the power to take their medical histories with them anywhere. As we'll see in Part 4, he's on the right track to the customer-led future.

I don't know how familiar you are with the Internet. You may be a beginner, as Dr Koop was in his seventies, or you may be able to send e-mail from your helicopter. This chapter has three main sections – the seven habits of online executives, the digest version of the Internet boot camp, and an important section on the chief net officer.

The Seven Habits of Web-Savvy Executives

Web-savvy executives are rare outside of Silicon Valley, California, and other high-tech clusters. The following seven habits come easily to web-savvy executives. If you find yourself resisting any of them, you'll have a gauge of how well you compare to your high-tech counterparts.

1 Kill the old systems. Many traditional companies use voice mail as a primary means of communication. At Goldman Sachs in New York City, it's not uncommon for a research analyst to get 75 voice mail messages in a day. What's wrong with voice mail? It's slow, retrieval is cumbersome, it can't be skimmed, it's almost impossible to annotate, it doesn't take attachments, it can't be archived easily, and it doesn't tie into any other kind of system. Voice mail may be useful for some things, but switching to e-mail will pay off quickly.

Internet standards – e-mail, web pages, web servers, and so on – are in the public domain. They are fast becoming the dominant platform for intracompany communication. These standards make additions and modification easy. Any company trying to enforce the use of proprietary products will be unable to take advantage of all the new web-based tools. To make the changes, the web-savvy executive must be willing to cause some pain, anticipate the complaints, and try to make the transition as easy as possible.

Many companies are constructing internal "portal" sites that search and categorize all the web sites mushrooming within the company. At General Motors, the internal portal – called Socrates and built at a cost of $2 million over two years – lists more than 500 internal web sites and serves over 400,000 pageviews per day to the 100,000 people in the company who have web browsers on their desks. Through the system, people can manage 401(k) plans, sign up for health-care options, take classes, and look for jobs. The 500,000 manufacturing employees will have access to Socrates through web-based kiosks in their plants. Socrates gets so much traffic that the company plans to sell banner ads to various divisions to help raise money for continued Socrates improvements.

2 Help people help each other. The web-savvy executive builds a supportive work environment where employees help each other move up the learning curve. Anyone who knows anything about the Internet gets a constant stream of beginner e-mail questions and phone calls from relatives, friends, and acquaintances. It's part of life online. As you learn more, you pay your debts by helping others. I can't count all the people – mostly total strangers – who helped me put my first web site together. You should have seen the stupid questions I asked! We've all been there. We all must take the time to give others a hand.

Employees can't help each other if they're not online. Everyone in the company should have Internet access. The web-savvy executive doesn't ask how much it costs to bring high-bandwidth access to every desktop – she asks how soon it can happen.

Employees should have Internet access at home as well as at work. The company should sponsor a group buying program and subsidize a certain percentage of employees' access fees. The more connected your employees are, the more they can help each other.

3 Encourage openness. It should be easy to get any employee's e-mail address from the company intranet or web site. Many companies are afraid to list individual e-mail addresses because they don't want to make it easy for competitors to woo employees away. But the benefits outweigh the risks. If employees enjoy their jobs, defections won't be a problem.

Anyone concerned about privacy or unwanted solicitations can set up an alias – an e-mail address that redirects messages to a person's real address. If the person wants to stop the messages coming to that address, he can simply create a new alias and dump the old one.

The web-savvy executive doesn't restrict Internet access. She knows the Internet is both a tool and a toy. After a few months of exploration, the novelty wears off, and people tend to concentrate on the areas useful to them. Any employee who spends an excessive amount of time playing online probably wasn't getting his job done to begin with. Does your policy let employees look out a window but not at a web site? If so, you might want to rethink that policy. For the employee who does make the Internet his distraction, the Internet isn't the problem.

4 Send a weekly message. A web-savvy manager sends a comprehensive e-mail message to everyone in the company once a week. Like the President's weekly radio address, a weekly e-mail "address" is a reassuring way to keep people informed of the latest developments. The message should cover internal and external issues. It should acknowledge a team for a job well done and mention an achievement that hasn't gotten the attention it deserves. It should always include a timely question. What question has she been asking herself lately? The message should include an answer or response to last week's question and any good e-mail snippets she received during the week. It should also include something personal – a thought, an anecdote, a book review – anything that helps people get to know her a bit better. This level of communication is time consuming, but it's part of the job.

5 Build a knowledge management system. I have a friend who's in a specialty service business. One day he told me on the phone that his company has only one competitor. While we were talking, I went to Yahoo! and found 30 small companies listed in his category. I started going to their web sites and telling him about them. In each case, he hadn't heard of the company. They were small, mostly regional players, but they all should have been on his radar screen.

Arthur Andersen, KPMG, and Cambridge Technology Partners, among others, maintain sophisticated knowledge databases that are accessible to everyone in the company. They also rent the systems to customers who prefer to get their own data directly. One percent of KPMG's global revenues now goes to developing knowledge-management systems.

Many companies make a mess of building knowledge management systems – they either don't finish them or people don't use them. Knowledge management systems make excellent tools and poor environments (we'll explore this further in Chapter 17). It's not a technology problem – it's a cultural one. When the web-savvy executive builds a culture that is empowering rather than threatening, the company's knowledge management system becomes one more area where employees will contribute.

6 Fix the org chart. Management is responsible for the shape of the org chart. If you ask any number of business veterans – from management guru Tom Peters to *Dilbert* cartoonist Scott Adams – they'll tell you hierarchies tend to reinforce established methods and stifle change. The best way to blow up the org chart is to encourage people to ignore it. Companies in the future will be much more like hives, with teams of people working with teams of customers around ever-changing business propositions.

The web-savvy executive knows she is the catalyst for breaking down traditional hierarchies. The first thing she does is make the web group autonomous. According to an Ernst & Young survey of Internet leaders and laggards, leaders have one thing in common: their Internet strategy drives their business strategy. Leaders' web initiatives are not typically run on the corporate level – they operate with their own leadership and their own budgets.

Clayton M. Christensen, author of *The Innovator's Dilemma*, has said that the only way for Old World companies to succeed online is to "set up a completely independent organization and let that organization attack the parent. If you try to address this opportunity from inside the mainstream, the probability of success is zero."

The best way to launch the web group is to hire a CNO – a chief net officer. This position is so important, I'm going to talk about it in more detail at the end of this chapter. The CNO will not only lead the web group, she'll recruit the entire company into it.

7 Institutionalize learning. The web-savvy executive pushes hard to integrate the Internet into everyone's job. She asks her employees to surf the Web at least 20 minutes a day and to work toward several common objectives. They should create a central directory of annotated links useful to the company. They should build their own intranet. They should start their own internal mailing lists and discussion groups. They could even build a carpool and ride-sharing network.

At Dell University, thousands of employees take classes, conduct discussions, collaborate, work on exercises, and extend their education online. The company conducts more than 80 percent of its training online and will soon have 100 percent of its courses online. Their online training costs are half of what the average computer company pays for training, and online training takes fewer hours than traditional classroom training.

Every beginner should have an intermediate who can field his questions, and every intermediate should know an expert he can approach for help. Many companies bring in consultants to set up online training programs. You'll find a set of excellent resources at Futurizenow.com.

The web-savvy executive builds an ongoing Internet education program that helps everyone in the company become an Internet expert. The following "boot camp" is an approach that is both challenging and fun. At Futurizenow.com you'll find a full complement of boot-camp exercises and tutorials.

Boot Camp

You've probably spent quite a bit of time online, but how expert are you? Simple tools, like e-mail, may be easy to use at first, but they are hard to use well. Are you getting the most out of your Internet tools?

The boot camp that follows will help you gauge your level of proficiency. It will challenge you to become more active and more informed. You don't have to become a webmaster, but if you want to achieve web superiority over the competition, understanding this material will help.

Note: This chapter contains only a small part of the boot camp. For the complete experience, go to Futurizenow.com. I only have room here to give you a taste of what is on the site. You'll also find updated links, tips, book recommendations, and references for each subsection at Futurizenow.com.

The boot camp is divided into three zones: beginner, intermediate, and expert. Each zone has three levels. Skim this section until you find your proficiency level, and start there. One way to determine your starting point is by the number of e-mail addresses you have:

Number of e-mail addresses	Level
0 – 1	Beginner
2 – 4	Intermediate
not sure	Expert

At the end of each zone is a quiz. I encourage you to challenge yourself and work all the way to the expert level.

Beginner Zone

Level 1: Setup

Hardware. You must have the proper equipment. You should have a high-bandwidth Internet connection, an 800 by 600 pixel (or higher) monitor that can display thousands of colors, and a way to input digital photographs.

Software. You will need to download several free fonts and plug-ins for your browser. You may want to find someone locally to install all this software for you and to do periodic maintenance on your system. Futurizenow.com will point you to sources online where you can find someone who can help.

Internet service provider. Not all Internet service providers (ISPs) are created equal. Some providers offer limited service or are prone to system failures. Some have poor customer service, some cause you to receive excessive junk e-mail. You'll want a reliable ISP, one that can support your online needs when you travel. Check Futurizenow.com for a list of recommendations.

> ### DVORAK KEY LAYOUT
>
> If you spend much of your day typing, you might consider switching from the QWERTY key layout to the Dvorak key layout, a more efficient assignment of keys than on a standard keyboard. It is available on all Windows-based PCs. For Macintosh and UNIX-based systems, you'll have to download software to customize your machine. The longer you've typed using QWERTY, the longer it takes to retrain yourself.

Touch typing. Many executives can't touch type. It takes about two weeks to master. If you want to speed up the process, you can invest in training software. Voice input is coming, but it's not quite ready for the average busy executive.

Level 2: E-Mail

E-mail. The number of e-mail messages worldwide now dwarfs the number of items sent by post. Most e-mail programs are easy to use, but hard to use well. Can you access your messages from home as well as work? Can you send and receive an attached file? Can your computer read a PDF (portable document format)? Do you know how to send e-mail to 80 people simultaneously? Can you find an e-mail message you deleted a year ago? Do you know if anyone in your company is reading your e-mail before it gets to you?

Misunderstandings. E-mail messages are sometimes frustratingly difficult to interpret. Though you would think that writing would clarify your message, it's quite common to discover that someone has interpreted your message in an unexpected way. What can you do to improve your clarity online?

Mailing lists. A mailing list lets a group of people send e-mail to each other efficiently, so that every person can read every message. It's a way of having a group conversation. When you send a message to a mailing list, everyone gets it. When someone replies, everyone reads the reply. It's not uncommon for a mailing list to have over 100 messages daily, so people often subscribe to the digest version and get all the messages compiled into one large message (that includes a table of contents) at the end of the day. You start out as a lurker – someone who just reads the messages without posting anything. Then, when you feel you're ready, you introduce yourself to the group. Many project managers use mailing lists to keep their project teams updated at all times.

E-MAIL DOS AND DON'TS

ONLY USE ALL CAPS WHEN YOU WANT TO SHOUT. Don't type whole sentences in capital letters. Use them sparingly, to emphasize a word or phrase.

Use asterisks to denote a *whisper,* to simulate italics: I was *hoping* Sofia Coppola would e-mail me.

Don't send long e-mail messages. Construct your messages as single-action items, so your recipients can easily manage them – forward them to others or delete them when they're done. When managing a project, set up a system of naming your messages and numbering your paragraphs so they are easy to sort and search.

Never send unsolicited attachments. They're not only impolite, they clutter people's hard drives. Put the document on the Web or on the intranet where everyone can access it, and send the location instead of the file itself.

Spam. After you get online, you will start to get all kinds of urgent – yet specious – e-mail messages: new anti-Internet bills about to go through Congress, a stock that's about to take off, a boy bitten by a dog, a Neiman Marcus lawsuit against a woman for baking cookies without rights to the recipe, a speech made by Kurt Vonnegut, and so on. The list of Internet frauds, scams, tall tales, nonexistent virus threats, chain letters, and e-pranks is long and sordid. Don't pass them on! Visit Futurizenow.com and test your knowledge of Internet hoaxes.

Level 3: Surfing

Surfing. Surfing the Web is spending time at web sites. You can look for specific things or see what you find as you wander around. An important part of surfing is building up a list of bookmarked sites or pages, so you can easily return to them. If you were picking up a friend at the airport, would you know which site posts the most accurate flight-arrival times? Can you find the best price on a cordless phone? Take an interest of yours (fly fishing, antiques, stocks), and spend time looking for sites that would attract people who share your interest. Initially, try to surf at least 30 minutes a day.

Browsing. You're browsing when you're following links from site to site. It's often undirected, unconscious, and fun. You never know what you'll find. Spend time on your company's site. Browse your competition. Browse companies that aren't in your business but have sites that appeal to your customers. Go to some directories, like Yahoo.com, Directory.netscape.com, Looksmart.com, and About.com, and compare their sections on the same subjects.

Searching. Searching online has several levels of proficiency. Search engines – like Altavista.com,

Inktomi.com, Directhit.com, or Google.com – change over time. Go to different search engines, and type in the same entry. Notice what happens when you use quotation marks or slightly different wording. For example, search for "Tiger Woods" both with and without quotation marks.

Researching. It's easy to make interesting discoveries on the Web. It's much harder to find specific information. You need to know the right places to look. The popular directories and search engines aren't always the answer. Sometimes you need a specialized directory or a mailing list of people who can help. Market research companies like Zonaresearch.com, Forrester.com, Collmktg.com are excellent sources. The people at Jupiter Communications (Jup.com) helped with many facts for this book.

Understanding domains. A URL is a web address, like www.highfive.com (capital letters don't matter in domains or e-mail addresses). A top-level domain is either a type designator (.com, .org, .gov, .edu) or a country designator (.us, .uk, .jp). A second-level domain is the last named part of a URL. In www.Sofia.Coppola-Siegel.com, "Coppola-Siegel" is the second-level domain. Do you know where you can find out which domains are already taken? Do you know how the government plans to allow expansion of the domain-name system?

Intermediate Zone

Level 4: E-Commerce

Technology. Technically speaking, e-commerce is fairly complicated. What's an application server? What's content management? What's load balancing? How do you get good measurements of your site's perform-ance? How secure is your site? Should your company use an instant e-commerce package or build a custom program? You don't have to know all the answers, but you should find someone who does. Ask ten experts how much it costs to build an e-commerce site, and you'll get ten different answers. Consider getting the help of a number of experts who can offer their advice without committing you to impractical and expensive "solutions."

Customer service. Many e-commerce companies don't realize what it takes to provide good service to thousands of customers whose only contact with a company is by modem and mouse. Customer expectations are high. How much of your company's resources should you throw into this area? How do you publish a catalog when you have 10,000 different suppliers? At Futurizenow.com, you'll find various ways to satisfy customers and preempt unnecessary e-mail questions and product returns.

E-marketing. A whole industry has sprung up around e-marketing, the topic du jour at many trade conferences. Companies are confused about the goals and how to achieve them. Buzzwords abound. How much does it cost to acquire new customers? Are auctions a good way to sell your products? How do you encourage repeat purchases? You'll need to teach yourself the basics and start slowly. Let your customers, common sense, and Futurizenow.com be your guides.

Level 5: E-Business

Newsletters. Unlike their paper counterparts, online newsletters are excellent listening tools because people can send feedback immediately. Many are free. Do you subscribe to *Iconocast,* the Iconocast.com newsletter? Do you get the 1to1.com newsletter, *Inside 1to1*? One of my favorites is *Consultations,* the newsletter from Consult.com.au. Want some consistently accurate stock picks? Sign up for the newsletter at Stockwinners.com, which arrives several times daily. Come to Futurizenow.com and sign up for more.

Extranets. If you're an e-business, you probably have an extranet, where customers can get access to their own private account information. Go to your suppliers' extranets and learn how they are set up to work with you. Consider tying your extranet to your customers' intranets. Dell does it; why can't you?

Customer communications. Everyone in your company should spend some time answering customer e-mail. High-level officers should devote at least half an hour per week to this task. The better you understand what your customers are going through, the better you can make their experience.

Level 6: E-Culture

Personal home pages. Millions of personal home pages reside on the Internet. Those pages speak volumes about their owners. Many of your customers virtually live in these online suburbs. The sites are worth exploring, and the people are worth meeting.

Communities. Are you part of an online community? Communities form around every topic you can think of, and several you can't. A friend of mine doubled her net worth last year by investing money with the help of other investors at Techstocks.com. With the proliferation of people trying to manipulate stock prices by touting stocks, that sounded risky. When I asked her how she knew whom to trust, she responded, "If you spend enough time there, you get to know which people know what they're talking about."

Counterculture. Businesses can benefit from watching what teens are doing online. Listen to a band you can't hear on a radio station play list. Read about people who spike trees or try to start their own countries. Learn to build a nuclear bomb or raise a wild duck. Go to events like Burning Man. (If you don't know what Burning Man is, go to Burningman.com and see the future as it's been happening for the last 15 years.) At The Cyberpunk Project, you can meet hackers, crackers, phreaks, netrunners, cypherpunks, otakus, ravers, transhumans, extropians, and even plain old nerds.

Mentoring. Many schools' alumni sites have pages where alumni can sign up to be an e-mail mentor to students. You may never meet the student, but you can answer his or her questions. Don't have time? It'll take 15 minutes a month. Who made a difference to you when you were a student?

Suppose you are a clothing retailer. In the physical world, your store might be in a suburban mall, next to a host of other stores that draw customers past your door. The low-priced outlet stores are a two-hour drive away. On the Web, however, the outlets are often positioned closer to your customers than you are, because they often come up first on search result lists. Many people use online comparison engines to help them find the best prices on goods. There are two types of comparison engines. What are they?

*

Affiliated comparison engines are really sellers' agents. They operate as referral services in the same way 1-800-DENTIST does. Your company pays the comparison engine a monthly subscription fee and a cut of every sale that results from their referrals. They try not to sign up direct competitors. Many surfers are wary of affiliated comparison engines because they list only the suppliers or resellers willing to pay them.

Unaffiliated comparison engines are buyers' agents. They work for shoppers, trying to get them the best deal anywhere online. They send out programs – bots – that visit your site, get as much information as they can, and put the information into their database. The customer usually asks for retailers to be ranked by price, but she could also ask for a listing by location or reputation, for example. While some unaffiliated comparison engines are subscription-based, many now rely on advertising revenues to pay for the service. If one of your competitors has paid a large amount of money for a banner ad, it's likely that a shopper will see the ad before she sees the search result listing your company's name and Internet address.

Expert Zone

Level 7: Group Collaboration

Intranets. Look around your office. Every single document you have in a ring binder or paper file can go on an intranet. Everyone in the company should use and contribute to the intranet. Get your suppliers and partners to take you through theirs. See what they have learned.

Play. There are thousands of games online. Do you play chess, bridge, backgammon, cribbage? Think you're pretty good? There are people online who will be happy to make you look like an amateur and plenty more who just want to meet other gamers who share their passion. They are waiting for you to make the first move. Think you'll skip this part? Not a good idea. Games are probably the most sophisticated form of real-time groupware online. Go out there and get beaten; then go back for more!

Groupware. Software that lets people collaborate on a project is called groupware. The two types of groupware are synchronous (everyone participates simultaneously) and asynchronous (participate on your own schedule). During the production of this book, the Siegel Vision team used an asynchronous service called eRoom to keep in touch with our publisher. It kept everyone up to date, with the right version of every chapter, and with all the comments and changes people wanted to make on any aspect of the book.

Level 8: Large-Scale Collaboration

Agents. Spiders (programs that automatically search the Internet), bots (programs that perform tasks on their owner's behalf), and other electronic agents make large-scale collaborations on the Web possible. Your personal agent, possibly represented by your chosen avatar (a picture and a personality you can design yourself), will make the Internet even more of a global village. In the next ten years, many of the systems you'll learn about at Futurizenow.com will become commonplace.

Community-based filtering. At the Massachusetts Institute of Technology Media Lab, researchers are working on systems that classify people, their conversations, their likes and dislikes, their previous actions, and many other social behaviors. The idea is to use this information to match people with other people, groups, services, and products.

Collaborative filtering is one example. It is based on the concept that if you like a certain ten films, then you probably have a lot in common with others who liked those same films. Collaborative filtering lets you see what else they liked. It's a great way to get suggestions for books, music, and other interests from people who are like you. The more you tell the system, the better it can match you with a subgroup with similar tastes.

Online events. If you think people don't get married online, you're several years behind. Everything from births to deaths to world's fairs have taken place online. There are dozens of events every week. You might even find yourself participating!

Clearinghouses. Clearinghouses are places where buyers and sellers – or their agents – meet. As online clearinghouses increase in popularity, more buying groups will form in real time. Customers will get together in big enough groups to have products custom-made to their specifications. Most online clearinghouses will take a percentage from the transactions they facilitate, some will charge subscription fees, and a few will be advertising-based.

Standards. Standards are essential to any form of large-scale collaboration. For example, people are working hard to establish public standards for all aspects of online commerce, allowing people to specify transactions via software agents. In Part 4, we'll examine the future with online standards in place. Meanwhile, you can explore sites like Commerce.net, Rosettanet.org, Ontology.org, X-act.org, Xmlu.com, and Xmlx.com.

Level 9: Living Online

Variety. Fetishes are in full bloom. Collectors are connected. Hundreds of people have 24-hour cameras in their homes, showing whatever they care to show to anyone who cares to watch. Many people lead full, expressive, alternative lives online, with alternative identities and an entire group of friends they will never meet in person. Dive in, and meet some denizens of the Web.

Identity. Each time a visitor registers at a web site, she gets to pick a new identity. Accountability and privacy issues fuel the identity argument, which I will explore in Chapter 28. There are potential liabilities to revealing personal information, but there are also rewards. Meanwhile, there is the hassle of trying to maintain all your identities. Software coming in the near future will change all that.

Trust. If you found a babysitter online, would you trust him? I once bought a watch from a man who had advertised it at Timezone.com. To prove he was honorable, he sent me an e-mail message of all his previous customers' praise. He could have fabricated that message and taken my money. Instead, he sent me the watch. In 1999, Andrew Tyler of Haddonfield, New Jersey, placed 14 bids for more than $3 million worth of merchandise at online auction house eBay. He won five of the auctions, including a Corvette convertible. The only problem: he was 13 years old and didn't have $1.2 million to pay for his purchases. He apologized, and the items went back on auction.

I hope this offline version of the boot camp has given you a taste of what to expect at Futurizenow.com. Before we move on to mapping out a customer-led strategy, I will finish this chapter with a more in-depth discussion of the chief net officer's role.

The Chief Net Officer

The chief net officer (CNO) is the person who really drives the customer-led approach. She will head the new business unit that will eventually become the New World company. Some people call this person the chief web officer, but the World Wide Web is only part of the larger Internet. E-mail, for example, runs parallel to the Web. So I call this person a chief net officer.

A really good chief net officer will drive the IT and marketing people crazy. By saying "no" to marketing's broadcast approach, the CNO will create a listening culture and begin the dialogue with customers on the company web site. By saying "no" to the channel-marketing people, the CNO helps them understand that the channel now goes both ways. By teaching people how to take advantage of the myriad tools available on the Web, the CNO may infuriate the IT manager, whose job it is to keep all desktops uniformly up to date.

The person best suited to head up your e-commerce effort isn't likely to be the best candidate for chief net officer. E-commerce is technical,

> **QUIZ 3: GATED COMMUNITIES**
>
> A group of teenagers spread around the world wants to start a teen-scene site. They don't want any grown-ups in there, especially their parents, but they do want new teens to join. How can they stop a sneaky parent from signing in as a teen and lurking? (If you don't know what lurking is, you skipped a section you should have read.)
>
> *
>
> The teens must set up a web of trust, in which new teens can enter only if sponsored by a member. Certain teens are designated as guardians. New members with no connections can exchange e-mail with the guardians for a while, to get to know them. After several exchanges, the guardians will be able to tell by the person's "voice" if he or she is a teen or not. Just as parents can tell when a teenager has something to hide, teens online can tell when a grown-up is faking it.

and more tactical than e-business is. The CNO must be a future-oriented risk taker, someone who is comfortable in new territory. She doesn't need a strong technology background, but she does need a strong sense of commitment to customers. She should be an intuitive.

You've probably heard of the Myers-Briggs Type Indicator, a test that categorizes people into one of 16 different personality types according to their positions on four basic scales. The test is based on the work of Swiss psychologist Carl Jung's pioneering work on archetypes. Thousands of companies now use this test to help improve compatibility, communication, and interaction.

One of the scales measures how people make sense of the world. On one end of the scale are the sensors – people who see the facts for what they are. On the other end are the intuitives – those who live in the realm of possibility and imagine what the facts may represent.

Sensors, who make up about 65 percent of the U.S. population, assemble facts in an ordered, sequential way. They use language as a tool and enjoy details. They are very good at procedural tasks. They understand e-commerce. Many executives are sensors. As you might expect, most sensors are anxious about the Internet because they can't see it or feel it. They tend to stay closer to the technical aspects, which they can understand and control.

Intuitives, who make up the other 35 percent of the U.S. population, see the world as a mystery. They revel in its complexities but also take pride in their ability to see beyond the individual elements. They usually can't be bothered with details. They are more likely to go to graduate school, because they are attracted to theoretical endeavors – making inferences and connecting seemingly unconnected things. They use analogies and complex speech patterns. They are usually much more interested in fiction than nonfiction. They have little interest in the past. They prefer to look ahead, to try to see the big picture.

Why have I brought this up? Because your CNO should be an intuitive. She needs sensors working with her, but above all she needs to be comfortable in situations where uncertainty and lack of details would inhibit a sensor's performance. She needs to take chances. She needs to be able to put failures in context. She must stand on general principles and be willing to throw tactical approaches out the window as soon as she sees they aren't working. And she needs the support of her CEO.

The customer-led executive encourages everyone in the company to understand personality types and place this information on an intranet, where everyone can learn more about each other. Each person in the company should have a personal page with information that will help others understand how she is motivated and rewarded. You can even implement team-building systems that use these factors to help people find each other and work together.

The CNO doesn't need to be a biologist, but it would help. A biologist sees the Web as a growth medium, where groups of customers and groups of employees cluster like cells – sticking to each other, creating new organisms, breaking apart again, shedding anything that doesn't stick, and constantly regrouping in response to changes in the environment.

Futurizing

If you're an executive or manager in a customer-led company, your job isn't to see the future. Your job is to create a listening environment and support employees in their conversations with customers. The best way to lead is to roll up your sleeves, grab your mouse, and participate. We can all learn to communicate more effectively. In time, we'll have much more sophisticated tools for both learning and communicating, but the basic principles won't change. The key is finding the balance between people and technology. When properly combined, they can be very powerful.

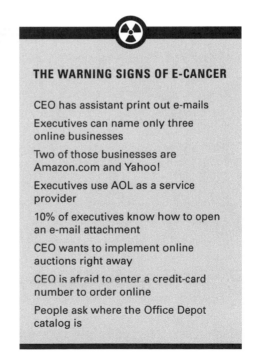

THE WARNING SIGNS OF E-CANCER

CEO has assistant print out e-mails

Executives can name only three online businesses

Two of those businesses are Amazon.com and Yahoo!

Executives use AOL as a service provider

10% of executives know how to open an e-mail attachment

CEO wants to implement online auctions right away

CEO is afraid to enter a credit-card number to order online

People ask where the Office Depot catalog is

The Customer-Led Web Site

CHAPTER 7

THE EXPERIENCE OF THE E-CUSTOMER begins with the company web site. Your customer-led strategy starts with the plans for a customer-led web site – something very few companies have today. Although this chapter talks about the web site, this isn't a web-site makeover. This is your next corporate re-org. In this chapter and the next, we will look at the entire process of transitioning to a customer-led company. The goal: to ask the right questions, get the right answers, and deploy a web strategy that will take your company to the New World.

A customer-led web site has specific areas for specific customer groups. To build the proper support system for a customer-led web site, you will need to conduct six important meetings. It will likely take two to four months to complete your strategy, including setting up the re-org I'll discuss in Chapter 8. Take your time. These are perhaps the most important meetings in your company's history.

Meeting 1	Commitment
Meeting 2	Customer Segmentation
Meeting 3	Active Listening
Meeting 4	Measuring Success
Meeting 5	Customer Modeling
Meeting 6	The Plan

These six meetings will lead to a new company philosophy. A customer-led strategy makes horizontal sites vertical, providing a natural growth medium for communities of interest. The customer-led web site is the first step in widening the communication bottleneck and listening to e-customers.

Meeting 1: Commitment

The company's first web site is an experiment that doesn't work out very well. In a panic to rebuild the site, the web manager promises it'll be ready on a certain date. She doesn't know much about the project, but she knows the launch date. Everything else fills in – backwards – from there, including the budget. The web manager and her team work hard and launch the site on time. The site doesn't get the desired results, and the cycle starts again.

How does this cycle get started? Executives extract promises from program managers, who immediately put their web teams into panic mode as they scramble to stay under arbitrary budgets. Executives don't want to know the details. They just want to stop reading in the press about what everyone else is doing online that they're not. This cycle may not be in progress at your company, but it is the norm. Every nine months, it starts again – with only the name of the program manager changing each time around.

My first advice is not to panic. You must first break the frenetic cycle of "ready, fire, aim." Then take a deep breath and start planning Meeting 1.

Make this first meeting an off-site strategy event for executives and key participants in the new effort. Allow about six weeks to prepare for the meeting and one to two days to conduct it. Top management must make a firm commitment to the effort. You can have the world's greatest web strategy, but it won't work unless managers have a stake in the outcome.

Second, forget about the company's current vision. Most companies – from start-ups to multinationals – have the same online mission statement: "We want to be the authoritative source for products, services, and knowledge in our industry." They have a vision for their site – not their business – and the strategy is just a matter of executing that vision. We've seen how that approach leads to wrong thinking, so leave your thick documents behind and come to this meeting with a clean slate.

Third, declare the chief net officer (CNO) and her team to be independent players – symbolically cut the cord and give them their freedom. Announce the team's new location and initial staff. Give them the budget they need to win their first customer group. Don't underpower this team! The CNO will bring in some New World people who've already been living online for years. Bring in a web researcher who can take the pulse of your customer groups online. Get a business development person with some web experience. Strengthen the team with managers who have good relationships with people in other divisions. The CNO will need a lot of favors, so make sure the team is credible in the eyes of the rest of the company.

In this first meeting, you'll want to see some tangible results. You'll want some answers. Resist those impulses! You've chosen your team. In this meeting, you only need to agree on what questions to ask.

THE WEB TEAM'S CHARTER

The charter doesn't have to be elaborate or unique, just enabling. Consider including the following elements. The web team shall:

Become a conduit for customers to reach employees

Facilitate learning

Have access to the resources of the entire company

Be an independent business unit

Become a catalyst for change

Transfer skills to the entire company over time

Ask the big questions: What would happen if we put every person in our company right on our customer's desktop? Which business areas are we open to exploring, and which are we going to avoid? Which parts of our industry are going online fastest? What changes do we expect from competitors? Which start-ups are going to put us out of business? Which of our competitors would make good partners? Which of our customers would make good partners? Who are our leading-edge customers? Who will our most profitable customers be in three to five years?

In this first meeting, you don't have to narrow the questions down, and you shouldn't try to answer them. Just get the questions on paper – I mean, into your notebook computer, so you can post them on your intranet.

This new e-business unit is different from the web team you have today. Its goal is to develop the customer-led strategy, deploy the site, establish relationships with customers, and then entice the entire company into the new divisions – one for each important group of customers.

At Meeting 1, it's important to note the reactions of upper management. If you suspect the executives aren't behind the transition to e-business, if you suspect they are having a hard enough time with e-commerce, now is the time to pull the red handle and discuss their resistance. These people must be willing to roll up their sleeves and get their hands dirty. You can start with an online training day – the first part of the boot camp – and get them interested in mastering new tools. If they *want* to learn about the Web – if they are still playing e-backgammon with someone in New Delhi at 11 P.M. – you're off to a good start. If online skill-building is not infectious and the top-level people aren't involved, none of this is going to work.

This meeting initiates the biggest transformation in the company's history, but it doesn't have to be the most disruptive. The CNO and CEO must give everyone a clear idea of the changes to come. *Today's web sites mirror their companies; tomorrow's companies will mirror their web sites.* The next several months will test the strength of the foundation you've laid in this meeting.

TWO PERCENT

Jeff Bezos, CEO of Amazon.com, has said on several occasions: "I bet we know two percent of what we'll know ten years from now." His is the right attitude. If everyone in your company works very hard for the next year, you might get up to four percent. Most of the customer-led changes will come in the second half of the coming decade. Your company won't be ready if you don't take careful steps now. A healthy level of paranoia, a bit of humility, and a slow start will be much more profitable in the long run.

Meeting 2: Customer Segmentation

Customer groups are the 800-pound gorillas of the Customer-Led Revolution. You should make every effort to give your top-tier customers whatever they desire. Start at the top of the loyalty pyramid, where you'll find your company's top 50 or more customers. If you work in a consumer company, it may be the top 500 customers. The beautiful thing about the Web is that you can find those people online. They're dying to get in touch with you. Invite as many of them as you can to this meeting. Your goal is to find out what you can do for them, and how you can help them help each other.

If some of your best customers do not have web browsers on their desks, buy them computers, set them up, and turn their default home pages to the personal extranet site you've created for them. Let them see a window into their accounts. No more faxing or sending documents. No more calls to check the status of something or other. Help them become e-customers. Once you get them all online, you can start leveraging their participation into something much more powerful.

Always name this club. Whether they are executive frequent fliers, Gold Club members, or the purple shirt gang, recognize them with a tangible symbol of their status. The people who aren't yet part of this special group need a clear hint of what they will gain if they take that next step toward the top.

Although it sounds counterintuitive, your customers often want to interact and help each other. Suppose you're in the business of leasing cars. Your top 50 customers, who lease many cars a month, would be interested in getting together to exchange information on which cars are best, to find the best rates, and perhaps even to pool their orders. Does that mean lower profits? It means greater customer loyalty, and that may be more important in the long run. If your customers are happy, they'll be walking billboards for your leasing service. They'll bring in their friends and get them to order cars, too. It's almost always beneficial to let your customers talk with each other, and it's a great way of keeping them close to you.

As for the rest of your customers, the question you should ask is: Which individuals are working their way toward top 50 status? It's important to identify both prospective and existing customers who have the highest potential to become members of your top-level club.

As an example, let's say you work at a bank. Banks make money when customers borrow money and pay it back with interest. Your first step would be to divide your customers into some standard groups: consumers, small businesses, medium-sized businesses, large businesses, and institutions.

That's a start, but it's not the whole story. Small businesses that stay small aren't nearly as profitable as small businesses that grow. Large businesses have dedicated specialists who can borrow at the best rates, so they're not as profitable as you might think. Growing businesses might be a better group to focus on. Growing businesses always need money, and they have to keep their eyes on their business, not on the capital markets. Credit cards are the most profitable product the bank offers.

So a long-term relationship with growing businesses, enabling them to use credit cards for as many purchases as possible, will be very profitable in the long run.

What else do growing businesses need? You might interview them and learn they would like a better relationship with a personal banker who can help them anticipate their needs, rather than simply react to financial emergencies. In most cases, these customers are on the leading edge of technology adoption, so they would be interested in being tied into the bank's computers as much as possible. You might learn they need itemized statements detailing each transaction. An online itemized statement would encourage them to use their credit cards even more.

Online, it's tempting to make the largest groups the most important. While the Web gives you considerable leverage, dealing with large numbers of people means dealing with large numbers of special requests. Some studies indicate that at least 20 percent of customers contact a company by e-mail at least once before buying. It's best to start with high-profitability groups that you can pay attention to and refine the system before taking it to a broader audience.

In this second meeting, you should clearly identify at least ten customer groups (15 to 20 is fine). Only after you've named them all should you come back and decide how many you can really satisfy 110 percent. The final number should be between one and four groups, maximum.

In general, count on at least ten full-time staff positions for each customer group. If you're going after four customer groups, you should have at least 40 people in your new online business unit.

Think that's too many? Do 80 percent of what you need to do, and 100 percent of your customers will go someplace else. How many people work at Amazon.com? At last count, more than 4,000. How many people are behind your favorite sites? Probably more than you think. The number one way to miss the boat is to spread your resources so thin that you can't challenge the competition online. With each customer group, strive for outrageous levels of customer satisfaction – don't settle for 99 percent.

It's fine to start with only one customer group, as long as you can give them an experience that makes them want to return for more. Two or three groups is a fine start. This means leaving some 70 to 90 percent of your customers on the sidelines for a while. Most mid-level managers are reluctant to take that path because they can't sell it to top management. That's why it's important to get executive staff to support this approach from day one. Temptations to try to satisfy more of your customers simultaneously will be great, but the goal of a comprehensive web strategy is to go after the secondary and tertiary groups only after the high-priority groups are securely attached to the company via the Internet. Only then can you confidently move on to the remaining customers and properly justify the effort.

The choice of customer groups is a visionary choice. It is perhaps the last visionary choice your company will ever make. Once you've chosen them, your customers will guide you in making strategic decisions. You must take into account demographics, social and economic factors, and the people inside your company. Decide who your most important customer groups are with an eye toward the future. Once you make the decision, your customers will lead you, and you will have to keep up.

> ## WHY SATISFIED CUSTOMERS DEFECT
>
> W. Earl Sasser is one of the gurus of customer service. In co-writing landmark *Harvard Business Review* article with Thomas O Junes, "Why Satisfied Customers Defect," Sasser points out that if you are letting one percent of your core customers slip through the cracks, that one percent has a huge negative multiplier effect. Online, word of mouth travels even more swiftly. One person can be responsible for hundreds – even thousands – of customers defecting or staying away.
>
> The only approach to reducing negative customer experiences is to institute a zero-tolerance policy. If someone is in one of your target groups, the company must do whatever it takes to make that person happy. Anyone on the edge of defection should cause a triage team to jump into action. Going the extra mile to bring a customer back can turn her into a dedicated member of your sales force. If you lose her, understand why and adjust accordingly.

Meeting 3: Active Listening

Now that the target groups have been identified, the newly empowered web team kicks off Meeting 3 with the question: "How are our online customers going to change our company?" Anyone who starts with that question is on the right track. The answers will come from your customers.

There are many methods of obtaining customer feedback. You can learn many of them from consultants and books. Since that is a matter of tactics, I'll leave the gathering of information to you. Here, I want to emphasize two things: scope and quality.

Scope. The future of your company is at stake. Don't start the big transformation by asking web-site questions. You're looking for your next business proposition, so start by asking customers – existing, new, and prospective – what you can offer online to get their attention. What would astonish and delight them? Think big here; don't worry about implementation costs. Forget about what the competition is doing. You're trying to hit a mark in the future, not in the present.

Blue Shield of California, an insurance company, didn't ask people how they could better sign up for insurance or make changes to their policies online. The company asked how people were using the Web to make health-care decisions. The result of their questions was Mylifepath.com, an enormous health-information resource that benefits all ranges of insurance customer, from pre-sale inquiries to online account-management tools. The site offers health advice, member directories, discounts on acupuncture, fat-ratio calculators, book recommendations, news reports, baby resources, online prenatal education, newsletters, and reference materials. The company has spent millions of dollars just to promote the site. It's a huge undertaking and a great start. Blue Shield understands the effort required to launch a large management-led site. Now, if the company opens its site to visitor contributions, Mylifepath.com will be on its way to becoming customer-led.

You are trying to determine how large an effort will succeed with a particular audience. If your questions are too narrow ("Do you prefer the red or blue color scheme?"), you'll never change the company fast enough. If your questions are too open-ended ("How can we better meet your ever-changing needs?"), you won't get meaningful suggestions. Customers would usually rather see a range of ideas and then critique them. Once they've voiced their opinions, they will usually continue to brainstorm with you. If they start to argue, that's a good sign.

Ask a series of questions designed to single out the people who are most forward-thinking, helpful, and willing to spend time with you.

Then really work with them to envision different scenarios. Start with 100 people, then narrow it down to 40 who'll give their time, then choose the 10 to 20 who can really help. You may have to start by listening to their complaints about prior service, but that's a great way to get the process started.

Quality. Questionnaires can be helpful in aggregating a group's choices, but the most important information will come from one-on-one conversations. Individual comments and personal suggestions from your customers are valuable research results. Encapsulating the responses in the form of stories or scenarios can help you communicate your findings to the entire company.

Learn as much as you can about the online habits of your customers – prospective, new, and committed. Where do they surf? How many hours do they spend online? What engages them? What turns them off? The more you know about your customers' behavior online, the better you'll be able to offer them something they'll want. This information will help you construct your customer models in the fifth meeting.

After a few weeks of dialogue with representative customers, assemble a customer advisory board. These people should come from several different demographic and psychographic customer groups. They should be eager to help. Find a way to reward these people, because you hope to get a lot out of them. Ask them to sign nondisclosure agreements. Make them feel special. Give them a stake. Encourage them to challenge you and make you feel uncomfortable. If you can put together an active 20-person customer advisory board, your chances of making it in the New World of business will double.

Executives who aren't used to the Internet are often afraid to bring online customers into their company because they're afraid of "giving too much away." Some fear the competition is logging on to the company's site and is extracting competitive information from its customer questionnaires. If necessary, set up layers of questions that qualify the responders as they move deeper into your site. The more they trust you and the more you trust them, the better both parties will feel about participating.

Don't take your cues from the competition. They haven't done the research for you. Many times clients have whispered to me, "This is a secret, but… you know that feature our competition has on its site? *We're working on one of those, too.* We just don't want to tip our hand to anyone right now." Imagine how surprised their competition will be when the company launches its big feature. Imagine how surprised its investors will be.

Meeting 4: Measuring Success

According to research company Jupiter Communications, only 24 percent of CEOs surveyed in 1998 viewed their web initiatives as an integrated part of their core business. Sixty-two percent measured web success by measuring visitor rates. What do those figures tell you? Unfortunately, they indicate that, as of that survey, at least 90 percent of all CEOs had no clear idea what their companies' web initiative was or where it was going.

Meeting 4 is for the chief net officer and as many of her people as she thinks is appropriate. The goal is to define the measurements that will drive each customer group forward. In this section, I'll talk about how the CNO can measure short-term results, what to look for over the long term, and what not to measure at all.

Don't measure the wrong things. What you measure can keep your company trapped in a particular business model. If the measurements focus on e-commerce, for example, your company won't become an e-business.

Don't measure server statistics. As you learned in Chapter 6, the number of hits the server receives has no strategic value. More appropriate measurements are number of pageviews, unique visitors, and visitors who register. You can measure stickiness by the number of pageviews per visit or the amount of time a visitor (or repeat visitor) spends on the site. Aggressive net companies break visits down by the hour and day of week. (Monday is the busiest day on the Internet; Sunday is the least active.)

For many Old World companies, near-term return on investment (ROI) is the driving force behind any web effort. This is an e-commerce mindset. Companies like catalog direct-market retailers have seen an immediate return investing in e-commerce. Many catalogs have managed to put their online divisions in the black in under 12 months.

Many chain stores, on the other hand, have seen their web projects spiral out of control. They end up paying ever more expensive consulting firms (or, worse, their own IT staffs) to fix the problems caused by the last group. Focusing only on ROI can be a trap – it's better to make a long-term investment, adjust it as necessary, and expect profits later.

Expenses in the New World aren't comparable to those in an Old World business endeavor. At REI (Recreational Equipment Inc.), the flagship store in Seattle has well over 300 employees. The online division has about 80 employees. Yet the two payrolls are almost the same. It's not going to be cheap to do this right. You'll need some hard-to-get people, and you'll want to put them in an environment (or give them stock options) that makes their friends want to work there, too.

Measure short-term business results. Many, but not all, business results are sales-related. What's the average order? What is the difference between kinds of orders? What time of day gets the highest orders? What add-ons do people go for? Who goes for them? Who generates the most errors? The most returns? Do customers make larger purchases if they have access to more information? Are they influenced by other customers' purchases? It's good to measure sales-related figures, but they are more relevant for e-commerce than e-business. They probably won't help you find new business propositions.

Tactically, server statistics can help you adjust course. Very sophisticated tools for analyzing web traffic and site performance are available. But to get consistently useful results, you must continue to ask new questions and challenge the meaning of your measurements. In the New World, a competitor might sell everything at cost, hoping to build up traffic and make money on ad sales. What will you measure then? The symbiotic nature of the web may make today's measurements obsolete tomorrow.

One of my favorite e-business metrics is an estimate of how many customers would be upset if your company's web site went down for 1) an hour, 2) a day, and 3) a week. How upset would they be? What would they do if your site stayed down? How long would they wait before they looked for something else? The more people who depend on your site, the better. If your site goes down at 3 A.M. and by 8 A.M. your switchboard isn't extra busy, that's a bad sign.

Measure long-term business results. An online bookstore could measure total revenues. An online stock brokerage could measure trade commissions. But sales to repeat customers are a much better indicator of profitability. A closer relationship with your customers will yield information on their buying patterns and habits, and the company can use that information to entice them toward the top of the loyalty pyramid. An automobile manufacturer would like a way to track prospects from the moment they enter the site to their final purchase. Why can't the company simply offer purchasers $50 to fill out a survey that reveals the steps they took and the decisions they made from the manufacturer's web site to the final purchase?

Long-term results are hard to quantify. In a presales or brand-building effort, you try to measure intangibles. What does it take to get site visitors to register? How deeply do they explore the site? At what point do they usually leave? Do they take advantage of the opportunities presented? Are they interested in meeting other people online?

You need different scales for different customer groups. A regular offline customer should be willing to do business with you online. If she isn't, find out why. On the other hand, new customers may drop in now and then, and that's a good start for them. Experts need to be measured on another scale altogether. With some groups, it isn't necessary to make a profit right away; for others, no early profit is a warning sign.

Your web-site plan should include a migratory path that gives all the important customer groups an incentive to register. If you've chosen your groups carefully, you should be able to entice them with something valuable and free – a newsletter, a discount, a chance to meet other people like them. Getting visitors on the site to register may require extra effort, but if it works, the effort will be well spent.

Registered users are the true currency of the Web. The company's relationship with the customer changes as soon as he registers at your site. The day he registers is the day the company begins to build a profile, and the more that profile contains, the better. You can measure the customer's propensity to click on red versus blue, banner versus link, left versus right, and so on. You can learn his habits and when he breaks them. You can change his environment slightly and see whether the effect is positive or negative. You can measure his session lengths and try to determine if he takes on different personalities at different times. You can start to ask more questions and get more answers. Introduce him to other registered customers. Initiate e-mail contact. Ask for feedback, and get him involved in designing his experience. Keep in mind that you must constantly give before you receive.

Don't just look for customers. Look for the *right* customers. Company investment in specific customer groups pays off when you find them attached to your employees at the hip. Learn how to measure each group's attachment and its responses to each new business proposition.

Don't think about pouring money into the site – think about investing in the customers. Tenure is one of your most important measurements. According to Jupiter Communications, 20 percent of first-year visitors purchase, 29 percent of second-year visitors purchase, and 43 percent of those who've been visiting for two or more years are active purchasers. Don't expect all your results to come in year two!

Every time a customer sees the company's name, it makes an impression. It may take 15 exposures to even register the name in the customer's mind, but each exposure counts for something. How do you measure the incremental value of each time someone sees your company's name online? In most cases, that's the wrong question. Word of mouth is always more influential than online banner ads. Measure word of mouth more than exposure. Insist on measuring the results that matter most, and you will find a way to get the numbers you need.

Meeting 5: Customer Modeling

Now that you've ranked your customer groups and you know what constitutes success for each group, it's time to get to know your customers even better. Use the information gleaned from questionnaires, videotapes, testimonials, and your customer advisory board to construct profiles of your top groups. You may want to profile several users per group, but I've always found it useful to boil it down to one or two representations per group.

Let's suppose you run an adventure-travel business. You've identified your top three customer groups: single affluent males, young couples without children, and semiretired couples in their fifties and sixties. For each group, you would construct an elaborate profile of a representative member. For single affluent males, we'll call our fictitious person Dan.

Dan is a 32-year-old stockbroker on Wall Street. He represents a group of about 1 million affluent single men who might be in the market for an adventure. Dan is at work by 7:00 A.M. every day, leaves by 4:00 P.M., and goes to the gym three times a week. He spends evenings socializing with friends and going out on dates. He plays poker every Sunday night with his investment-banker buddies. Dan makes around $120,000 per year, which means he has plenty of money to indulge his desire for cool stuff. He buys sports equipment, fancy watches, and art, and he loves to take adventure vacations.

Dan spends almost every hour of his workday staring at computer screens, but he still enjoys getting online. He sends 20-plus e-mail messages a day from work – everything from notes to his clients to confirmations of racquetball dates with his friends. He reads several sports sites, gets sports scores on his pager, and is very active in several fantasy-sports leagues. He keeps in touch with his family through e-mail and often buys presents for his family members online. He subscribes to *The Wall Street Journal* and *The New York Times* online. He subscribes to several weekly magazines, which he reads on the subway. He watches two hours of TV a week and typically spends one night a week online. He's been surfing the Web regularly for three years; he probably goes to fewer movies and watches less TV than he did before discovering the Web.

Because Dan doesn't really exist, you should take extra pains to make him come alive in your mind. Does he read all the way through his magazines? What grabs his attention? Has he ever been on a singles vacation before? What is his vacation history? The more complete your picture of Dan, the better. You should be able to imagine how Dan would react to almost anything. If you can find an actual person who represents your core audience, or if you can work with a number of dedicated customers who represent the target group, that's fine, too.

Next, construct an entire part of your business around Dan, starting with the web site. How will he find you? What keywords might he type into a search engine? How much time will he have when he gets there? What's likely to draw his attention? What can you offer him online?

Start Dan as a beginner on the site, and imagine what it would take to keep him coming back. Entice him with experiences he would like to

Dan (Single Affluent Male)	Action Or Need	Web Site Feature
Beginner	Discovery	Co-op ads and deals with sports sites
	Interest	Emphasis on singles adventure vacations
	Entry	Photos of people having fun
	Exploration	Easy navigation by type of vacation rather than by locale
	Inquiry	FAQ (Frequently Asked Questions), opportunity to communicate with guides by e-mail
	Looks for images he can relate to	Photos of extreme sports and places visitor may recognize
	Looks for images that catch his interest	Photos of exciting expeditions visitor has never experienced
	Looks for an objective point of view	Testimonials and reviews of past trip participants
Intermediate (Looking for a Trip)	Learns about vacation opportunities	Newsletter, new offerings, updates on bookings
	Works with his schedule	Scheduling tool
	Looks for people like him	Buddy-matching with someone who's been on previous trips
	Looks for opportunities to meet single women	Page where people who are considering a trip can meet those already signed up
		Page where trip members can plan the trip even before they've met
		System for matching visitors with similar profiles
	Looks for entertaining or interesting artifacts	Adventure postcards
Expert (After the Trip)	Opportunity to review his vacation	A subsite where the trip participants can see photos of the trip and make their own journal entries
	Opportunity to keep in touch with new friends	A reunion subsite where trip participants can hook up as they travel
	Mementos	A store where trip participants can review photos and order custom items: T-shirts, photos, posters, etc.
	Looks for more adventures	Opportunity to be a trip captain on a custom trip with friends to a destination never offered before (and a discount for organizing it)
	Special requests	Assistance in planning a special trip

The feature matrix assigns features to a given customer's needs. The list helps prioritize site features and makes sure the customer has something to look forward to on each level.

repeat. Introduce him to people with whom he can identify. When he starts interacting with other customers, he becomes an intermediate. Get him to bookmark the site and depend on it for something he values. When he finally starts contributing, he's an expert. How can you take him through all those levels?

With Dan's profile firmly in mind, construct a feature matrix for him, describing him as a beginner, intermediate, and expert at the site. Because the site is organized vertically (based on psychographics, not demographics), you'll want to steer him toward a top-level community of like-minded adventurers.

If your company has an active customer advisory board made up of individuals from your target groups, you can use real people rather than fictional characters like Dan to construct a feature matrix. The more specific you are about what it takes to win an audience, the better.

Obviously Meeting 5 is not going to be a short meeting. For each customer need there must be a response, and in each response you must include content and features that engage the visitor. Those features must fit within the visitor's requirements and surfing habits. You can't do everything, so after brainstorming feature ideas, you must prioritize the feature list. Each feature should have its own set of metrics for determining success. That list sets the agenda for the business model and the specific results you can reasonably achieve.

The deliverable for Meeting 5 is a prioritized list of features, broken down by release, for each customer group you want to satisfy. If you have a large travel company and are serious about tapping into your online markets, you can see that it is going to take at least ten people to make each customer group happy. That's a huge undertaking, but it pays off if you view it as a long-term investment.

You can't know how many of these features constitute critical mass for your target customer group. Your competition will set the minimum requirements. It often takes more features than you'd imagine, because customers want to feel they have plenty of choices. They want to feel they're at a full-service resort, not a cabin in the woods. Yet some of the features are much harder to accomplish than others, so you create a release schedule.

The release schedule is one of the most powerful tools your site manager has while producing the site. It lets her earmark each feature for releases 1.0, 1.5, 2.0, and beyond. When it seems there's an endless list of things to do on the site, the release schedule helps the site manager prioritize them properly. It allows her to say she'll take on a task but not until everything for the upcoming release is up and running smoothly.

The difference between e-commerce and e-business is that e-business will transform your company. Thanks to a deep feature matrix, the site gives Dan's real counterparts a way to meet other people – both employees and travelers. And it won't be long before those customers get their friends to use the site to construct their own adventures.

Meeting 6: The Plan

The only thing left is to map out your strategy for a customer-led experience online. On a content-driven site, everyone in the company wants to monopolize the home page for his own purposes. But a customer-led web site breaks the logjam on the home page by sacrificing it, killing the sacred cow, and putting the customer first.

The home page of a customer-led site should direct visitors in the target groups to their own neighborhood pages. In the example I've used, an adventure-travel company's page would have some catchy news items, a brief statement about the company and its reputation, a couple of quotes from people who took recent trips, and some contact information. The most prominent items, however, would be the links to various neighborhoods. A neighborhood is an area of the site that caters to a particular customer group.

Don't put detailed information on the home page! The space should be reserved for newcomer directions and a few vital statistics. Don't give any visitor a reason to bookmark the home page. Someone like Dan should want to bookmark his neighborhood page, not the home page. Design the web experience carefully so that the visitor doesn't feel he's missing anything by bookmarking his subsection of the site.

A neighborhood page should be friendly, informative, and tailored to its customer group. Real people should reside there – people the average group member can relate to. The host – the company's representative – is welcoming, personable, and always available to answer questions.

A typical neighborhood home page accommodates beginners (50 percent of surface area), intermediates (40 percent of surface area), and

Customer-Led Architecture

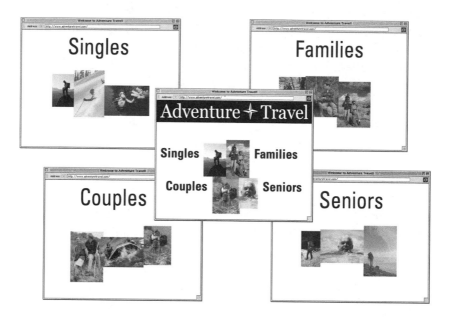

A customer-led site uses its home page as a way to direct visitors to neighborhood home pages, where they can meet people like themselves.

experts (ten percent – a search window and a link to the expert realm). Those priorities are expressed in something I call a page map. Page maps identify 1) the percentage of the total area dedicated to each level of customer, and 2) the percentage of those areas allotted to each feature.

While that sounds like preliminary design, it's not. Design comes later. The page maps are information architecture – they map the structure, not the presentation, of the page content.

Now, after six intense meetings, you finally have a prioritized laundry list of things to work on for a particular customer group. The rest, you may be happy to learn, is execution. For that, you need a budget, a set of execution documents, contractors, and staff. There are books on the market that tell you how best to handle those elements. I've written one. Check the Futurizenow.com for a complete resource list.

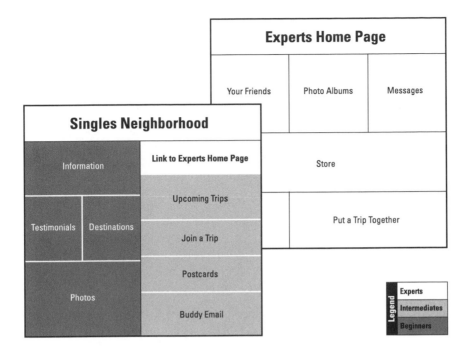

Experts Home Page

| Your Friends | Photo Albums | Messages |

| Store |

| Put a Trip Together |

Singles Neighborhood

Information	**Link to Experts Home Page**
Testimonials	Destinations	Upcoming Trips
		Join a Trip
Photos	Postcards
	Buddy Email

Legend
Experts
Intermediates
Beginners

Page maps. Beginners, intermediates, and experts on a neighborhood page have unique interests. A page map doesn't dictate which features go where on a neighborhood page. It dictates only the amount of surface area dedicated to the features. Beginners, for example, are much more interested in content than in tools.

After all that effort, however, don't expect immediate results. No matter how big your brand is offline, you shouldn't expect to launch the company web site on Monday and see big revenues by Friday. What's important is that you are moving customers and potential customers along the path from beginners to intermediates to experts. Even those categories have finer distinctions. The more you understand where your customers are in the continuum, the more you can listen for what's missing and adjust accordingly.

If you've been taking notes throughout the six meetings, you should have a document with about 10 to 12 pages dedicated to each customer group, plus appendixes containing survey results and comments. If top-level management has been involved in every step of the process, you are on your way to a successful e-business.

Futurizing

The customer-led strategy is deep, not wide. The six meetings outlined in this chapter are a huge investment. You must conduct them in the spirit of open, collaborative inquiry. If you simply run through the meetings mechanically, treating the steps as tactics, you are wasting time and effort. Done properly, the entire process forces you to think critically about your products and services. It will motivate you and your company to make the adjustments necessary to accommodate online customers. When you have a well-crafted business strategy, backed up by a well-crafted web site and an enthusiastic staff, you'll have the fundamentals for your journey to the New World.

In the next chapter, I'll discuss the internal organization issues that will combine to make the customer-led site a success.

THE WARNING SIGNS OF E-CANCER

Company thinks "customer-driven" means customer-led

Employees get more voice mail than e-mail messages

Management has completed Meetings 1-6, and company is still in the same business

CEO's assistant *still* prints out all e-mail messages

Web team is afraid to tell CEO she is clueless

Board of directors thinks the web site is not its concern

CEO thinks "gift givers" is a customer group

Company's top managers all have this book, but no one has read it

The Customer-Led Company

CHAPTER 8

BACK IN 1996, at my request, the head webmasters of the divisions of a very large company got together around a conference table. It may have been the first time they'd ever been in the same room. Each division had its own web-design contractor – my firm, in fact, had been one – and each site had its own navigation scheme, look-and-feel, language, and purchasing protocol. When I called the meeting, I had hoped to discuss making the company's site a more cohesive, easy-to-navigate experience for all customers.

The webmasters had other ideas. They explained that the company was very proud of the autonomy of its divisions. Each division had its own income statement and was in charge of spending money in its own way. Headquarters had little influence on their operations. Each division had made its own mark on the web, and the webmasters all admitted to competing with each other to create the coolest or the best part of the site. One of them summed up our brief conversation by saying, "Forget it. You might as well try to herd cats."

To this day, the internal competition on that site continues. Customers looking for the company's products buy them through online resellers, not at the company's cyberstore. Should the company try to present a more united face to the customer? Or does internal competition actually bring out the best in all the divisions? That is what we are here to find out.

The Need for a New Approach

Most web projects fail for political reasons. If you work in a large company, you know that most reorganizations also fail for political reasons.

Divisions face off against each other rather than turning to face the customer together.

In most companies, it's impossible for the web mission to win because it runs over too many toes. Why? Too many companies see the web site as a threat, a liability, or a contest – not as a new way of doing business. If the company's goal is to look as if it knows what it's doing online, the result will be nothing but endless rounds of musical chairs.

Companies that have been successful online give their web divisions space. They take more of a start-up approach, setting up a ".com" subsidiary with its own initial funding, a few key managers, and a mandate to hire web-aware personnel. Unfortunately, few have been able to transfer the web divisions' experiences back into the parent companies.

The chief executive and the chief net officer must create an environment that supports everyone in learning what the web division learns. Together, they must learn to herd the cats. In this chapter, I outline some of the important ingredients in creating that environment. The CEO helps the CNO build the web team into a multidivision business unit gradually, starting with the appointment of the key company contact for each customer group: a host. As we'll see, the hosts play three important roles – in the company, on the site, and on the Web. The CEO and CNO build divisions around the hosts based on the needs of customers in each group. Finally, they set up systems that allow the company employees to control their own destinies. In this chapter, I'll show that progression – from the web team to the final New World company – in action.

Championing the Customer

At Herman Miller, the hundreds of e-mail messages the office furniture company gets every week go through Carol. Carol has a background in technical writing and customer care. She tirelessly tracks down requests for information on furniture. She helps people find parts, refinishers, and appraisers. She listens to the problems of people whose chairs don't fit and discusses possible solutions with the engineers. She is both the company's representative on the web site and the customer's advocate within the organization.

The first step in realigning any organization with its customers is to empower an employee like Carol to serve each customer group coming to the company's web site. Each group has a neighborhood page. The host of that neighborhood serves as concierge to the members of the group. She is the face on the neighborhood page, and she owns that part of the site. She is responsible for keeping the content current, the discussions lively, and the visitors coming back.

Rather than being an editor on a content-organized site, she is a host dedicated to helping a particular customer group. She works for the customers in her group.

The host actually plays three roles, all of which are part of representing her chosen customer group: 1) Inside the company, she is the customer champion, helping customers get what they need and connecting customers with employees. 2) On the web site, she's the concierge. She puts her name on the customer-group neighborhood pages and lets visitors know she's there to help them with anything they require. 3) Online, she is an ambassador. On other sites, in other communities, and in discussion groups, she represents the company. She participates and contributes alongside people who are potential site visitors.

Customer Champion (inside the company)	Concierge (on the web site)	Ambassador (outside the company)
Helps customers get what they want inside the company	Gives customers what they want	Goes to sites and events where the company or its products are being discussed
Connects customers with employees	Connects customers with other customers	Sets up kiosks or help desks at other sites
Conducts focus groups	Conducts promotions and events	Provides content and updated information to other sites
Tracks demand for new features	Draws visitors to the site	Watches where her customers congregate and what they do online
Measures and reports on success in the customer group	Helps solve problems	
	Helps improve the customer's experience	
	Asks questions that help the company understand customer need	

The customer-group host plays three important roles: in the company, on the site, and on the Web. A New World company pairs a host with a manager to form each customer-led division. The host becomes the key facilitator for an entire neighborhood on the site.

In smaller companies, one person can often handle all three roles. In companies with hundreds of thousands of customers per target group, several people may share the roles. The hosts and their three roles are crucial to the formation of the new customer divisions. By focusing on these three distinct roles, companies will better understand what it takes to serve customers.

A host has no agenda other than to know her site visitors and serve them well. The host is not a customer rep, an account executive, or a salesperson. She works for all the people who come to her section of the site. She reaches into the company and finds what her customers are looking for. Whether it's an e-mail inquiry or a request for a bid, she makes sure the right person steps in or gives her the information to relay.

When someone in the company is thinking about adding a new feature to the web site or investigating a new business proposition, the host enrolls customers to help work on the project. Rather than being a bottleneck, she is a facilitator. She connects people outside with those inside.

The host's role as a concierge is perhaps the most important. Suppose you've started an online brokerage. One way to identify your customers would be based on their investment goals. Another would be based on frequency of participation. As an example, I'll show how customer divisions would form around four kinds of customers, based on their frequency of buying and selling stocks: 1) monthlies, 2) weeklies, 3) dailies, and 4) hourlies. The web site would have four main areas, each with its own theme color or other visual identifier. In each area, members of the group can see the concierge's home page, learn how to contact him or her, and get all the personal attention they need. Let's take a look at the concierges for the four groups of customers.

Daryn hosts the monthlies customer group. She has an online page that includes her photo and a brief bio. She's fairly conservative. She understands the concerns of investors who have long-term financial plans and aren't interested in trading. She helps them find resources for mutual funds and tax planning. Daryn watches for the beginners, putting information on the site that helps answer their questions and providing help information on every screen. She loves interacting with the intermediates in her group, because they're usually enthusiastic learners. And she enjoys matching the experts up and letting them discover common interests. No marketing person tells Daryn what message to get out today or what products to push. Her job is to make the monthlies feel at home – period.

Kayla helps the weeklies customer group. Weeklies are often people in transition. They come to the site more interested in learning than trading. Kayla directs them to all kinds of resources: an online bookstore, links to newsletter sites, and tutorials on investing. She helps people meet each other. She spends time with the beginners in a weekly Q&A chat session, holds phantom stock-trading contests, and helps them graduate into real stock-trading clubs. She also sends out a weekly e-mail newsletter to her group members filled with interesting investing stories.

Nathan and Nina are the dailies' hosts. They've got news, stock updates, trends, analysis – everything for the information-hungry e-trader. The intermediates and experts in the group have access to some fairly sophisticated trading screens. Nina maintains a long list of what people want or need – mostly tools for customizing their trading "dashboards." Nathan helps them set up discussion topics and exchange information. If a customer makes a trading mistake, she can push a panic button, which activates Nathan's or Nina's beeper. Because of the trading volume, Nathan and Nina need an assistant every weekday morning until 11 A.M. or so.

Jordan supports the hourlies. He gets up every morning at five o'clock along with many of his day traders. These investors want all the data and rumors they can get. He doesn't substantiate any rumors; he just sets up links to all the sources he can find. He wants everything to be right there, one click away, so day traders can get the most out of their experience with his firm. He has worked hard to construct a special interface for his customers – he calls it the cockpit – which comes complete with several sound channels for news, updates, reminders, alerts, and even customer-to-customer connections. For these insatiable customers, 60 seconds is an eternity, so Jordan is always trying to provide them with the latest, fastest tools on the market.

A Jupiter Communications report on account management emphasizes the importance of "face time" with online customers – 40 percent of Jupiter's respondents said they would be more comfortable with online purchasing if there were more human contact. Jordan meets his customers' need for contact by answering about 300 e-mail messages a day.

Aligning by Customer Group

Customer-group hosts are the faces that will be most evident in an e-business. As I said in the previous chapter, however, you can count on hiring at least ten people for each customer group. That number is simply a guide for making sure you have enough people in your new web division. For example, if your company plans to focus on four customer groups, as illustrated in the brokerage example, you'll want to start with at least 40 people. You may need hundreds more, depending on your business proposition, but you won't want to start with fewer than 40. Whatever the size, probably half of the people will work to build the system, and the other half will work on the customer experience. It goes without saying that each customer division must have a sympathetic general manager, who empowers the hosts to help guide the division and provide the agenda for new business opportunities.

Rather than creating horizontal divisions for different products or services, the customer-led company first and foremost organizes its new online business unit around customer groups. In our brokerage example, the company might have had presidents for retail stocks, mutual funds, capital markets, marketing, branch offices, telemarketing, research, Europe, Asia, human resources, and information technology. The customer-led approach, however, results in four divisions –the monthly, weekly, daily, and hourly investors – and four presidents. All other company functions would support the customer-led goals. (As I mentioned, there are other ways to select these groups – trading frequency may or may not have been an appropriate selection criterion for the company.)

The customer-led approach is really an evolved service structure. Most service companies, like consultants, have been using the horizontal-vertical matrix approach for years. Many product companies, on the other hand, have focused on and structured themselves by product groups (like workstations and printers) or by distribution channel (like retail and education).

But an organization that fosters sacred cows will no longer work. In the New World, the companies on top will consider their customers more sacred than their products or even their channels of distribution.

The company that applies e-customer categories to the traditional service matrix will be better prepared to follow its customers. It's important, however, to choose those customer groups wisely. As I noted in Chapter 3, Microsoft's realignment according to its top four customer groups (IT managers, knowledge workers, software developers, and consumers) reflects a lot of thought toward the nature of their customer relationships. Microsoft did not pursue traditional industry verticals such as finance and health care. Rather, the company looked hard at its individual customers, and the real customer groups emerged.

As management focuses on the chosen target customer groups, other customers will inevitably be left out. That's fine – they will become part of another company's target group. Your company must focus 100 percent on the groups it can serve best.

Office Depot is a good example. The company is divided along three customer groups: individual consumers, small businesses, and contract customers (generally large businesses with several locations). Each group gets its own catalog. Officedepot.com is administered by an independent web division. The main web site targets the first two customer groups, tracking their purchasing habits and offering special deals to high-volume accounts. A separate site handles the contract customers. Office Depot understands the false economy of managing all catalogs or all web sites under one administration.

Responding to Customer Needs

The customer-led company has a broad interface across which all employees can get to know their customers. Employees invite customers in to collaborate on new products, support systems, and methodologies that work for both sides. Facilitating those interactions will take new communication skills, new tools, and the ability to move people in and out of project teams easily. Rather than planning these project teams, however, you must set up the conditions in which they can form organically. It will take a sophisticated and flexible system to be able to match your resources to your customers' needs.

With a growing number of offices around the world, consulting firm Viant has built an innovative system, called STARRS, for managing and forecasting staffing needs. Every employee in the firm can see and use the system, which has real-time access to information on offices, clients, projects, and consulting assignments. When a project manager needs a certain kind of programmer, she looks at the system to see who's available in her office. If no one is, she checks the other offices. If she sees someone she can use, she puts in a request. Each week, the staffing captains from each office conduct a conference call to work on the current requests.

Project managers and employees themselves build and maintain most of the information, updating it daily. Anyone in the company can see who's working on what, and who's available and when. Anyone can see which projects are short-staffed and how critical the situation is. Project managers don't have to go through an intermediary to find someone they need. This internal market system empowers everyone to see holes and try to plug them creatively.

As the customer-led company evolves, the different customer groups take the company in new directions. Using our earlier brokerage example, the brokerage will find that monthly investors aren't interested in becoming weekly investors at all. They are more likely to pull the company toward annuities, leisure planning, trusts, travel services, and the like. The day traders could take the company in an entirely different direction.

Those new opportunities are really the goal – not just the by-product – of a customer-led company. To bring management into the future, there must be a straight line from the CNO or CEO to each customer-group division. As Peter Senge demonstrates so lucidly in *The Fifth Discipline*, these lines are lines of responsibility, not command. Management's job is to give each business unit the leverage to move away from the others and toward the customer. The divisions must also be strong enough to stand up to the CEO and bargain on behalf of their respective employee and customer groups.

Reinventing Human Resources

Ask a few employees of large corporations what percentage of their time they spend doing work they would rather not do. My guess is you'll hear some pretty high numbers. People get stuck doing unfulfilling tasks because hierarchies tend to enforce the status quo. It's hard to innovate when management tells employees not only what to do, but *how* to do it.

In the New World labor market, the legal definition of an employee will have to change – at least in the United States, where free agents are becoming more powerful by the day. Just as the e-customer is changing the rules of business, the e-employee is changing the rules of work. The master-slave relationship between company and employee won't last in the truth economy.

Disintermediation – the elimination of middlemen in transactions – is working its magic in external markets. Travel agencies, stock brokerages, and employment agencies reincarnate themselves daily as web sites. As web tools improve, human resource departments and much of middle management will also disappear. Today, human resource departments build enterprise resource planning (ERP) systems that can put teams together dynamically and make sure every resource is utilized. Are these systems efficient? Yes. But they are also doomed to fail because the most important ingredient has been left out: desire. Soon, employees will organize themselves, with no need for *adult* supervision or coordination. The culture of the e-employee will relegate ERP systems and the people who administer them to the dustbin of history.

Instead, open labor markets will prevail. Soon job markets will be relative rather than absolute. Call it the labor tornado. Labor will be priced at market value. Employees will be free agents. They'll do the work they want to do, and the market will fill the gaps.

These New World employees will go to the company intranet to see what projects or work they have to choose from each day – or what they feel like doing. It's also the place they'll find out how much money they'll get paid for doing the work. At home, on the train, or at their desks, they'll be able to log on to the company intranet. There they'll read the major news stories, visit a few sites, check out the livelier gossip sections, and then head to the labor auctions. The auctions will be a virtual marketplace of labor supply and demand. Anything anyone wants done goes into the job auction system – from preparing for a corporate event to writing a white paper or building a design team.

The intracompany auction system combines features of an online auction, the stock market, newspaper classified ads, Hollywood's independent producers, and today's best ERP software. The intracompany labor market will be divided into three main categories: labor, jobs, and projects.

Perhaps 30 percent of the company's work pool will be in the short-term market. Many jobs will be auctioned at 5:00 P.M. one day and filled by 8:00 A.M. the next. A contractor scans the jobs offered. She accepts one or, if she doesn't like any of the choices, turns over and goes back to sleep, forgoing the money. She also has the choice of expanding her search.

Another 30 percent of the job pool will want more stability. These contractors are the "bond" section of the labor market, taking a potentially lower salary in exchange for the security of a single-year or multiyear contract. But they don't complain because they know they can always get back into the auctions and look for a better situation.

The remaining 40 percent will be in the market for project-based work. A group of employees and their customers may write a project description and put it on the intranet for approved outside contractors and internal people to bid on. People inside and outside the company form teams to bid on the project and deliver it on time and on budget. In the future, many of today's employees will be independent producers.

The technology behind the open job market – called auction-based or real-time resource planning – will take into account previous performance, project oversight, and safety issues. The systems will be run by employees, not by human resource managers, because employees will want to set the rules. This e-employee future will lead to the most customer satisfaction and the most shareholder value.

Meritocracies Rule

Virtually anything can be subcontracted. Don't want to fill out your own expense reports? You can always pay someone to do it for you. If enough people don't want to fill out expense reports, someone will see the opportunity and find a way to make money doing it for everyone. The more repetitive, dull, and predictable a task is, the more ripe it is for subcontracting. If all the administrative assistants in a company start subcontracting all their boring work, the company will end up with more contractors and fewer administrative assistants. If that works, it saves the company money. If it doesn't work, then the market will pay for administrative assistants who are better suited for the work they need to do.

Companies will encourage intrapreneurship – the ability of employees to start new businesses. If an account rep discovers a better way to help people with their Internet connections while on the road, he can start his own service inside the company. As it becomes bigger, he can turn it into a business that serves other companies. That happens today, though with more secrecy and discontinuity.

Labor auctions create flexibility and fairness. They also expose bottlenecks. They pay people for what they do, when they do it, according to talent and availability – not what they negotiated last year or how long they've been with the company. Because the system is not command-based, there are no masters and no slaves. The system frees people to do what they find enjoyable, and it rewards people for taking on undesirable work with an entrepreneurial spirit.

Intercompany auctions will also become commonplace. Companies will trade contracts, subcontracts, teams, and even individuals who are interested in being traded. This flexibility will give project managers more tools to get their projects done on time and on budget. Imagine needing someone for a project and getting help from a competitor. This will happen more often than you might expect. Why? Because the competitor might want credit the next time it's overloaded and needs help. When everything is connected, new symbiotic relationships form.

An auction system isn't dehumanizing – it's empowering. It asks groups and individuals to take initiative. It lets people find their own

---

THE GOLDEN RULE

In business, the Golden Rule is seriously flawed. Rather than treating people the way you would want them to treat you, treat them the way they want to be treated! Why give people more money if they would prefer more time or better conditions? The new tools that sprout from our intranets will facilitate communication and understanding. They will let us specify what each person has to offer and what she wants in return.

niches and change their requirements over time. It gives employees direct responsibility for balancing the needs of the company and its shareholders with their own needs and those of their customers.

The auction labor system is not a substitute for management. As many middle-management positions disappear, leadership and mentoring will become even more important. Workers still need to learn, be recognized, work out problems, and discuss plans. Managers still need to help workers help each other, and workers and management need to work together to improve the labor-market system itself.

Larger companies will be first to implement these intra- and inter-company systems because their sizeable job markets resemble a familiar forum – the classified ads in the local newspaper. Finding project work will be just like finding a job. Smaller companies will group together to create their own markets, and more people will enter the real-time labor pool.

Workers have more than just economic motivations. They want the system to reflect their individual priorities. In places like Silicon Valley and San Francisco, where average salaries are among the highest in the country, these processes are already emerging. The trend will continue as New World companies start to show increased productivity and legislators open up the labor law debate.

Herding Cats, Revisited

Should you herd the cats, or should you let them do as they wish? If your company has a separate division for each product or service category, you should try to reorganize those cats. Once you have a "cat" for each of your important customer groups, let them do as they wish. Without this customer alignment, your Old World divisions will be hopelessly lost as they go up against New World competitors.

Any cat owner will tell you that a can of tuna will solve almost any behavior problem. As your customer-led divisions evolve, the rest of your employees will see the customer-led approach working. They will see the efficiencies of internal labor markets. They will see that people do less of what they don't want to do and more of what genuinely interests them. The customer-led business unit with its customer-focused divisions will become a magnet for people who thrive in a meritocracy, attracting the people you most want and leaving the late-adopters behind.

After several of the new customer-led divisions are thriving, the company reaches the end game. By now, most of the good people have abandoned the old routines and only the bureaucrats are left, stubbornly defending their territories. You should think about proceeding without them, rather than trying to teach them to adapt to New World realities. The New World is in a state of constant flux. The stragglers will only hold you back.

Letting Go

This approach to reorganization is more an exercise in letting go than it is in setting an agenda. If done properly, this will be the company's last major reorganization. After that, each division will naturally grow around its customers in a way that prevents further musical chairs. Management's job is not to make all this happen, but rather to let it happen.

While very few companies are ready for the kinds of internal freedom I describe, most companies will adopt new tools – the same way they have adopted cell phones and pagers. But the cultural shift is more difficult. Your employees may not be ready or willing to reorganize around your customers. Your company may be one of those that won't make it to 2010. If it looks that way, you must decide whether you can make a difference. And if you *can* make a difference, are you *willing* to? Of all the people who read this book, many will take the challenge and try to futurize their companies.

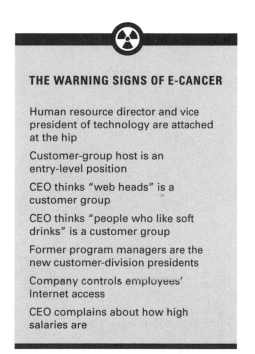

THE WARNING SIGNS OF E-CANCER

Human resource director and vice president of technology are attached at the hip

Customer-group host is an entry-level position

CEO thinks "web heads" is a customer group

CEO thinks "people who like soft drinks" is a customer group

Former program managers are the new customer-division presidents

Company controls employees' Internet access

CEO complains about how high salaries are

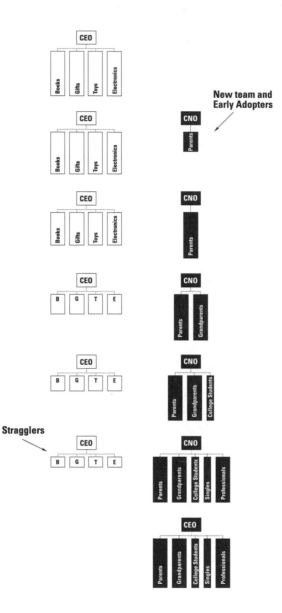

The transformation begins when the CNO establishes the new online business unit, hiring a small team of new people to help get it started. The web team quickly forms customer divisions around its hosts and division managers. The divisions continue to grow as more people emerge from the boot camp and the CNO adds new customer groups. Finally, the old company is left with only stragglers, who get left behind as the company enters the New World. At that point, the CNO is out of a job – she either stays on in a new capacity or goes to her next company.

Others may decide their best choice is to find a company that is already heading toward the customer-led future. That's an important part of why I wrote *Futurize Your Enterprise*. If you think your company can turn only one degree per year, you may not want to stick around for the next 180 years to see how it turned out!

Futurizing

The path to becoming a customer-led company involves radical changes. Each new step moves you deeper into the realm of the completely networked, pilotless corporate environment.

The chief net officer is the chief executive officer's partner in change. As the CNO hires one or more hosts per customer group, the customer divisions start to take shape. The customer-group hosts facilitate the dialogue between the company and its customers. Project managers follow by assembling their own teams to better serve their customer groups. New company divisions emerge following the customers' lead. Soon, labor laws and intranet systems provide the means for a real-time labor market and – *voilà!* – your company has made the leap from being management-led to being customer-led. Middle management disappears, executives are paid for results rather than for being executives, earnings continue to improve, and the stock market rewards the companies that dare to transform themselves in this radical way.

Old World companies partner with customers to achieve company objectives. New World companies partner with customers to set and achieve mutual objectives. That can be done only if you hitch your companies' divisions to their customer groups and let them go. Don't worry about them too much. They'll be fine without the usual amount of supervision because they're letting their customers lead the way. Besides, as we're about to see, you still have more work to do.

Cyber Synergy

CHAPTER 9

PICTURE YOURSELF WALKING THROUGH an old-growth forest somewhere in central Montana. Spruces and bristlecone pines that sprouted in the eighteenth century tower into the sky. Each inch of soil takes over 200 years to form, and there are 36 inches below your feet. The seasons change drastically but predictably. Trees can withstand temperature extremes of 150 degrees Fahrenheit, but only if the transition is slow. In the entire state of Montana, there are perhaps 5,000 species of plants, insects, birds, and animals. Higher in the canyon, a glacier glides down from the peaks at a pace of three feet per year.

About every 400 years, the trees become so tall that they prevent most of the sunlight from reaching the forest floor. Many of the smaller species die out. The trees become dry and brittle. Eventually, there is a fire. The resulting ash provides a fertile medium for surviving seeds to sprout, and a few new species introduce themselves. The new trees begin their upward climb, restarting the long, slow cycle of the temperate forest.

Now get on an airplane, get off in Ecuador, and take a ten-hour jeep ride to Yasuni National Park. Things are very different here. The tree canopy is 300 feet above your head. The ground is almost pitch dark. The soil is only a few inches deep. Sitting on the banks of a rushing stream, you can see over 700 different kinds of trees and *over 40,000* species of plants and animals. Roses grow as tall as giraffes. Grasses grow up to three feet *per day*. Two hundred feet above the ground, you can find flowers that store enough water to bathe in. And there are crabs – yes, crabs – that live in these treetop "tanks." There are spiders that eat birds, frogs that eat rats, flowers the size of pickup trucks, rodents that weigh as much as a teenager, snakes that fly, gnats that suck the blood out of mosquitoes, ants bigger than your thumb, bats larger than a ten-year-old child, and moths the size of this book. Opened.

Compared to the temperate forest, the rain forest is a completely different world – dazzling in its complexity and ferocious in its pace of change. Diversity is the key to survival. The rain forest causes its own turbulent weather. Most species spend their entire lives without ever touching the ground. Nothing lasts very long. Trees shoot up, mature into multiton giants, then crash to the ground or disintegrate, creating opportunities for thousands of species to compete for the additional sunlight. The ever-changing environment gives birth to a new species *daily*, even as humankind extinguishes over 30 rain forest species in that same 24 hours.

The Internet Is the Rain Forest

The temperate forest and the rain forest illustrate the differences in business climate between the Old World and the New World. Before the Web became a mainstream medium, business conditions were fairly stable, punctuated by revolutions that changed the playing field for many years at a time. By the mid-nineties, much of the focus was on cost reduction, rather than topline growth. Although the climate fluctuated drastically throughout the year, the dominant "species" in each industry were able to predict seasonal variations. Distribution bottlenecks made it hard to challenge the giants in a given category.

On the Internet, symbiotic opportunities are everywhere. Size is no longer an advantage. People build this month on what others built last month. With your friends *and* your enemies this close, it's hard to know where your allies are.

One way to find your allies would be through link analysis. Anyone can send programs – called spiders – to go out and visit every site on the Web. It takes a few days, but pretty soon you have the text of the entire Web on your hard disk. Now you can perform a reverse link analysis. By following all the links on the Web, you can find every site that links to your site. Among those sites that link to yours, you can find the top 20 other sites that are most commonly pointed to. These 20 sites are your virtual neighbors. You might think about finding them, approaching them, and discussing options for partnering, since you share a common visitor base.

Affiliate programs are an effective way for businesses to make friends online. An affiliate program is a referral program in which you reward people for sending web traffic to your site. When a visitor follows a link (from the affiliate's site, or even an e-mail message) and makes a purchase, the affiliate typically receives 2 to 20 percent of the sale. When people sign up to market your products to their friends, your reach on the Web expands considerably.

Referral programs are everywhere online. You can earn five cents every time you refer someone who signs up for Jokes4u.com, a free daily joke by e-mail. At Mypoints.com, you can buy points to give away to your customers. Frequent shoppers in the network can redeem points for prizes. Netcentives' Click Rewards program lets your shoppers earn frequent-flier miles for eight major airlines.

Pennyweb.com is a completely automated site that lets you choose the sponsors you want, host their banners in rotation on your own site, and receive ten cents every time your visitors click through the banners. Lendingtree.com will send you $14 for every visitor you've referred who completes the first five pages of their loan form. Iown.com will pay you $25 for each loan application your visitors complete. And Credit-cards-online.com will pay you $175 for every business you sign up to use their credit-card clearing service. Finally, if you don't want to set up your own affiliate network, Clickbank.com will do it for you in a few minutes.

Partnership opportunities exist on all levels. People who are good at business development – partnering with other companies – are now worth their weight in beryllium. Let's see how customer-led companies can look for appropriate partnership opportunities online.

Fitting In

Throughout this book I've talked about the power of e-customers and how they like to see each other, meet each other, and communicate. But there are many businesses that can't have relationships with customers after the sale, simply because their customers aren't interested in working their way up the loyalty pyramid every time they purchase. Companies like that must look for symbiotic partners on the Web.

Let's look at a mattress company's business proposition. Every five to ten years, you are in the market for a new mattress. You try some, you buy one, you take it home, and you get rid of your old one. If things go well, you forget about the product until it's time to get rid of it. You don't want to be in a mattress community, share your mattress experience, or trade tips on getting the most out of your mattress. You're perfectly capable of dealing with your mattress without group support. Am I right?

A mattress retailer says: "We want to be the authoritative source for information about mattresses online." The company wants to build a web site with a sleep center, where the Sandman can answer their questions; an online testing center, where you can bounce on the virtual beds all day; a product-comparison feature; a linen gallery; and other features. Then, to drive customers to the site, the retailer will buy banner ads and search keywords at all the portal sites.

It should be clear by now that this approach wastes money and annoys e-customers. They want the big picture, not the big pitch. How can an online store harness the power of e-customers? Lets look at the whole customer and how a mattress store can fit into the online ecosystem.

People shopping for a new mattress might be looking for a new bed, they might be remodeling or redecorating, they might be building or moving to a new home, or they might have a medical condition like sleep apnea or a back problem. In each of these cases, the mattress company can partner with other web sites to increase its exposure. Because the other sites have return customers involved in a longer process, they can build a critical mass of customers and content where the mattress company alone cannot.

In the context of discussing their home-remodeling project, some people are very interested in sharing their opinions about beds. Now they are no longer bed shoppers but home remodelers. They have much in common and enjoy helping each other.

Some sites focus on students and their housing needs. Some focus on people relocating. Some are very popular health destinations. In all these cases, the mattress company's expertise fits right into the ongoing conversation.

For a lot of people, convenience is very important. Sites that offer regular conveniences like ordering groceries or drugstore items would make excellent partners. As easily as they order office supplies or groceries online, people can order a mattress using a wizard that asks them questions. They can have the new mattress delivered and installed and have the old one taken away. They'll be guaranteed a good night's sleep or the company will come back tomorrow with another mattress.

Start-ups use these guerilla tactics, but few larger companies do. An important part of your strategy should be to send ambassadors into the lives of your potential customers online. Participate in their activities. Why make them come to you? Set up kiosks around the Web and help other sites make their discussions a success. When visitors ask for more information, invite them to your site. By working from the outside in, you'll attract qualified people who are ready to do business.

Microsyndication

Partnerships online are the rule, not the exception. If your audience would like to read a daily newsletter, someone is ready to provide it. If you have daily coverage of a certain subject, chances are someone is willing to license it.

When books and magazines talk about syndication, they usually mean expert content (advice, columns, and articles) or large data sets (weather, sports scores, etc.). We've already seen how About.com uses hundreds of volunteer and paid guides to help people find information. Here, I'd like to focus on customer-generated content that has value in the marketplace. I call it microsyndication.

One company that has been microsyndicating for years is Geocities.com (now owned by Yahoo!). It's a customer-led community of over 4 million people who want to build their own home pages and become part of a larger community. The company pays for the service with ads that pop up when visitors come to the sites. The residents provide the page inventory and Yahoo! makes money on the ads.

In the past, people building home pages at Geocities were happy just to have their sites hosted and be part of the community. But the company makes a lot of money on the ads. The next step is for the company to share revenues with its residents. When they do that, people with popular pages will be encouraged to create even more content for their audiences.

The important thing about microsyndication is that you don't need anyone's seal of approval besides that of your readers. You don't need to become an editor or work your way up to syndicated columnist. Like Matt Drudge and Harry Jay Knowles, all you need is an audience. If people are beating a path to your door, there will be several ways to charge them for consuming what you produce.

Distance learning is microsyndication. Teachers put up courses and get paid by the number of graduates. Many services online are good examples – advisories, horoscopes, newsletters, stock tips – people will pay for many services by the click.

Much to the government's disappointment, it's not just traceable cash that will trade hands. People will earn scrip, chits, credits – even shares of stock – all by the click. There will be clearinghouses for exchanging everything from frequent-flier miles to massages, and whenever you refer a customer or cause an ad to be displayed, you'll earn something.

Now turn this around. What if someone is willing to spend time looking at photos of properties for sale in Florida? If he qualifies, he might actually get paid for spending time on an advertiser's site. Suppose someone else clicks through a banner for home appliances. If she's in the market and looks at five of their top offers, they'll actually pay her, or make her eligible for some "fabulous prizes."

The future will be filled with people paying each other to go to their web sites, contributing content, and clicking on ads, forming a huge circle of payments that may well net out at zero. The costs of microsyndication are much lower than those of traditional syndication, and the results are often more satisfying.

Through networks, many people will become knowledge workers – adding to, annotating, verifying, and linking for a living. This expansion of the knowledge worker's role in society will continue the spread of the online ecosystem until everything is completely interconnected.

Expert City

Recall that About.com has over 600 chosen guides, who receive 30 percent of the revenues from their sections of the site. In the following scenario, I'll take the About.com model one step further – to a place I'll call Expert City.

Expert City (not to be confused with any actual web site) is an alternative web directory where people can proclaim their expertise on any subject. Its front page looks like a standard web directory, with a search window and a number of top-level categories.

Suppose someone named Tom goes to the site and looks at the dog trainers category. He notices there are no experts on training dogs for the movies, which happens to be his specialty. So he clicks "add a new subcategory," adds his list of movie-dog links, and – *voilà!* – he's just become an expert. He might want to introduce himself, talk about his qualifications, and ask visitors for feedback. He annotates his list for easy reference and keeps it up-to-date. He publishes a weekly newsletter, *The Canine Star,* at the site, leading people to films featuring his dog stars. Pretty soon, people are sending him links to their movie dog sites and asking him how to get their dogs noticed by producers.

If Tom's category is popular, Expert City can sell plenty of ads on his pages. The ads can be more targeted, since the level of customer refinement is quite high. Experts use the service themselves, which is one of the traditional hallmarks of a good multilevel marketing scheme. Every day, new experts arrive and expand the directory.

If you're looking for advice on taking a ski vacation, you may find six different experts who all have extensive lists of links to various ski resources online. You can choose one you like and sign up to be notified when her list changes.

It gets more interesting when there are more experts. You might be looking for a political interpretation of the week's events. There are so many political experts in the system that you decide to go with a meta-expert – someone who monitors the experts and directs you to the expert with the most insightful thing to say that day. Both the meta-expert and the expert of the day receive revenues from your visit. In this way, people can get the opinions of people they relate to, and the opinions of those opinions, too.

The company that runs this microsyndicated directory can charge more for ads because the visitors have bonded with their experts and trust them. Their search results are more relevant. People are more likely to click on an ad if the expert helps the advertisers fine-tune their approach. The company rewards its experts with a significant share of the ad revenues. Experts whose links are popular and whose pages produce the best results for advertisers will be able to make a comfortable living simply by maintaining their links. In a completely competitive market like this, experts may try to discredit each other, merge and cooperate, or try to jazz up their offerings to improve readership. Whatever they do, the audience decides who gets the money. Advertisers are happy. Visitors are happy. And the experts who can keep up with the competition are happy, too.

Expert City is all opinion. But like any brand of journalism, the line between fact and opinion is broad and blurry. Experts make money in this system by getting visits, not by being right. The more popular someone's pages are, the more money she will make. She can tell jokes, lies, link to humor sites, or give straight answers – whatever it takes to get people to click through those ads and see what is on the advertiser's sites. This model is the same as the phone-sex or phone-clairvoyant business – you get paid as long as you keep people interested.

Viral Marketing

There are hundreds of online résumé banks. At some point, someone will figure out that posting résumés is much less efficient than having people turn in their friends to collect the bounty. Imagine going to Bountyhunters.com (again, no relation to any actual web site), where you find job descriptions. If you get $500 for turning in your friends (assuming they take the job and stay six months), you might get more involved with that site.

This recruit-your-friends model is an example of viral marketing – a cousin of microsyndication. In viral marketing, you tap into something people want to tell their friends about. When they do, the word spreads exponentially. All the multilevel marketing schemes we saw in the Old World are just the beginning. Online, one person might be involved in dozens of referral schemes, ranging from credit-card initiation to playing online games and cashing in points.

A marketing scheme is viral only if it taps into people's basic desires, not if it rewards people for doing things they wouldn't ordinarily do. Not all online marketing techniques are viral, but that doesn't keep them from being profitable.

Permission Marketing

Among web sites, people trust some messages more than others. If someone in one of your regular groups says a certain movie is great, you're more likely to see it than if ten strangers tell you it's good. If someone you know trusts someone else, you're likely to trust that person, and you're also likely to trust whomever she trusts. If you have a relationship with a company, you may give that company permission to tell you things you wouldn't like to hear from other companies. In all these cases, a personal connection is much better than a targeted message. Enter the world of permission marketing.

I'll bet you've had an experience where you were shopping in a store, and another customer – an expert – happened to overhear your conversation with the salesperson. When the customer took you aside and gave you his unsolicited recommendation, how did you rate it against the salesperson's? The customer didn't have a stake in the transaction, so you probably gave his recommendation more weight. The salesperson's message was on the left side of the permission line, and the customer-expert's message was on the right side. Everything to the right of that line is in your permission space.

The Permission Line

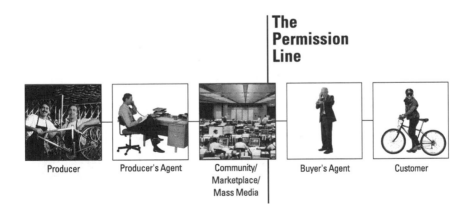

| Producer | Producer's Agent | Community/ Marketplace/ Mass Media | Buyer's Agent | Customer |

The permission line crosses the supply chain on the side of the market nearest the customer. People trust messages that originate closest to themselves. The permission line separates their home turf from random messages in the public marketplace.

Market messages are on the far left edge of the permission marketing spectrum. Trusted messages are on the right. In the middle, people look for signs of allegiance to one side or the other. The closer to the customer, the more trusted the message.

Affiliate programs are a first step toward permission marketing. The Web enables movie studios to set up an affiliate system for referring your friends to the movies you like. If they read about a movie you recommend on your site, click through it to a site that lists show times, and buy tickets, you'll receive a small credit in your movie account. Just by reviewing films and telling your friends, you could easily never have to pay to go to another film again.

Another form of permission marketing involves an infomediary. An infomediary is a trusted third party that lets you keep your information private yet usable online. For example, you may not want to tell an online pharmacy everything about yourself, fearing that your private information will be sold to unscrupulous marketers. So you contact the infomediary, and the infomediary helps you manage your relationships with several online pharmacies. The infomediary acts as a filter, hiding your identity and expressing your interests. Through the infomediary, you can turn off the relationship any time. In this way, you might learn about products and services you're interested in without having to endure unwanted messages.

As you can imagine, people inherently trust messages that come from the right side of the permission line. A community site, like Women.com, starts out in the public marketplace, but intermediates and experts at the site may form their own groups that take them into their own private domain. In this space, the company can't run the same ads it runs on the front page. This is why, for example, there are no ads at Yahoo!'s games site.

On the customer's side of the permission line, the customer drives the relationship. Companies that don't listen can't make it on the right side of the "P" line. The more customers believe that the company is on their side, the more loyal they will be.

Futurizing

The New World is much more like the rain forest than the temperate forest. Residents of the rain forest are tribal – they band together, pack lightly, and can move on a moment's notice. Tribes are much better suited to conditions in the rain forest than armies can ever be. Tribal behavior – territoriality, allegiance to small groups, interdependencies, trading, and mobility – will become more common.

Microsyndication and permission-based marketing make your customers your partners. Without relationships, your company cannot survive online. You don't need big deals with all the established players to be successful. A broad, small-scale approach works better than mass messaging. Work your way into communities of interest around your customers – your neighbors online – and see how they would like you to participate in their online lives.

THE WARNING SIGNS OF E-CANCER

CEO thinks mass e-mail is "viral"

Marketing thinks affiliate programs are easy to implement

Company is proud that its affiliate program hardly pays out any money

Executives think the current business development team can get online and start making deals

Company thinks the distribution channel is moving online

Company relies on ad agency for web strategy

Executives think chat rooms are listening devices

Company relies on "thought leaders" for web strategy

Company measures partnerships in monetary terms

Navigating in the New World

CHAPTER 10

AT CONFERENCES, the number one question people ask me is, "How much does it cost to build a good web site?" What do these people want to hear? They want to hear some low number, so they can go ahead with their plans. They expect me to say something like, "Well, for a small site, it's this much; for a medium-sized site with a shopping cart, this much." They want to hear the secret to saving money. Instead, I give the same answer every time: "How much does it cost to have a baby? The lifetime cost of keeping your commitment is much higher than the initial cost of delivery."

I'm looking forward to the day when the most frequently asked question is, "What does it take to build a good web *business*?" To ask this question, you must be in a completely different mindset. To answer this question, you must be willing to commit to the care and feeding a customer-led organization requires.

After you've built a customer-led web site, and after you've reorganized around customer groups, how do you keep the engine running? How can you expand this effort so it takes over the entire company? In this section, I'll outline the six forward-looking questions a customer-led company continues to ask itself.

What Will Our Next Business Proposition Be?

Listening to your customers naturally leads to new business propositions. Over time, the customer-led company increasingly becomes a total-solution provider.

A perfect example is OnStar, GM's integrated tracking service that puts a personal assistant at your fingertips. The service combines a global positioning system receiver, a cell phone, and a 24-hour call center to give you directions, unlock your car remotely, help you in an emergency, and track your car if it's stolen. They can even call an ambulance if your airbags deploy and you don't answer your phone. The price is reasonable. They protect your privacy. And they put the names of some of their customer-service agents on their web site. Combine this service with the Internet, and GM will have a powerful new platform for keeping in touch with customers. And the customers are happy to pay for all that contact! Pretty soon, they'll be using OnStar to let customers talk with each other as they drive.

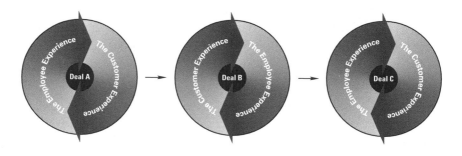

New business propositions continue to move the company forward as the company and the customers roll from one business proposition to the next. Eventually, you can't tell who's leading and who's following.

OnStar is an example of a business proposition that will last for years. As technology improves people's abilities to communicate, your next business proposition may last only a few months. If you have one that works, you might get a chance to refine it. Or the company may be dragged off toward a new one on a moment's notice. It depends on your customers and how they respond. They decide what quality is and when they've had enough.

There are bad ways to move from one business proposition to the next. Magazines and industry pundits may not be the best indicators of your next opportunity. Whatever is supposed to be the next big thing usually isn't. About the worst approach is to look at the most popular web sites and try to add their functionality to your site. Your customers can already go to those other sites. Why would they want to get the same experience from you? Does it really strengthen your brand? No. Just because some web company went public and is now worth billions doesn't mean you should try to copy their business model.

How do you get from one business proposition to the next? Simple. Just listen. As Marriott, Dell, and Microsoft have already realized, customers are more than happy to tell you where they want to go. You don't have to try to come up with the next cash cow. If you're working with your customers, the ideas will bubble up. All you have to do is listen for them, try their ideas out, and pursue those that get the best results. Remember that those at the very top of the customer-loyalty pyramid are the people you should empower to lead you into the future.

How Many Customer Groups Should We Try to Satisfy?

I emphasize a depth-first approach to satisfying your customers 110 percent. Any particular customer group can keep you endlessly busy with new demands. Instead, turn your customers into walking billboards for your company.

Many companies do fine with only one customer group. For example, Priceline.com aims for bargain-hunting nonbusiness travelers. Neimanmarcus.com caters to affluent families. Williamssonoma.com is aimed at home chefs. These companies stick to their customers like glue rather than trying to broaden their horizons to please everyone.

But at some point, you will reach some measurable goals, and you'll know the fire is burning well enough with your initial groups that you can go start more fires. You may want to diversify.

My advice is to start slowly. Think of the business plan for each new customer division as a marriage proposal for a lifelong relationship. Most companies won't have more than four main groups. It will be too hard to compete if you don't have the resources. Following Microsoft's example, it's okay to have 20,000 people plus subcontractors dedicated to only four groups of customers.

Taking on a new group is simply the same exercise all over again. You dedicate a team of people, go back to Chapter 7, and start listening. As you bring on more customer groups, you'll be able to take advantage of tools and processes you've already built. And you'll be able to extend the support layers horizontally to better serve each business unit.

You may not have the resources to create a new division for every customer group you'd like to serve. As your customer-led strategy evolves, you may want to go after new customer groups. This could be set up as a separate incubator operation or remain within the core company.

You may also find that one of your large customer groups really wants to split into two separate divisions. For example, by splitting your senior market into senior men and senior women, you may find these two divisions departing for territory they couldn't cover while combined.

If you can't get completely behind a customer group, you'll do better to say no than to offer less and hope for more in return. The competition will force you to choose your groups carefully. Today, you're probably holding on to at least a couple of groups you would be wise to release. It may be painful, but remember: if you're satisfying your main groups only 99 percent, you're too distracted.

How Can We Transfer New Knowledge to Everyone in the Company?

The CNO must support all her employees as they work their way through the boot camp. The first major milestone is when 20 percent of the people in the company are enrolled beginners. The next is when 20 percent become intermediates. And you know you're really on your way when 20 percent become experts. By then, most of the people should be in boot camp – helping each other, learning, building web sites, and having fun talking with customers.

The CNO should pay most attention to the intermediates. They start new projects and need help implementing them. They teach the beginners. They are enthusiastic about communicating with customers. They build the intranet that leads to more team-building and recruiting flexibility.

The CNO should keep a helpful eye out for members of the upper management team who break through into intermediate status. Many executives may never become experts, but if they are all strong intermediates the company will learn much faster than if a fraction are experts and a fraction are still beginners. Another trick is to pair executives with customers. Give a few expert customers their own pet executive to get to know. When the executive relies on the customer for support, you know there is a lot of learning going on.

The learning process should have built-in incentives. When employees graduate from beginners to intermediates, the CNO should recognize them. When intermediates become experts, the company should give them some special honor. The process doesn't have to institutionalize a rigorous training program in which everyone learns exactly the same thing. Becoming an expert should be more like being a graduate student – people should be able to work on a project and complete it, understanding how it could be improved before going on to graduate school.

Setting the web division up in new offices is an excellent way to make the change real to everyone. It's important for people to understand that to enter this division is to enter the New World. They must physically leave their Old World desk behind. In the new e-business unit, there is a new and nimble human-resources group. There are new support people. Things are run differently. People use new tools. Everyone has an employee "buddy" and a customer "buddy." Every so often, there is an incoming class of beginners. Each incoming class has a project to do.

Should We Implement a One-to-One System?

In their groundbreaking work, Don Peppers and Martha Rogers outline an approach that promotes a one-to-one relationship between the customer and the company. In essence, they advocate that companies build profiles on each customer and use those profiles to offer better service. In business-to-business terms, it means customizing extranet site tools for each customer. In consumer terms, it means giving people their own custom home page on your site. The more your customer tells you, the better you can serve her. All of this takes place on the customer's side of the permission line.

As your customers get to know you, they will be willing to tell you more about themselves. Manufacturers will find it harder to establish one-to-one relationships than magazines or retailers will. Service businesses can often get a head start by building customer profiles as part of their first contact with customers.

Experts in the customer-loyalty pyramid will most likely demand a highly personalized approach. They'll want to keep track of their accounts. They'll want to be notified with personalized e-mails. They'll want you to remember them every time they contact you. They'll want to set up their use of your web site so they don't have to repeat actions you can automate for them. Even intermediates are usually interested in a one-click checkout when shopping online.

While the one-to-one approach involves powerful tools for improving the customer experience, the customer-led approach involves people interacting with other people. A customer-led web site attracts groups of people who are interested in meeting each other. A customer-led company encourages customers to help each other solve problems. Ultimately, customers gang up on the company and get involved in the development of the products and services they want. People are much more powerful in groups than as individuals. As effective as the one-to-one approach is, it's just a tactical part of a customer-led strategy.

What Other Skills Will We Have to Improve?

Companies beginning to implement a customer-led strategy find that many of their Old World habits become liabilities. Your company may simply become a single web site with thousands of people behind it. In the New World, that's not something to be afraid of. Once your company commits to the Web, you won't get many second chances to make a good impression online. A few reminders here underscore the fact that becoming customer-led isn't business as usual.

The use of plain English is a competitive advantage. Most web sites are full of jargon. Copywriters sanitize their corporate communications until they become meaningless. Most companies communicate using the passive voice, rather than an active, personal voice. They use a formal writing style that both complicates and generalizes their messages, then they wonder why no one takes the time to read them. We can all learn to write better. With hundreds of employees sending thousands of messages daily, a series of seminars on simple, clear writing might be an excellent investment.

Make your presentations web-based. PowerPoint is an Old World tool. It reinforces the kind of linear thinking that stifles innovation. Look at every document in your company and see if it really serves its purpose. People making presentations today usually prepare a sequence of blue-

and-yellow slides, each with a title and 4 to 7 bullet points, then they read the slides to their audience while their audience takes a nap. Sound familiar? Any time a diagram or chart pops up, the 3-D "graphics" turn the data into a rocket ship, a rising pizza, or a set of barrels and boxes connected by yellow arrows. Better tools exist, and even better tools are coming. You'll see some examples in Part 3.

Team communication is not a natural gift. Teamwork usually suffers if team members have never communicated with each other in person. Team members should work side-by-side for a period before breaking into virtual teams. A company can set up a training campus, where new teams can come together for weeks at a time to sharpen their skills and learn to work together efficiently. It's also a great chance for project managers to form their own groups and support each other in sharing new knowledge.

Understanding others is a skill you can learn. I have already mentioned the failure of the Golden Rule in business and the usefulness of the Myers-Briggs tests for understanding temperaments. Still, deep down, it's almost impossible to know what motivates individuals. The less you assume about your customers and co-workers, and the more they tell you about themselves, the better.

Women will be key players in your new administration. In times like these, when your transition to a customer-led company is critical to your survival, women may turn out to be better listeners, who are more attuned to customers' needs than men are. They are often better than men at cooperating, communicating, sharing, and collaborating under pressure.

Men who have achieved high levels of technical proficiency may hold on to Old World notions much longer than women. They may believe that most of what they need to learn is technical. They may unconsciously think of the Internet as a "guy thing," because it involves complex technology. But the Internet is actually very egalitarian, and the higher levels of New World learning are all about communication. In the New World, I expect customer-led companies to have more women at the top than most companies do now.

Consultants can and should support your tactical decisions. While you can develop your overall strategy with your customers' input, you should rely on outside consultants to help implement many of your customer-led programs. You will want to call on web site auditors, e-commerce specialists, information architects, designers, writers, groupware gurus, and many other specialists who can come in and help build your online business unit. Consultants are New World people who left their day jobs to help other people learn what they have learned. Helpful consultants ask helpful questions. They will help you turn your existing employees into New World collaborators. Poor consultants, on the other hand, are full of solutions. Beware the Old World experts! Look for coaches, not answers.

Let integrity guide your actions. Integrity is one cylinder of the engine that will power your transition into the New World. The truth economy is already in motion both inside and outside your company – the cost of misjudging people continues to climb. It's easy to make assumptions about what people need to know and what they don't. Archiving employees' knowledge in databases doesn't make them expendable. The Customer-Led Revolution will result in everyone being treated as individuals rather than cogs in a machine. Patience and openness will be your allies as you move your company forward.

Tell the truth sooner and more often. When interviewing a candidate for a position, you can usually tell within the first few minutes if a person isn't right for the job. You try to get it over with as soon as possible. What do you say at the end? Something positive. Something hopeful. Now think about business deals. Don't you hate it when you make a proposal and other people put you off, saying it's going to take more time to decide? How many times have you said, "If they would just tell me the answer is 'no,' that would be fine. But this indecision is really costing me." People are often indecisive when they are trying hard to avoid saying something negative. They hope that in time you will go away.

It's often uncomfortable to tell the truth, but you can learn. I've found one approach that helps – giving percentages. If you give someone a percentage chance that something will happen, you're able to be much more straightforward. If it's zero percent, you can always say ten percent, and you're covered. If you're conscientious about telling people what the percentage chance is, and if you can stay away from the dreaded 50/50 prognosis (no real information there), you can prevent a lot of second guessing.

Acknowledge mistakes. If people aren't making mistakes, they aren't learning. I once heard of a restaurant owner who rewards the employee who makes the biggest mistake of the month with a special parking space for the next month. When there is no stigma or punishment attached, everyone can learn from a mistake in a positive way. Better to make a mistake and be recognized than to pretend to have all the answers and let something build into a real problem.

Recognize the competition. Most companies recognize the competition in a spirit of combat rather than respect. How many companies have mission statements that talk about "doing things right," "putting the customer first," and "being market leaders"? How does that set them apart? Understanding and respecting your competition should be a cornerstone of your corporate culture. If your competitors are much better at something than you are, telling your customers to trust you with the task makes you look silly. Your competitors deserve your respect. If you're going to take market share away from them, pick your customer groups carefully and make it clear through your actions, not your claims, that you are the obvious choice.

Make cultural issues a number one priority. Whether it's in mergers or day-to-day management, a CEO sets the tone of the company. In a customer-led company, executives think of themselves as one of the flock. They take responsibility for the customers who are the biggest pains in the neck. They set an example by supporting the Internet boot camp and evangelizing alongside their customer champions. The word will get around – via e-mail, on the intranet, in the virtual hallways – "Our boss is really committed to this stuff!"

Following customers doesn't mean the company loses its ability to compete. On the contrary, following customers rewards employees for investing their time in customer relationships. There is a customer out there for every employee, and there is a customer-led strategy for every group of employees willing to follow, rather than lead. Can you imagine people like Henry Ford or Larry Ellison saying, "We get our corporate vision from our customers"? Probably not. But that's what they say at Microsoft, FedEx, and most companies leading the way into the New World.

Learn to give before you get. E-customers expect a lot. You must invest in your relationship with them and not expect immediate financial returns. Most companies are still scrambling for market share. Some companies spend quite a lot of money to acquire each new online customer; they tell themselves the payoff will come later. But rather than trying to push more people into the bottom of your customer-loyalty pyramid, why not pull them up through the pyramid from the top? It might be better to add people who can establish personal relationships with prospective customers than to spend more money on ads.

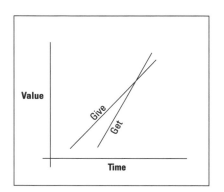

How Can Employees Get More Online Experience?

Companies going online focus way too much on e-commerce. If you are serious about making the transition to the New World, I suggest you think about giving something to the Internet community without asking for anything in return. No matter how large your company is, you can identify a suitable project and do it simply for the reward of seeing it succeed. You might need to find partners. You might need to raise money. You might need to learn things you never thought you'd learn.

There is no shortage of exciting project possibilities online. From identifying land mines to helping refugees to finding lost children to mapping the surface of Mars – there is a project out there right now that could use your help. Some companies are willing to sponsor a project in return for a banner ad and some good press, but that's not what I mean. I would like to see every company in the Fortune 2000 participate by building goodwill online, contributing to a specific worthwhile goal. Come to Futurizenow.com – we'll start you with a list of projects that could use your help.

If you're dedicated to helping, listening, and learning, your company will turn into a customer-led company faster than you expect. Next thing you know, you'll be surrounded by seasoned experts.

NETAID.COM

An easy entry point to giving online is Cisco and the UN's Netaid.com project, a clearinghouse for people trying to eradicate poverty in the world. This online training ground is an excellent way to bring people up to speed, have them bond with others around the world, and raise money for an important cause. With companies like Cisco leading the way, there will be many such efforts in the years to come.

Futurizing

It's the CNO's job to close the gap between beginners and experts until he or she is out of a job. Companies like stock brokerages, banks, software companies – maybe even toy stores – are quickly evolving into big web sites with thousands of dedicated people behind them. Management has no time to waste in preparing the way for the entire company to come on board.

The view from behind is crystal clear. Following our customers allows us to take a more relaxed, Zen-like attitude toward the tsunami that is engulfing us. We can swim in the New World. We had this ability all along! We no longer need to hold our breath. We can relax and go with the flow. What looked like a weak strategy – *following* – actually turns out to be the strongest choice for the turbulent times ahead.

THE WARNING SIGNS OF E-CANCER

Company's budget for copiers exceeds budget for networking

Company's budget for networking exceeds budget for listening

CEO thinks CNO doesn't get regular calls from venture capitalists

Company thinks investing in the Web is building a web site

Company is in same building as before

Company is in same business as before

Paint on walls is the same color as before

People's heart rates are the same as before

CNO really does not get regular calls from venture capitalists

By 2005, thousands of companies will have a much narrower customer focus and internal structures that reflect their choice of customer groups. Who your customers are – not what your mission statement is – will define your company. In fact, all customer-led companies have the same basic mission statement: YOU'RE IN CHARGE.

In the next section of the book, I invite you to practice being your own consultant by applying customer-led principles to a range of different businesses. I hope it will help you hone some of the skills you've learned so far. But most important, I hope these scenarios will help you clarify your own goals and inspire you to take the plunge into the customer-led sea.

PART 3

Prototypes

Everyone thinks of changing the world, but no one thinks of changing himself.

– Leo Tolstoy

Introduction

In Part 3, we'll look at eight fictitious companies – a bank, a steel fabricator, a bookstore, a grocery store, a start-up, even a giant pharmaceutical company – as case studies. The sample companies sell substantially different products and services, but all apply one or more of the customer-led principles described in Parts 1 and 2 as they shift from being management-led Old World businesses to customer-led businesses of the future.

Each chapter in Part 3 illustrates at least one customer-led principle. In almost every case, the company must re-examine its customer groups. Identifying a company's primary customer groups in the new customer-led environment – and then following their lead – is the most visionary aspect of transforming the company. Keep this in mind as you read the case studies. They may not represent the particular business you're in, but the lessons they offer are relevant to your own customer-led strategy.

Grocery Store

CHAPTER 11

THE STOCK OPENED DOWN, then it sank like a rock. By noon, the executives at Whole Harvest, Inc., had seen its market capitalization drop 20 percent. They were in shock. Their company had been the darling of the early 1990s stock market. They had opened 16 natural food stores around the country in the last 12 months. Earnings were right on target. What had happened? An analyst in New York had issued a release saying the grocery business was entering a new era and that Whole Harvest wasn't prepared for the fight.

Meanwhile, in an office park near Sacramento, California, two brothers were celebrating. They were looking at the left column of the front page of *The Wall Street Journal*. The headline read: "The Future of Upscale Retail." The article told their story. Six months after getting their venture capital, the brothers, an MBA and an online marketing consultant, had launched a web site called Yourfoods.com. The site catered to high-end customers who wanted organic food, cruelty-free products, hypoallergenic vitamins, recycled paper goods, and kosher products.

Yourfoods.com had one web site and a staff of just 80 people (compared with Whole Harvest's 38 stores and 2,200 people). The company had no inventory, no warehouses, and no trucks – yet it was making deliveries to customers within hours of their orders! Yourfoods.com's margins were better than Whole Harvest's, its prices were lower, and more than 300,000 customers had signed up in the first six months. The brothers were already talking about a public stock offering!

Back at Whole Harvest, the executives had just convened an emergency session when the phone rang. It was David the Vegetarian, calling from his cell phone. The CEO, wondering how this guy had managed to get past his assistant yet again, listened to David complain about the meat department cooking free samples in the Whole Harvest store where David shopped. As usual. But this call, David said, would be his last, because he was through with Whole Harvest. David said he was taking his business elsewhere. He was going to start shopping at Yourfoods.com. *Click.*

Too Little, Too Late

Whole Harvest *had* an Internet strategy. The company even had an e-commerce site, where people could order supplements and canned items. Management had farmed out all the web tasks as the consultants recommended. They had cut 20 percent off the list price for online shoppers. The site had a store locator, investor information, and news articles about current legislation affecting the food-supplement industry. The webmaster even provided a form customers could fill out to send an e-mail message to their congressional representatives! The company was doing a reasonable business online, though it wasn't yet making any money. What was wrong?

Whole Harvest, like hundreds of thousands of businesses today, was looking behind, not ahead. Its CEO hadn't spent much time on the Web. He wasn't even aware that Yourfoods.com existed, though his customers were finding it easily. Whole Harvest's executives considered the Internet to be a shift in technology, not a shift in the company-to-customer relationship. They were wrong.

Many of Whole Harvest's customers were already online, demanding a high level of service. Because online Whole Harvest didn't have courteous sales personnel handling people's requests, as it did in the stores, it should have gone out of its way to provide not only exceptional service but also complete information about the products they sold.

Whole Harvest wants to get back in the online game before it's too late. The company is willing to do everything the online competition is doing and more. But competing successfully online is not simply a matter of the logistics of stocking, picking, packing, and delivering perishables, or of hardware and software infrastructure. Whole Harvest's executives need a winning strategy for "owning" the high-end customers the company enjoys in its retail stores. They need a coach. Or maybe a whole coaching staff. Let's see what we can do to help as the Whole Harvest executives plan their future online business.

The Whole Harvest E-Customer

First, we gather information about the Whole Harvest customers, both on their site and elsewhere online. After spending a day coming up with questions, we use small product giveaways to entice people to answer those questions. (We've learned from experience that big prizes don't attract the right kinds of people.) We also spend several days in the stores asking customers about their online buying habits. Soon, we have enough information to draw some conclusions.

> **BUSINESS ASSUMPTIONS FOR THIS CHAPTER**
>
> Whole Harvest will deliver orders to customers' doors by the end of the next business day
>
> Whole Harvest will provide both safe boxes and refrigerators either at cost or on a rental basis, or at no charge to customers who maintain a certain minimum monthly order balance
>
> Whole Harvest will provide a drive-up window at its retail stores for order pickups
>
> Whole Harvest will set up a customer-service number to receive orders and handle complaints

As we suspected, the people who shop at Whole Harvest aren't generally looking for the best price. In fact, price is their sixth consideration, behind health, safety, quality, convenience, and individual shopping preferences.

Next, we divide the customers into smaller customer segments. That's where customer modeling comes in. Let's look at some typical Whole Harvest customers, based on the responses from the questionnaires:

Andrew and Shelli have two young children. As parents, they are very concerned about the purity of the food they buy. They are interested in buying the least processed foods possible, and they want to know when an organically grown alternative is available. They don't want synthetic hormones in their milk, antibiotics in their chicken, or pesticides on their vegetables, and they're willing to pay more, if necessary, to avoid them.

Greg and Marcie keep a kosher household. They need to know whether a given item has dairy products, meat products, or neither. They want to design meals from a large database of recipes, indicate how many servings they need, and have all the ingredients for the meals packed and shipped together.

Tereza has severe allergies; her husband, Doug, has asthma. For Tereza, knowing whether a product contains peanuts – even trace amounts – is a matter of life and death. She knows from experience that package labels don't always tell the whole story. Tereza is also allergic to wheat and is always on the lookout for breads and pastas made with other grains. Certain foods and preservatives can trigger Doug's asthma. He is active in asthma groups online and prefers herbal remedies to prescription drugs.

Sabine has a new baby. After her baby is weaned, Sabine wants to feed him organically grown food. She wants to know which baby-food companies, if any, use organically grown vegetables and fruit. If she can't find a source, she'll make her own. She also wants advice on homeopathic remedies for children's health problems, such as earaches. She'd like to buy diapers that have the least impact on the environment. She buys lots of books on nutrition, health, and healing.

David is a strict vegetarian. He wants to say what kind of vegetarian he is, and he's interested only in products that don't contain items on his exclusion list. He would be happy to order from home because he finds the meat counter at the store distasteful.

Annuschka is concerned about her kids eating too much sugar. She wants to know how much sugar is in everything she buys. She wants product ingredient lists with sugar ranked as a percentage of total calories. She is very interested in health articles about food-related diseases and preventatives.

Scott and Amy are animal lovers. They want to buy pet food that is good for their pets. Amy wants cosmetics that have not been tested on animals, and they both want dolphin-safe canned tuna and other cruelty-free foods and nonfood items. If a product isn't labeled cruelty-free, they're unsure about buying it.

Dan and Gail live in a condominium. They want to organize a food-buying club in their building. Dan and Gail lived in a housing co-op when they were in college and enjoyed buying and sharing food with their neighbors. They discovered that getting together to order and divide up the food was a real community builder. Another motivation is saving money – bulk purchases will keep their food expenses down.

Mary is an information addict. She's willing to pay retail prices if she can learn everything about the various products she buys and is able to make her own comparisons. She's often frustrated by store clerks who don't know much, if anything, about their products. She also prefers to cook by recipe – she wants to be able to put her own recipes into the system and use them to order from.

People with the preferences and concerns these Whole Harvest customers expressed add up to more than half of all Whole Harvest customers. They all care about *something,* and they want a retailer who cares that they care.

If You Build It, They Will Come

At first glance, it seems impossible that one store could satisfy all the Whole Harvest customers' very specific preferences and requests. Whole Harvest's suppliers and distributors have very little of the information the customers want. It would also mean increasing the amount of information the company presents online by a factor of at least ten. Whole Harvest can't meet its customers' requests for information until someone finds and enters that information into the system and vigilantly maintains it. That could take years!

But these aren't ordinary customers. These are *e-customers*. They can lift ten times their body weight in information! They would be happy to help the store help them. They will put time and energy into making this store the place where they want to shop.

First, we match the most profitable ten customer groups with enthusiastic, like-minded hosts inside the company. Second, we solicit ten customer-group representatives to help organize the categories (the people named in the scenarios above are all willing to accept this role).

Third, we put all the hosts and customer representatives in a hotel conference room for a weekend and ask them to come up with a plan for each group and how they would coordinate their efforts.

Helping allergy sufferers. Tereza, the allergy sufferer, knows better than anyone on the Whole Harvest staff which products are likely to contain peanuts or peanut oil. She would be happy to help build and maintain the peanut-content database. Her host helps her start a peanut-allergy discussion group on the Whole Harvest web site, and everyone in the group contributes to compiling a product list. Whole Harvest offers Tereza access to its product database, as well as the aid of a company host who spends four hours a week typing in ingredient lists.

The customers who handle this neighborhood of the online store will create their own content, send out alerts, and keep the database current. Tereza and members of the peanut-allergy community worldwide – even those who will never buy from the company – all work together to maintain the database and keep an eye out for new products that might be problematic.

The Whole Harvest database soon becomes a world-class source of information. People start to use the site for research purposes. Tereza and the host begin linking to allergy-related sites and sending out newsletters to all peanut-concerned cybercitizens, many of whom will begin to shop at Whole Harvest. Groups that track walnuts and other allergens begin to form. Tereza eventually becomes a customer delegate to the company.

Supporting a cause. Scott and Amy, the animal lovers, are involved in the cruelty-free movement. Many items that are not labeled cruelty-free actually are cruelty-free. Some items that are cruelty-free come from companies who do animal testing on other products. Scott and Amy are probably more familiar with these intricacies than any Whole Harvest employee. The company would be wise to help Scott and Amy share their knowledge with others who have similar concerns.

Scott and Amy are also interested in supporting businesses that raise food animals in humane conditions. They would be thrilled to set up a discussion group on the topic. Amy, in particular, is familiar with the local farms that raise free-range chickens and with the family-run dairies in the area. She would be willing to do profiles on the producers for the Whole Harvest web site in the hope of building a market for those products.

Cooperating with co-ops. The condominium building Dan and Gail live in has 130 units. They've convinced their owners' association to provide a storage room with shelves and a refrigerator for grocery deliveries.

Dan wants to be sure the produce is fresh. Does he need a web-cam to scan the broccoli for freshness and a robotic arm to test the avocados? No! He'll specify how he likes his produce and then trust Whole Harvest to provide it. Because Whole Harvest is making an effort to be customer-led, they'll do their best to choose fruits and vegetables that meet Dan's requests. Once Dan trusts the company, he convinces other people in the building to add their orders to his. The company can also offer the buying group first choice on odd lots and special purchases.

Whole Harvest can offer the buying club an extranet site to make purchasing more convenient. Once customers trust that a company will deliver quality merchandise, they are likely to trust it on other matters of judgment as well. A number of people in Dan's building are interested in organic produce and enjoy getting whatever is in season. Whole Harvest can offer them a special place on its web site to discuss their needs. On the extranet, buying club members can collaborate on orders, plan special meals and events, and share recipes and kitchen tools – all activities that will build community.

Eventually, the group gets its buyer involved with meal planning and trusts her to send entire dinner kits based on the number of people eating on a particular night. The buying club establishes recurring orders that are the basis for its weekly delivery. By preselling recurring products on a monthly or seasonal basis, Whole Harvest enjoys better inventory control and can better match its orders to demand.

Consumer watchdogs. Mary, the information addict, likes to comparison shop. She wants Whole Harvest to set up an unaffiliated comparison engine that compares Whole Harvest's products against those available elsewhere. In this scenario, the company becomes a true infomediary, giving its customers the tools and the privacy – and therefore the confidence – to shape the store according to their wishes. If Mary learns that Whole Harvest's competitor offers a better product for a better price, she can link to that company's site. Obviously, that would signal Whole Harvest that it should consider carrying the product!

Similarly, if enough people want to boycott a product for any reason, they should be able to inform other customers about the boycott on a prominent page on the site. Boycotts that gather momentum send a message to Whole Harvest about suppliers it should weed out.

Customer Democracy

The Whole Harvest scenario illustrates how a company can work with any customer group it cares about. The online system is flexible and easy to use. If one person is in several groups, he can use the system to configure a custom home page that makes him a "resident" of several neighborhoods simultaneously. Once the first ten neighborhoods are running smoothly, the company doesn't have to delegate any more hosts. Any customer with a particular interest or concern can start a new neighborhood, and it only takes 200 like-minded shoppers to get their own host and a link from the home page.

To help facilitate the various neighborhood discussions, Whole Harvest can publish a customer's bill of rights as well as guidelines on how customers can form groups to influence company policy. The more involved the customers are, the more they will help maintain the site.

Whole Harvest should expect some controversy. There will be mistakes in the research and some overzealous customers. The company may lose a few suppliers who aren't interested in the scrutiny provided by these enthusiastic volunteers. The hosts will get to know individual customers, at least by reputation, and will have to weed out the few troublemakers.

Customers will provide all the filtering information for the site. They should be able to ask to see products ranked by overall popularity or by popularity within groups that have achieved a level of credibility on the web site.

New groups form easily. Customers can gang up on the company and ask it to carry new products. Done properly, the customers will perform the buyers' roles so well that the buyers simply become facilitators.

Whole Harvest's customer advisory board is made up of delegates who represent the targeted customer groups. These energetic people are often willing to work for recognition, but the company can also show its appreciation by offering them shopping credits, special deals, referrals, and invitations to the annual convention. The company can ask them to write articles for the web site and to partner with other health-conscious online businesses to attract new customers.

At the end of every year, Whole Harvest may want to give a certain percentage of its profits to local charities. Which charities? The customers can decide. Customers receive a vote for every dollar they've spent at the store during the year. The customer advisory board compiles the final list of candidate charities, one of which may even be a rebate to all Whole Harvest customers. The company then distributes the profit allotment according to the customers' wishes.

Expanding the Business Proposition

The Whole Harvest web site is now a very "sticky" environment, presenting an ideal opportunity for cross-selling. Whole Harvest customers throwing a party should be able to shop for the whole event online, from a decorated cake to a wine that matches the meal perfectly.

Many Whole Harvest customers are interested in environmental issues – the company could offer special eco-tour packages and adventures. Customers interested in the combined benefits of diet and exercise will be interested in exercise equipment, fitness videos, workout clothes, and more. Now that customers have banded together, the company can help customers form buying groups for long-distance telephone service, entertainment packages, travel, and other goods and services.

The customers should be able to take Whole Harvest in new directions. If they ask for clothing made with organically grown cotton, or if the company offers some and gets a positive response, Whole Harvest could find itself in the clothing business. If the company discovers that the bulk of its customers are families, Whole Harvest may want to redefine itself as a family store or spin off a separate business. It's much better to follow a school of fish and adapt to their movements than to stand still with your content "nets" and try to catch new customers as they happen to swim by.

Organic Changes

How does this new external environment change the company internally? Customer profiles and customer groups become the primary tools for running the business. The company never wonders what to do next, because the hosts help prioritize a customer wish list for each group. People in management, accounting, human resources, and information technology must cater to the needs of the groups. Some groups will be more fussy than others. Everyone – including management – will have to adjust accordingly.

The annual Whole Harvest customer convention helps adjust the course and set new objectives. It should be a huge all-day event, with plenty of opportunities for the hosts to meet and talk with their constituents. The neighborhood hosts should be empowered to deepen their relationships with their customer delegates, give them awards, and let customers air their views on where to take their part of the company. The convention should be an important part of the company-customer dialogue that everyone looks forward to.

A static, supplier-based company can transform itself into a dynamic, customer-led one. Allowing customers to lead creates a dramatic shift in power within the organization. That shift in power is the real key to making any company a New World success.

What happened to the two brothers at the beginning of this chapter? As a pure play, they were able to take a lot of the Northern California market. But Whole Harvest – with a complete turnaround in thinking and fast action – held on to first place in the lucrative Bay Area market. A year after that eye-opening *Wall Street Journal* article, the executives at Whole Harvest were featured in the left-hand column with a story of their own.

OLD MISSION STATEMENT | To offer the widest selection of the highest quality natural food products.

NEW MISSION STATEMENT | To partner with our customers in providing for themselves and their families.

Magazine Publisher

CHAPTER 12

I WAS ONCE PRIVILEGED TO SPEAK at a conference organized by a company that publishes dozens of magazines, mostly centered around home themes: family, garden, architecture, interiors, remodeling, crafts, woodworking, travel, and so on. The company is a large media conglomerate, with books, videos, television, and other properties. The conference was centered around the company's response to the Internet.

My talk and others' were about web sites and the systems to build them. Everyone seemed preoccupied with creating the technical infrastructure that would let the various magazines serve their content on the Web. Most of the people were young and energetic. They talked about outbound e-messaging, constellation sites, interstitial ads, sticky channels, vortex marketing, portal power, and content management. They were concerned with banner ads, click-through rates, real-time rate cards, creating a network of sites for various visitor groups, "vectoring" readers from the magazine into the site, and the business model behind their online brand-extension programs. All very cutting edge.

But the most interesting presentation came at the end of the seminar. An unassuming middle-aged guy named Tom stepped up to the lectern. He showed a sequence of simple slides, mostly graphs. Tom is a full-time demographer. He was talking about the aging baby boomers and how they were going to affect the company's magazines. He was explaining that in 1900, the average American died at age 50. Today, that number is 80 and rising. The quarter-century increase isn't just tacked onto the end. These extra years now come after child-raising and family years, but before old age. Most people won't run into serious health problems until they are 70. For the first time in history, he said, we have a cohort of people – the 76 million u.s. baby boomers – who will add those 25 extra years between the ages of 50 and 75.

Modern medicine and a host of other socioeconomic factors have combined to give this generation 25 additional years of good health, wealth, and a strong desire for adventure and activity. Tom explained how this was going to impact the company's business.

And then he said one of the smartest things I've ever heard in a corporate environment. He said, "From our first magazine in the 1920s to the 60 million readers we reach today, this company has grown to keep up with the changing needs of our readers. I've always believed that our job is helping families keep their commitments."

It struck me that if a company has even one person who truly understands what business the company is in and can communicate it that well, that company is in better shape than most. This company could have hired an army of hotshot consultants to work on mission statements and e-commerce initiatives, and they wouldn't have come up with that simple statement. *Helping families keep their commitments* has stuck in my mind as a mantra that serves the company very well.

Keeping Commitments Online

That's a true story. To continue the discussion, I'll focus on a fictitious company called Allmag, which is similar to the company I just described. This time, however, I'm going to put Tom in charge of the effort. Tom doesn't know much about technology, but he surfs the Internet often. As a demographer, he's fascinated by the opportunity to listen to people.

The first thing we need to do is translate Tom's focus on customers into a coherent strategy for going online. Rather than trying to figure out how to make an e-business out of the company's existing magazines, let's start by understanding who their core readers are.

Allmag comes into a couple's life when they buy their first home. Most couples buy three homes during their lives, each corresponding to the changing needs of their family. Some couples buy a third house when the woman is in her early- to mid-50s (the age at which she stops working). But most stay and remodel the home where they raised their families.

Allmag's readership is women, from the time they get married until they are into their 70s. From a demographic point of view, American heterosexual couples go through the following life stages, as measured by the woman's age:

Women get married for the first time at about age 25

Women have their first child at a median age of 26.5

Couples generally buy their first house when the woman is 28 to 30

Couples buy their second house when the woman is 39 to 42 (the kids are in their teen years)

Children are normally out of the house by the time the woman is 49 (80 percent of 49-year-old women are working)

These facts drive every aspect of Allmag's business strategy. Tom identifies three markets for the company's major magazines: families with young children, families with teens, and seniors (also called empty nesters). As the baby boom generation ages, the third market will grow dramatically. By 2020, the number of women ages 50 to 69 will increase from 26.5 million to 40.7 million – a staggering 54 percent jump.

A media company needs to understand how it fits into its readers' lives, and Tom – the guy who doesn't understand technology – has a pretty clear idea. According to him, people have three zones of communication.

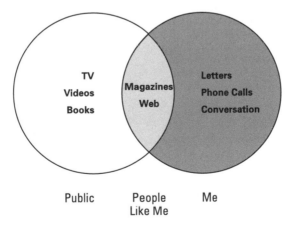

Everyone has different ways of talking to strangers, people in affinity groups, and friends and family. Each medium has an appropriate audience online.

In this view, magazines and the Web are on a continuum that emphasizes people's connections to other people they don't know. Magazines, like web sites, filter information. By choosing to read a certain magazine and the sections inside it, you are filtering information from the outside world through people that you have begun to trust. Tom has thought about this process and has conceived Eight Cs that describe online relationships. The Cs work together to create a cycle of satisfying, repeat experiences for the web visitor.

THE EIGHT Cs OF THE WEB

Community: I can meet and interact with people like me.

Continuity: I can go from one session to the next easily, no matter how much time has elapsed.

Convenience: I can get what I'm looking for quickly and intuitively.

Customization: I want to see what I want, I don't want to see what I don't want – most of the time.

Commerce: The web makes transactions easier.

Content: I want very deep content, and I want to be able to mine it to get what I'm looking for.

Commitment: I want to know that you will help me in the future. If you don't have what I'm looking for, you'll go get it for me.

Control: I want to control our relationship. I want to turn it on or off, and anything you do with my information should be with my permission.

Internal Alignment

Allmag has been focusing on its three main markets for years. How is Allmag organized internally? Allmag has both vertical and horizontal products (a quilting magazine and a Southwest-living magazine, for example). Although the company has many more vertical products, the horizontal monthly magazines have traditionally been the heavyweights.

Any magazine that sells to 2 million people is going to be a sacred cow with firmly entrenched staff. The smaller, more targeted brands rise and fall with consumer interest.

The company has a separate research department that is built on its huge database of subscriber and sales information and reader input (letters, phone calls, events). Allmag mines the data to look for trends and signals. This balance of brand-based affinity and broad spectral analysis gives Allmag the ability to launch new products more successfully than its competitors. The question is: How will Allmag keep up with its e-customers?

The company either stays with its current approach – brands plus overall research – or it follows groups of customers through their life stages. In futurizing the company, should Allmag align with *people,* whose commitments change over time – or should it align with *commitments,* whose people change over time?

We'll spend the rest of this chapter on that question. To do that, we'll look at the company's three large horizontal markets: families with small children, families with older children, and empty nesters. In each section to follow, we will investigate how Allmag can help people in these three groups keep their commitments. Along the way, we'll ask questions about brands, loyalty, and business models. At the end of the chapter, we'll return to this question and decide which alignment would make the most business sense.

Families with Young Children

Most couples buy their first home when the first child is under five years of age. That's when they show up on the Allmag radar. What does Allmag know about these people and their commitments? What challenges do they face in keeping them? And how do they behave online? We need to know more about these people before we can give them any answers.

Fortunately, my sister Carla serves as a model customer. Today, she is 36 years old, is in her first house, has two children and one on the way, and still has the husband she originally started with. She works at home doing bookkeeping for her husband's and her stepfather's businesses. She is the family chef and bookkeeper as well. She does a lot of community and charity work, and she is very active in her boys' education.

Needless to say, Carla has a lot of commitments: family, house, job, health, school, community, friends. One of her biggest commitments is to save enough money for all the things she wants to do in the future: preparing for the new baby's arrival in a few months, sending her kids to private school, taking family vacations, getting a bigger house some day, buying a new car next year, etc. She and her husband have many activity-related commitments: to their car pool, soccer club, Little League, the local community center, and spending time with their friends.

Carla subscribes to several Allmag magazines. Her favorite subjects are parenting, entertainment, travel, interior design, cooking, and kids. She often buys magazines off the rack that address a near-term event or problem.

Her online time is spent either in the morning after the kids go to school or late at night after they are asleep. Her "food" on the Internet is, in this order: world news, local news, shopping, financial news, health tips, cooking (tips, techniques, ideas, recipes), weather, movie reviews, entertainment news, and travel research.

What would she like to see on a single site? Carla can imagine having a personal magazine that has all her content right in one place: relevant news; research tools; a database of home, family, and activity tips; recipes and menu ideas; shopping tools; local events and weather; and so on.

For Carla, the focus must be on content. The site must be deep and searchable. She isn't interested in having to visit five different sites to get everything she's looking for. Her site would revolve around her top five areas of concern and eliminate just about everything else. If Carla is going to click on a "pets channel" button, she isn't going there to browse. She's going to have a very specific question on her mind. If the question isn't answered, she's gone.

In cases where one brand's content is narrow and deep, Allmag could be very competitive. For example, Allmag may have more recipes in its database than any other site online. On the other hand, all back issues of Allmag's parenting magazine may constitute a significant body of information, but by now it probably pales in comparison with what people can find at some of the early parenting web sites that have now matured. And Allmag isn't in the news or weather business, so the company will need to find partners for that content if it wants to keep Carla on its site.

Carla's two boys keep her very busy. She spends most of her day in "kidworld." She has a close group of friends, many of whom also have children, but she is interested in staying more in touch with the rest of the world and subjects that used to interest her. She wants to be in touch with people like herself and *not* talk about kids. She would probably be willing to spend another hour a week online just to interact with other people like her. A community of parents would give her the opportunity to meet people, make new friends, join a discussion, read books and talk about them, or do projects online together – as long as she could do her part asynchronously (on her own time).

People say they want information, but busy people like Carla often want advice. If Carla wants a new cell phone, she knows whom to call. It's not 1-800-CELLPHONE. It's her friend Gino, who knows everything about cell phones. He'll listen to her needs, tell her what to get and where to get it, and the next day she'll have a new cell phone. Allmag has a chance to become a source of trusted advice. That's something the search engines can't offer. Rather than having some fancy database of knowledge, the company could sponsor experts on its site – people who can help Carla answer her questions about personal finance, health, and other topics. And, Allmag should facilitate Carla meeting other people like her so they can help each other and form a network of support. Allmag should think about creating its central brand for parents of small children around both information and advice.

Carla proves one of Tom's theories – even though people say they want exactly what they ask for, they're often pleasantly surprised to find something else. Tom estimates that people like Carla allow you to offer them 70 percent what they want and 30 percent new material. If they're even occasionally receptive, you can keep experimenting to see what things they go for and what they ignore. If they stay away from everything, reduce the new material to 20, or even 10 percent, and see if you can target them more specifically.

Families with Teens

It might sound a little *too* convenient that I happen to have another sister who's 38, has two daughters entering their second decades of life, is in her second house, has a full-time job as a teacher, has an au pair who helps take care of the kids, does most of

> ### BRANDWIDTH
>
> If the executives at Allmag understand how much brandwidth their customers have online – how much time the customer can give all their brands combined – they quickly realize that their universe of magazine brands doesn't translate straight onto the Web.
>
> Instead, a company with many product brands should try to merge products that serve the same audience, either by simplifying, combining, or creating a new online brand altogether. The effort required to sustain one brand online is often more than companies initially estimate. It's better to build your visitor base to critical mass before expanding to more brands later.

the household planning, and still has her original husband. But it's true. Lisa is facing the expansion of her family activities as her two daughters enter their teen years and the corresponding expansion in her commitments.

Lisa's day is extremely structured. Virtually every minute is accounted for. If she takes any extra time for herself, it comes out of her nightly 6.5 hours of sleep. Her daughters are into everything, from gymnastics to tap lessons, and school trips to ski vacations. They require transportation and coordination. Lisa finds herself doing a lot of repetitive tasks. She's in the carpool. She's in the PTA. She has to pick up something somewhere every day. She's concerned about nutrition, so she does all the food shopping.

Lisa spends a few hours a month online, mostly using e-mail and shopping for gifts. She would spend another minute online if she could gain two minutes by doing so.

Lisa doesn't need as much content or advice as Carla does. She needs more help in the "me" category than in the "people like me" category. While she would love to have the luxury of being in several online communities, it's just not possible. She needs execution. She needs *tools*.

Lisa needs two kinds of tools: those that give her access to information, and those that give her access to services. Most of her life revolves around schedules, and those schedules have a habit of changing at the last minute. The question is: What can Allmag offer Lisa online that would help her manage her schedule? She needs tools she can access from her cell phone. She needs local tools – tools that help her find an electrician or a plumber. She needs tools that help her prevent emergencies, get things delivered or picked up, and tools that help her work toward long-term objectives in the face of day-to-day demands.

Let's assume that the company spends time with a number of women like Lisa and comes up with a prioritized list of tools they need.

THETRIP.COM

Thetrip.com is an excellent example of a tool-based site for busy business travelers. The site features a flight tracker that is more accurate than most airlines have (the information comes straight from the plane itself), destination guides, itinerary planners, maps, currency converters, driving directions, fare alerts, and other tools. If you have a digital pager, you can even arrange to have your pager tell you when a flight lands – that's a cool tool!

One of the top concerns is financial planning. Lisa and her husband have a consultant to help them save, invest, plan for taxes, and so on. Having a professional look after their investments is well worth the expense. But communication with their planner still consists of phone calls, faxes, and face-to-face meetings.

If Allmag built a family finance tool that let people work with their finances online, with or without a personal financial planner, Lisa would probably use it. If Allmag hosted a database of financial planners, with qualitative comments and meaningful ratings of each one, visitors would be able to choose or switch financial planners – or feel more confident with the one they have. As more people rate their advisors, the database grows. It changes the playing field for financial advisors, who now have a strong incentive to achieve results – which happens to be the best kind of marketing in the online world.

How can Allmag's web team build such a system? Simple. It already exists. All they have to do is look for financial tools online and license one that works for them. They may want to modify it a bit, add some community features, and create a brand for it. Once it gets going, the people and their comments – not the technology – become Allmag's strategic advantage. Allmag can do the same with local businesses, so Lisa's personal yellow pages – with comments and ratings from others like her – are always at her fingertips.

Once a customer like Lisa has started to use a few tools, she can graduate to a system that sends her alerts when anything changes. These power tools will help her avoid extra trips and save time, making her more loyal to the Allmag brand.

Seniors

Our demographer friend, Tom, describes these people – ages 50 to 75 – as empty nesters. They are ready to dip into the pot of gold at the end of their rainbow. These people are healthy, wealthy, and looking for adventure. They control some 77 percent of the country's financial assets and are now responsible for 40 percent of all consumer spending. They shop online as eagerly as younger people do.

Over 10 million seniors are already online. They know just enough about technology to communicate with their friends, meet new people, learn new things, and find places to go and things to do. As one of the fastest growing populations on the Web, they are drawing advertisers to targeted sites in droves.

Seniors need tools, too. They want to keep in touch with family members and see photos and videos of their grandchildren. They also need financial and health-maintenance tools. What makes this group different from the others is that they're actively looking for *experiences*. From discussions to education, from volunteer opportunities to vacations, seniors are interested in *doing* things. Often, that means doing things with other people.

Seniors have a strong desire to participate. They are often good writers, smart business people, creative artists. They have a myriad of skills and the desire to help others. Give them the tools, and they'll build huge web sites.

Because these people are getting online quickly, Allmag should consider folding its paper magazines aimed at seniors into just one remaining title and put the rest of their effort into one huge site for seniors online. They can buy an active site with a thriving senior community and set up a framework for seniors to create their own content. They should pour resources into it until it's the largest participatory publication in the world. Since Allmag is strong in travel, it should buy and expand a site that lets people discuss popular destinations, travel tips, sightseeing, and so on.

They can start by letting most of the editorial staff go. The company should let seniors create all their own content. They can write essays, recommend books, put up paintings and drawings, show off their photography, offer advice, lead projects, and more. Allmag will have a small staff for this site and thousands of volunteers.

Realignment

Allmag will benefit from an organization that has less emphasis on properties and more on customers. Let's reassess the options.

Life stage alignment. Life stage alignment creates separate divisions for families with small children, families with teens, and empty nesters. The company's real customers are its advertisers, and advertisers will be well served by a division whose salespeople can help them adjust the mix within a particular life stage, rather than having separate salespeople for each brand. In this so-called "spectral" approach, the company will need to try new experiments with the baby boomers now becoming empty nesters while cutting down on the number of properties aimed at young career women.

Cohort alignment. Cohort alignment creates separate divisions to lock on and stay with certain groups as they go through their life stages. It aligns the company with customers more than with advertisers, which may benefit the company more in the end. In the New World, customers prefer this kind of focus. They don't want what's best for the advertisers. They want to talk with *each other*, and this alignment makes the conversation easier. If Allmag staffs each cohort division with people from that cohort, it will be able to try new products and adjust to the turbulent change their customers are going through. If Allmag executes well, the advertisers will be knocking down its doors to get in on the action.

Cohort alignment encourages more trust and more one-to-one contact between employees and customers. Upper management should strive to create an environment in which people from each of these groups naturally gravitate toward working on the products that serve people in their own group. This makes the conversation easier. While Allmag shouldn't expect employees to stay with a cohort for 20 years, the knowledge and energy inside the company stay with its intended target group, providing a consistent interface to a constantly changing audience. This structure is more agile and less subject to the internal disruptions cohorts can cause as they work their way through each life stage.

These two possible alignments are both better than Allmag's current property-driven structure. Both Tom and I would argue for cohort alignment over spectral alignment, since the conversations and relationships will deepen over time. The cohorts are a great source of people who can potentially staff Allmag employee-customer interface positions.

Moving at the Speed of E-Customers

The Internet isn't a good place to sit on your hands. Allmag can chase its customers' rising expectations by focusing on few brands and blurring the boundaries between the people who work there and the people they serve. Those companies should consider switching to a cohort-aligned structure. If Allmag's executives decide to take this approach, they should be prepared to take it all the way.

Companies that want to succeed online can all use a demographer like Tom. Sure, they need technologists and consultants. They need to pay attention to what their advertisers want. But in the long run, knowing your customers personally – knowing them by name – is more important than anything else. People don't come to your web site and ask what technology you have. They ask what you can do for them and what you have done for them lately.

OLD MISSION STATEMENT | Helping families keep their commitments.

NEW MISSION STATEMENT | Helping families keep their commitments everywhere, all the time.

Steel Fabricator

CHAPTER 13

YOU LIVE IN COLUMBUS, OHIO. You're the CEO of Essex Steel, a mid-size (fictional) steel products company with 2,200 employees. In the last ten years, Essex has been one of the few companies to prosper. It has survived by making specialty goods to order, particularly for commercial and public buildings. You have taken the company from $140 million in sales ten years ago to more than $250 million in sales today. Your accounts range from boat builders in Maine to high-rise contractors in Brazil.

You command respect among clients (you always call them *clients*, not customers) because though you had never set foot inside a steel mill until you took over the company ten years ago, you now know the business inside and out. It's a service business. Competitors who thought they were making products have been reduced to toxic cleanup sites.

Your chief information officer has been in place for four years. Eight out of ten desks in the company have computers on them. Designers use computer-aided drafting software to control giant water-jet cutting machines. Robots do much of the welding, cleaning, finishing, and painting. Automated carriers whisk parts to the assembly bay. A state-of-the-art computer system logs orders, tracks them, and schedules shipments. You can convert an entire assembly line to manufacture a new product in under 48 hours – down from the six weeks it took when you started as CEO. Profits are up, and for the first time since the 1960s, people enjoy working at Essex.

That was a year ago. Before Essex Steel became an Internet company. Before you fired your CIO.

What Happened?

In the last year, you turned the company 180 degrees with one simple decision. It started when the CIO announced a plan to expand Lotus Notes from 450 desktops to 1,100 – the company's entire computer-based work force. Although the CIO's plan sounded good at the time, you decided to get a second opinion from your friend Nicole, who was working in California as a systems architect for Cisco Systems. She spent a week looking over the concept and came up with a different idea. "Let me do this right," she said. "We'll start by scrapping Lotus Notes."

The CIO – who knew nothing of Internet protocols or web-based systems – objected, saying Notes was the most cost-effective way to expand the company's knowledge base. The Notes server could even be integrated with various Internet applications and serve the company's web sites. Besides, he said, everyone already had Notes – it would be costly to implement a new system.

"Hogwash," said Nicole. In her opinion, Lotus Notes was an addictive, unhealthy habit at too many companies because it didn't work seamlessly with all the new software based on common Internet standards. She argued that continued use of Notes would lead to e-cancer – it would be the limiting factor in most IT decisions, preventing the IT staff from using the best products in each category. The more you invest in Lotus Notes, she said, the more you have to keep patching the system to accommodate new features.

It was probably the fire in Nicole's eyes and her willingness to move to Columbus that sealed your decision. It wasn't easy, but you let the CIO go and brought Nicole on board as chief net officer (CNO). Now Essex Steel leads the industry in project turnaround time and quality. You and Nicole even made the cover of *Business Week* last month, after receiving the Futurizenow E-Customer Alignment Award in San Francisco.

A Key Decision

Hiring Nicole changed the entire company. First, she set everyone up with an e-mail service that delivers secure e-mail through an Internet browser. Because the service is outsourced, Nicole doesn't worry about maintenance. Employees have as many e-mail accounts and mailing lists as they like. They can send and receive documents as easily from a client's site as they can from their desktops.

Nicole then looked at workflow – a project's progress from the initial contact with the client to the final delivery and subsequent follow-up. She wanted to make it as easy as possible for all the different people Essex deals with to share information. Although many CNOs in Nicole's situation would see Essex as the hub of the process, with suppliers on one side and clients on the other, she saw Essex as an important part – but still just a part – of the client's complicated world.

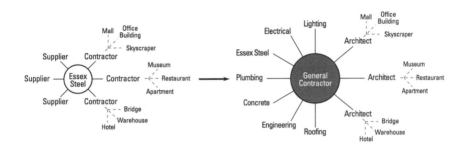

A change in viewpoint puts the client at the center of Essex's world for each project. This shift drove Essex to explore new ways of communicating with its clients and suppliers.

Not only is every client different, but every project has its own unique needs. Nicole realized she would have to go to each client individually and create a new model for their relationship. She started with a visit to Gencon, a large (fictional) general contractor in Atlanta.

Constructive Collaboration

Gencon currently plays a lead role in the construction of a prestressed concrete high-rise in Malaysia. Six top-level contractors are working on the 162-story office tower, a project that will take six years and $780 million from initial concept to the opening gala. For the first time, an entire building is being built in one place – on a server in San Diego. Teams from all over the world check into the server, not just to get documents and messages, but to actually design the structure online – a virtual building. They work in a real-time collaborative environment using new design tools, some of which didn't even exist when the project began.

On screen, all the collaborators can actually see the building coming together. More than 800 contributors work in teams to design the electrical, mechanical, and data and communications systems; the structure and interiors; the utility services and safety features – all in the same virtual space. Any part of the project can be checked out, worked on, and returned. The implications of any changes then ripple through the system. A change to the specifications for a lighting fixture might affect a single fixture or the entire electrical and fire-safety system. Elevator shafts are being designed in concert with wind-simulation vibration studies. The system can not only monitor air pressure in the simulated building as different components are added, it can *predict* air pressure under various what-if scenarios, giving designers more flexibility to try new ventilation designs even as other teams simulate the thermal effects of different paint colors. The system automatically monitors impacts on the budget, the environment, and the construction schedule.

The software that makes all of this possible is based on Internet standards. It's a completely open process. Everyone has access to everyone else's information. Simple menus and search tools guide participants to any part of the project. Anyone can raise a concern on the message boards and take that concern to the highest levels if she feels it's critical to the building's integrity, safety, or the quality of life for future inhabitants.

Essex won the bid to work with Gencon based on Nicole's presentation. Nicole figured Essex would need a team that could plug seamlessly into the process and into Gencon's system.

In the following months, Nicole and her counterparts at Gencon bonded, assembling software tools that would let both teams collaborate online. They quickly developed a system for using web sites to communicate design decisions to Essex. Within 24 hours of an architect's putting a digital sketch into the system, Gencon and Essex could respond in unison, saying what the structural and logistical requirements would be.

Communicating with dozens of other teams can be messy. By using standard Internet components and hooking them up through web servers and middleware to translate data, Nicole was able to keep up with the changes. Nicole hired a researcher who does nothing but prowl the

Internet for new tools and methods to hook teams together. The standard web-based interfaces give Essex's people a feeling of continuity from one project to the next, though the tools underneath continue to change. Gencon had one client who was using Lotus Notes, so Nicole quickly deployed a Notes-based system on Essex's central server to help integrate the team into the process with minimal disruption.

Nicole wanted a place where Gencon and Essex employees could just hang out and discuss anything they wanted. In addition to adding more face-to-face time to their schedules at conferences and kick-off meetings, she organized some special bulletin boards the two companies could share. Although that was just a few months ago, employees spending time at each other's physical sites are already helping each other with travel tips, restaurant suggestions, even house swaps. That is exactly the kind of interaction Nicole was hoping for. The intercompany bulletin boards give people a chance to bump into each other in the virtual hallways.

Nicole knew from experience that teams work best when they know each other personally, so she insisted that Essex design teams go to Atlanta to spend two weeks working with Gencon people before connecting via the powerful online tools. There were bumps along the way, but the more the teams worked together, the more they were able to suggest their own solutions. Nicole – the information technology guru – surprised everyone by bringing in an Outward Bound group to teach communication skills through outdoor exercises while she had the teams

---

GROUPWARE

Groupware is a term for any software tool that lets people collaborate. E-mail is the most basic type of groupware. Repositories, or asset-management systems, are another step up. But groupware that helps people communicate is still in its infancy.

Synchronous groupware usually involves conferencing or other real-time collaboration. The telephone is a good example of a synchronous appliance. Remote surgery is another example. New tools are in development for conferencing, simulations, creative collaboration, composing music, and even operating sailboats via the Internet.

Asynchronous groupware is flexible. Like a telephone answering system, it lets people check documents in and out on their own time. A participant does his part and leaves messages for others to pick up the next time they log on. More sophisticated systems can send out alerts or warn a project manager if any aspect of the project changes.

together. But they loved it. Sharing physical challenges and problem-solving fostered an online atmosphere of friendly, helpful collaboration.

Onward and Outward

After getting the Gencon project on track, Nicole visited the rest of Essex's clients. She saw that each had unique needs. A shipyard needed government-procurement software. A sign company wanted to get its order-to-delivery time down to two weeks. An architectural firm wanted the specs on the latest coatings without having to call Essex every time a new product came out. Nicole held a two-day workshop with each client to learn what their respective wish lists would be if Essex could deliver anything the clients wanted.

Nicole's team grew to 85 people during the year as she deployed people to analyze clients' processes and tie them into the online tools Essex had found most useful. By the end of her first year, Nicole had set up a modest web site that featured her monthly newsletter on IT solutions for large-scale projects.

Thanks to Nicole's work, clients are lining up outside Essex's door. But she isn't stopping. Nicole is currently working on a common scheduling application that lets Essex and all its competitors disclose when they are at capacity and when they will be able to take new work. Not only does this help clients find the right steel fabricator, it helps Essex identify partners to work with when the company needs extra capacity. Online bidding has cut four to eight weeks off the traditional proposal process.

Nicole's focus on job-specific systems integration rather than deep infrastructure and custom applications is the key to all the progress Essex has made in the last year. Nicole has been able to charge systems-integrator prices for every project she's done with clients, giving her the cash to grow her team and serve clients at the same time. Her department has the highest margins in the company.

Nicole has made and continues to make a positive impression on a stodgy industry. She has the willingness to help people communicate and to give them tools they can modify according to their needs. Back in California, where Nicole began her career, that's the way start-ups do things, but in Columbus, Ohio, it all sounds so new and different. Nicole comes from an environment where speed and flexibility count more than muscle and market dominance. She looks at IT as a service function, a place where project leaders can get help – not static.

Nicole puts it this way: "This industry has huge problems with inventory and supply bottlenecks. Every job we do can be done better. I ask each of our clients one question: 'What if our entire company were located right across the street from yours? How would our relationship be different?' In most cases, the client responds that the two companies would have a lot more informal contact, which would be very beneficial."

A New Frontier

Hiring Nicole didn't rescue Essex. No crisis loomed. But asking her to fix what wasn't broken – to apply a start-up attitude to an industry that creeps at a snail's pace – put Essex in the driver's seat. Everyone at Essex can now see the value of using the Internet to align the company with its clients. Employees are lined up to take evening computer classes.

Nicole's mindset – that the client is at the center of a dynamic collaboration – was the shift in thinking that propelled Essex into the New World. Ten years from now, Essex Steel may change its name to Essex Consulting. General contractors will always need structural products. But in the future, they are going to need to *communicate* about structural products even more than they do today.

The point of this story is not that you need to seek out someone amazing like Nicole. You already have people like Nicole working for you. Your job is to create an environment in which they can flourish.

OLD MISSION STATEMENT | The highest quality steel products at a reasonable price.

NEW MISSION STATEMENT | We fit into your process, from concept to installation.

Real Estate Clearinghouse

CHAPTER 14

A GROUP OF FRIENDS QUIT THEIR DAY JOBS in real estate to look for gold on the Web. Their goal was to become the dominant source for commercial real estate sales and rentals in the United States. Unfortunately, the founders landed in many of the traps entrepreneurs fall into when starting online companies. My goal in this chapter is to show how well-meaning entrepreneurs can salvage a solid e-business idea from a very bad customer experience.

Our fictitious online real estate company is Realnet.com (not to be confused with any actual web site). Because Realnet.com is a pure play – it lives or dies by its web site – this chapter focuses more on the site than on the organization. Let's start by looking at the Realnet.com site; then we'll break up that site into three sites to serve the company's customer groups more effectively.

The Entrepreneurs' Dream

Realnet.com started in someone's living room as a concept for an online clearinghouse. The founders wanted to build a searchable database of commercial properties for sale and for lease. At first, the listings would be free. When they had enough listings, they would begin charging a fee for each transaction.

After consulting with several web design shops, the founders decided to do all the site design and construction in-house to save money. Everything was done in a hurry so that the founders could get the next round of financing, and it shows. A quick look at the Realnet.com home page tells you this company either isn't serious about creating a positive customer experience or doesn't know how to. Icons occur on the page in the order in which their services became operational. A column of advertisers' logos makes it even harder for buyers and tenants to figure out how to locate property.

The Realnet.com home page is an unbranded, unfocused hodgepodge of icons that mean nothing to a visitor. The site has scaled poorly – adding more content has made things worse.

Why does the home page give visitors the options of searching for property, listing property, *and* getting a job as a broker? Because the founders have fallen into the trap of wanting the site to do everything for everyone. Their webmaster said that people only bookmark home pages, so they felt it was important to make sure everything was there for anyone who came by. Yet only ten percent of the people who came to the home page clicked on anything at all. The web strategy here is typical – there isn't one. Who's responsible for the strategy? Nobody. Everyone in the company likes the site because the animation effects look so cool.

Realnet has three divisions, each run by a company founder. One division helps people find properties to buy or lease. Another division tries to get brokers and owners to list their properties for sale or rent. And the last division tries to sell advertising, recruit new hires, and do deals with major brokerages.

Unlike many start-ups, which are usually divided along product lines, this company's internal structure is sound. It's based on the company's two categories of customers: buyers/tenants, and sellers/landlords. The problem is the principals – they keep fighting over what to put on the site. The solution – break up the monolith into three separate web sites, each with its own unique web address. Realnet.com is where tenants look for space, RealnetBroker.com is where landlords list their properties, and RealnetCorp.com is the administrative site.

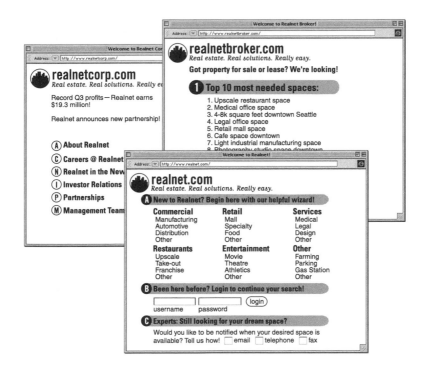

Three sites from one: By breaking up one site into three, the company's divisions can now focus on their separate objectives. Visitors coming from search engines will be directed to the correct site based on whether they are tenants or landlords.

The three autonomous sites prevent the squabbling founders from interfering with each other's business objectives. Each group is now dedicated to serving its own customers on its own site. Each has its own budget and its own objectives. As we'll soon see, they are not all created equal.

The Customer's View

The Realnet.com division is now focused on customers looking for space to either buy or lease. The division's goal is to help businesses find the space that's right for them. Assuming Realnet.com advertises appropriately and receives good media coverage, what should the staff do with the visitors once they arrive? What kind of people might come to the site? And what might they be looking for?

Investors looking for property to buy could be looking for different kinds of buildings. Rather than dividing this large group according to building type (office, medical, retail, etc.), the Realnet.com staff would do better to look at the investors' reasons for buying commercial property. Three main reasons emerge: income, appreciation, and tax benefits.

Business owners looking for space to lease are interested in one of three types of space: office, operations, or retail/restaurant/entertainment (which I'll simply call retail). Business owners usually have a pretty good idea of the kind of space they want. Size, quality, price, and location are at the top of their list of concerns. Manufacturing facilities may be concerned about city ordinances and access to major transportation routes. Retailers want to know about foot traffic, parking, amenities, and complementary businesses in the area. They are often flexible on price, since a higher price often corresponds to more traffic.

Although investors are a profitable group, let's leave them aside and concentrate on commercial landlords and tenants. Using a customer-led approach, we'll examine how the company should respond to the specific needs of a tenant named Michelle, an e-customer looking for a retail storefront.

Finding a Retail Space

Michelle is looking for a new home for her juice bar. Because fresh fruit smoothies are hard to ship, she knows her business lunch won't be eaten by some web site. She needs a small storefront with plenty of afternoon traffic. How can Realnet.com best help Michelle find her dream location?

We can imagine two scenarios for Michelle – either she comes to the Realnet.com site, finds a list of places, goes to see them in person, and rents one; or she comes to the site and doesn't find exactly what she's looking for in the listings. In either case, the Realnet.com site should offer Michelle a way to reduce the list of possibilities by applying her criteria for a space. A help utility, called a wizard, guides Michelle through the step-by-step process of eliminating what she doesn't want and homing in on what she does. Because Michelle is a beginner – that is, a first-time visitor to the site – a wizard is much easier for her to use than a long form.

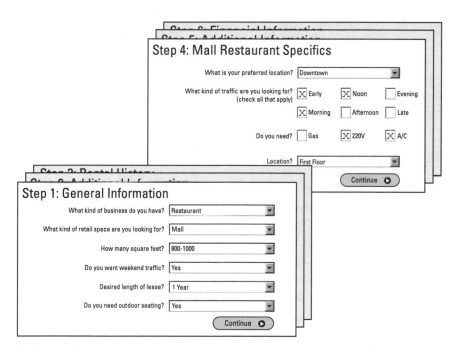

A wizard is helpful to beginners because it lets them narrow the scope of their search in logical steps. The order of questions is important; wizards should begin with general questions and progress to more specific questions, showing a manageable list of properties as soon as possible in the process.

Once Michelle has narrowed her search, she sees a list of properties sorted in her order of preference. If the people at RealnetBroker have done their job, the database contains enough listings for her to make comparisons. The last thing Realnet wants Michelle to do is run all over town looking at properties that don't work for her. So the more information she can get, the better.

Listing realtors like to control the amount of information they disclose on a property. The people at RealnetBroker must extract from the listing realtors all the information a prospective renter might want. Michelle is interested in the history of the property, sales per square foot, parking, weekend versus weekday traffic, evening versus afternoon traffic, and a list of all retail establishments within two blocks.

Although real estate agents may prefer a long description of each property, it's much more efficient to define subcategories like retail.snack, retail.restaurant, retail.hair, and so on. The tenants in each specific subgroup can fill out wizards that ask them questions pertaining to the space they want to lease. Realnet.com's comparison engine can then match tenants with properties without any phone calls or faxes. Having comprehensive comparison data for many groups is Realnet.com's secret weapon because it guarantees each customer the most relevant search results.

The Buy Side

What if Michelle doesn't find her dream location in the database? Realnet must keep her from going to other sites to look for additional listings. Realnet.com must be her one-stop solution.

What should Realnet's staff do? They'd better search the competition's sites! They should search the classifieds! They might want to drive the neighborhoods looking for signs – whatever it takes to get Michelle her dream space! Realnet must do everything it can to bring Michelle the best prospective locations as quickly as possible, because Michelle isn't going to wait passively. Realnet.com must become a buyer's agent, not a seller's agent. We split the site into three so Realnet.com could serve Michelle better, not to give the interface a face-lift.

Realnet.com should send urgent messages to its cohorts at RealnetBroker, asking them to put the word out through their network to find a great space for a juice bar. As soon as a possible space pops up, Realnet's alert staff sends e-mail to Michelle, pages her, or calls her. With any luck, Realnet will find Michelle the perfect space quickly and make her a happy customer. If she finds someone else doing a better job with Realnet's data, she'll be telling her friends about another, more agile start-up.

Over time, as people hear about Realnet's incredible service, the site will attract more buyers and sellers. Then the power of the database will start to take over. More buyers and sellers mean fewer special requests and a higher first-time success rate. The word will spread to others in the industry. Soon, a business owner looking for space will be able to visit Realnet.com at 10:00 P.M., send e-mail messages to the listing agents, and have a set of appointments by 9 A.M. the next morning. Today, tenants don't do that. Not because they don't want to, but because they can't.

Follow-up is very important. The company should survey every renter at least once a year to learn how well the property has performed, including information about foot and car traffic, parking, landlord and neighbor problems or plusses, and so on. By measuring what tenants care about, Realnet.com stays closer to its current customers and provides even more information for the next customer. If Michelle moves to a new location, the company is better informed about the property than before she leased it and has gained information about the property no other site has. Because the people at Realnet work for the tenants, they have no conflicts in trying to get the most accurate information possible. Because tenants like Michelle get better service from Realnet, they are willing to fill out the surveys that help the next tenant make a better decision.

The marketing people at Realnet.com decide which types of properties they want RealnetBroker.com to bring into the database. For example, they may focus first on retail, then consultants, then service bureaus, then medical. The founders should determine this order by doing market research and analysis. They also need to go after the big categories that will get more people talking about the site. By going for depth over breadth, they will make Realnet.com a category winner.

The Supply Side

Now let's look at the broker's site: RealnetBroker.com. Because we've separated the supply side from the buy side, this group of former real estate agents can focus on rounding up properties and serving the broker community. The buy side has decided, for example, to go after restaurants, general retail, gas stations, and retail and professional services. The supply side must now respond. It must concentrate all its energy on getting every quality property in the region into the database.

RealnetBroker.com should focus on both brokers and property owners, understanding their respective concerns and addressing them. For example, if owners want to list properties without paying a broker's commission, the company will want to build a self-serve model into its site. The company should give property owners their own extranet pages so they can monitor all their properties easily. The company may want to create an online marketplace for ancillary services owners can use to market their properties themselves.

Property owners may be uncomfortable about having so much information about their properties online. Once Michelle enters her comments about her leased location, the property owner has lost control of the message. This is an educational issue, not a business conflict. In the long run, both RealnetBroker.com and the property owners work for the renters. The people at RealnetBroker.com must educate sellers that if they want to reduce the time their property is vacant, they must provide complete, accurate information up front and make their properties searchable online. In the long run, what works for the buyer will also work best for the seller.

The listing agents the company is so eager to sign up may also resist at first. They may be reluctant to give prospects so much detailed information on their listings, preferring instead to try to close deals themselves. The RealnetBroker staff should plan on spending a great deal of time and energy educating realtors in this new, more effective way of doing business.

Like all processes, the sales process can be made dramatically more efficient with online tools. The comparison criteria allow sellers to respond more efficiently to all questions up front – rather than later in the process, when conflicts can undermine deals. In fact, the people attracted to Realnet.com are serious, qualified renters who do business only after their need for information has been satisfied. For RealnetBroker.com, the e-customer presents a new sales challenge, a challenge any site in this market will have to meet. Realnet's online education and offline seminars will become a competitive advantage.

Home Base

The RealnetCorp.com site is dedicated to various business partners and other audiences like the media, prospective employees, mortgage companies, and so on. By making it a separate site, the company keeps all those messages off the other two sites. RealnetCorp.com will be listed with different search-engine keywords so the site will generally not turn up on tenants' searches.

If the buy side is in the driver's seat and the supply side is in the passenger's seat, the advertising sales team is in the back seat. The team should sell ads only to the RealnetBroker.com site, not Realnet.com. The people at Realnet should remind themselves that they are not trying to become a portal. Portal sites are ad-driven, and for most of them, their strategy is to distract people from their original search goal.

RealnetCorp's business model is to become a service that can charge a percentage fee on each sale. As soon as the traffic on Realnet.com puts them in first place, they can start charging property owners for listings or for a percentage of each transaction. The first goal should be to increase traffic, not satisfy advertisers.

Making the Rules

Realnet must focus on dozens of customer subcategories. To satisfy retailers, restaurateurs, consultants, and other subgroups, Realnet must phase in the subcategories it goes after. The company will probably want to relaunch the site with at least ten subcategories of customers and try to add several more each month. If Realnet can stay ahead of the competition with a deeper – then broader – database, the company will set the pace and make the rules for everyone else.

The company's crown jewel, however, isn't the database. It's the critical

THE WEB RESEARCHER

I always encourage companies to hire a full-time web researcher and statistician – someone who can read the tea leaves and tell which way the company's customers are drifting on any given day. These people observe and participate in various online communities. They can tap into research resources that help keep up with daily changes in the industry and send an internal newsletter to all employees. A web researcher can watch for new competition and signs of customer defection. This person is an early warning device against surprises that could crop up later and kill a small company like Realnet.

mass of repeat customers who enter information about the properties they lease and own. By listening to customers and continually refining their criteria, Realnet ensures its customers get the most out of the system.

Realnet's founders started with a "ready-fire-aim" attitude toward the Web. The site they built was confusing and conflicting. In trying to do everything for everyone, Realnet wasn't pleasing anyone. In trying to please its investors, the company failed to realize its valuation was tied to the number of buyers and tenants relying on the site for their next properties. Now that the founders can see the business proposition from their customers' point of view, they can all focus on making Realnet.com the most successful of their three sites.

OLD MISSION STATEMENT | Bringing buyers and sellers together at our web site.

NEW MISSION STATEMENT | Helping business owners grow their businesses.

Book Superstore

CHAPTER 15

IN 1997, AMAZON.COM teamed up with author John Updike to write a community-based short story. Updike started "Murder Makes the Magazine" with a few paragraphs. Over the next 44 days, Amazon.com asked visitors to continue the story by contributing original paragraphs. Each night, the staff picked out the most promising entries and sent them to Updike to choose the best one. Each morning, the winning entry was posted, and the process started over again. The daily winner received a $1,000 prize. After the final entry, Updike wrote the closing paragraphs, and the company gave away a $100,000 cash prize to one lucky writer. The final short story still lives at Amazon.com.

How many people submitted continuing paragraphs for the story? Amazon.com received between 5,000 and 12,000 submissions *per day*. Over the 44 days, the site received more than 250,000 submissions – probably over 1 million paragraphs! All of them came from Amazon.com's online audience: people who love to read books.

In this chapter, we'll take a customer-led approach to the online bookstore scene by playing consultants to a fictitious company called Justbooks.com (no association with any actual web site). It's modeled on a combination of today's online bookstores, but any online retailer can use the customer-led concepts to tap into the energy of its customers.

The Content-Driven Bookstore

Justbooks established its brand early, building a reputation on three elements important to book buyers: selection, service, and price. Astutely, Justbooks invited customers to participate in the business. First, the company encouraged customers to comment on individual books and displayed the comments near each book's description. Second, visitors to the site could rate any book, using a rating system from one to five. Justbooks also noted how many people had submitted ratings for each book, which helped calibrate the ratings. Third, Justbooks implemented community-based filtering – each book was accompanied by a list of other books purchased by customers who had bought that title.

The fourth and perhaps most ingenious way Justbooks let their customers participate in the business was through an affiliate program. The program gives people the opportunity to set up their own book-

---

FILTERS

Filters allow anyone looking for something to find relevant results in a sea of possibilities. The five basic types of filters can be applied to searching the Web or any large data set. I'll illustrate each one by imagining you're in the mood to buy a book, but you aren't sure which book would be right for you.

Rule-based. Find a book whose title contains a topic or theme you're interested in. Keyword, category, and concept searches use simple rules to separate candidates from non-candidates. They are usually based on a single taxonomy – an ordered division of items into groups. Rule-based filters usually offer too many random choices and few relevant results.

Inference-based. Find a book written by an author whose books you have bought before. If a system has information about your past purchases, an inference-based filter presents suggestions based on your history. Sometimes the results are comical: the software doesn't know you in the same way your favorite neighborhood bookstore does.

Expert-based. Find a book recommended by a certain critic. By relying on people whose opinions you respect, you can filter out a huge percentage of the books you're not interested in. Let experts do the work for you. It can be more advantageous to look for an expert on a topic who can recommend a book than to search through hundreds of titles.

Community-based. Find the five most popular books among people whose demographics or psychographics match yours. A community-based search – or popularity filtering – recommends books based on the past behavior of a community of people. With a very deep data set, community-based filters can be surprisingly effective. With a wide variety of data, the results are often less useful.

Expert systems. Find a book chosen by a book-reviewing software program. These programs process thousands of book synopses and apply various forms of artificial intelligence to come up with a list of books. Programmers often interview experts and then create software that models as many of the rules, nuances, and instincts of their thought processes as possible.

---

stores on their own sites all over the Web and link them to Justbooks.com. Justbooks handles the actual transactions and returns 14 percent of the sales price to the referring sites. It didn't take long for *all* online bookstores to copy the idea. Now many sites participate in multiple affiliate programs, giving their visitors a choice of stores.

What's Wrong with This Picture?

The original Justbooks.com web site and Justbooks' management structure were based on the static, content-based model of a physical bookstore. There were sections for different kinds of books: Biography, Business, Computers, Cooking, Health, History, Home and Garden, Fiction, Mystery, Nature, Nonfiction, Parenting, Religion, Science, and so on. Each section had a full-time editor who featured new books for her section of the store, wrote book reviews, arranged events, and handled visitor feedback. These experts functioned much like their counterparts do in a physical bookstore.

In looking at the traffic patterns on their site, we learned that a surprising number of visitors came to the home page, clicked on a category page, and left the site. Justbooks hadn't realized the important difference between an online bookstore and a physical bookstore – physical bookstores *have* to do it that way. The content-based design of Justbooks' site inherits all the frustration of searching through a physical bookstore as well. The company continued to add new content-based features, rather than ask how well the site met the needs of e-customers.

Beginners are browsers. They tend to use the home page as a source of content, just as people do with the display window of a physical bookstore as they walk by. They read the page, perhaps are enticed to explore a bit, and then they leave. If they see an interesting book, they might buy it. Otherwise, they will come back another time to see what's new up front. For them, the site isn't very sticky – it doesn't draw them in unless they just happen to be strongly interested in a particular category of books.

Experts are searchers. They type in a title (or an author's name or a subject), find a book, order it, and leave. Occasionally they buy a related title that catches their eye. What happens when they learn that another site carries books at cost – significantly below Justbooks' prices? Even though the brand is strong, the business proposition isn't very sticky. Experts will be happy to go to another site, type in keywords, and buy books at lower prices.

Where were the intermediates? There weren't any. No one is a business book person or a biography person. Even mystery-novel addicts read other books occasionally. The site, organized by content category, didn't have anything for intermediates to do, except review books and participate in the occasional contest. How many people left the site because they didn't feel at home? That was impossible to measure. Justbooks had tried everything to get people to venture past the top two levels and nothing had worked.

Even though Justbooks.com was a huge success, management decided to fix what wasn't broken. The company had captured early market share, but specialty sites were giving beginners a deeper experience and sending their book buyers to any site that paid the highest commissions. Price-cutters were taking the experts. Management knew the current strategy wouldn't defend the company against those competitors.

So Justbooks' executives hired us (you and me) as consultants to walk through the company corridors, audit the web site, ask questions, and make suggestions. Little did they know we would soon be talking about their internal culture, organization, and philosophy. But we focused on the web site first, because that's where the customers were.

A year later, the site is a completely different place – a combination of a club and a pub, a place where people gather to discuss books and pay money almost incidentally. Let's see how we helped Justbooks reorganize its web site and, in the process, the entire company.

Welcoming Beginners

In e-commerce, visitors only give you one or two clicks to show them something appealing. In e-business, however, your visitor's interest in other people draws them into the site, forgetting how many clicks it takes. Once they find places they enjoy, they are happy to set a bookmark and return for more. To give beginners a browsing experience they can relate to, we decided to ask them to make one click on the front page – a click that took them into a neighborhood of people they can relate to. By dividing this huge site into these 15 categories, beginners could take the first step onto the customer-loyalty pyramid and continue on a natural progression toward becoming experts.

HOME PAGE

Enterprise People (Stacy)
  Managers
  Project managers
  Administrators
  Lawyers
  Human resource personnel
  Public relations personnel
  Information technology
    personnel

**Small Business People
(Jessica)**
  Service providers,
    manufacturers
  Retailers
  Consultants
  Technologists, web
    developers

Entrepreneurs (Hershel)

Seniors (Dane)
  Couples
  Singles

Lifestyles (Fisher)
  Singles
  Gay
  Lesbian

Travelers (Valerie)
  Drivers, motorcyclists
  Campers
  Adventurers, explorers
  International travelers
  Students

Cooks (Marc)
  Nutritionists
  Professional chefs
  Homemakers

Sports Enthusiasts (Claudia)
  Baseball
  Basketball
  Soccer
  Football
  Hockey
  Golf

Sports Participants (Rodney)
  Golfers
  Bowlers
  Tennis players
  Hikers
  Bikers
  Fishers

Children (Jennifer)

Teens (Jason)

Parents (Aviva)
  Expecting
  Parents of children
  Parents of teens

Teachers (Ian)
  Elementary school
  Junior high school
  High school and vocational
  College

Fans (Joelle)
  Mysteries
  Romance
  Science fiction
  Movies and actors
  Music

Hobbyists (Estelle)
  Collectors
  Tinkerers
  Artists
  History buffs

The 15 major neighborhoods of an online bookstore are further broken down into subneighborhoods. The subneighborhoods are dynamic – they form as the demand for them rises and disappear as they fall into disuse. Large neighborhoods or subneighborhoods need many hosts.

The customer-group breakdown was based on data gathered from questionnaires filled out on the site and customer discussion sessions. Notice there's no section for people who read novels – practically everyone reads a good novel once in a while. Instead, we looked for broader interests and like-minded people. We decided, for example, that corporate lawyers are much more like lawyers at large law firms or other corporate workers, whereas independent lawyers had a lot more in common with small business owners and consultants. Anyone who is interested in entrepreneurship can spend time at the entrepreneurs' section and meet the entrepreneurs who will gather there.

The customer-service people – soon to be hosts – were very excited. They helped us write scenarios we could pitch to Justbooks' executives. For example, Stacy, the team-player host for the enterprise neighborhood, wanted to grow horizontal subneighborhoods. She wanted beginners who are project managers to meet each other. She also wanted to match people who had expert knowledge with writers who could help them prepare proposals and collaborate on books. Each of the 15 neighborhoods would start with the set of obvious subneighborhoods we listed, then the hosts would be free to modify or add new ones as necessary. This targeted approach would give beginners an immediate path toward becoming intermediates and starting to participate on the site.

Jessica, the multitalented host for the Small Business neighborhood, knew that her customers wear many hats. They want to increase their skill sets and learn where to get help when they need it. They view books as tools, and they are willing to pay for good tools. Most of their needs are common to all small businesspeople, so beginners to this neighborhood would see a lively mix of discussion and advice. They would be able to exchange ideas on everything from accounting systems to building web sites. Jessica wanted to set up forums for reviewing and discussing books grouped by topic, letting customers compare books head-to-head and vote for their favorites.

Hershel, the enterprising neighborhood host for entrepreneurs, knew that if he tried to separate his visitors into subgroups of venture capitalists, engineers, marketers, and so on, these people would simply spend their time in each other's areas, trying to learn what everyone else was doing. He would draw beginners in by setting up a single online mailing list where customers could talk about exciting new books and ideas, and where authors could interview entrepreneurs. He wanted to share content with the fast-moving magazines entrepreneurs read. And he wanted to reward his active customers with new books on the day they were published, so those people could get the scoop ahead of everyone else.

For beginners, the hosts will be the most important part of the Justbooks.com experience. The host for each group makes everyone feel welcome and connects each visitor to the discussion groups, tools, and features that will eventually make that person feel the neighborhood is home. Once beginners are settled in, they become intermediates.

Every neighborhood host would welcome new group members into an entry-level discussion that is "the daily read" for that neighborhood. Discussion topics might include current events, reactions to new books, rumors about upcoming books, and so on. The daily read would give newcomers a chance to participate in the neighborhood right away – an entrance to the inter-mediate discussion groups.

At the launch of Phase 1, we proposed to reconstruct Justbooks.com to include enticing links to the different neighborhoods. Because that would be a radical change for surfers, we planned to introduce the links at the bottom of the page and then move them toward the prime real estate at the top over a two-week period. Each neighborhood would have a simple web address, like www.Justbooks.com/entrepreneurs. By the end of Phase 2, the front page of the site would be a place to do a quick search for an item or dive directly into the neighborhoods.

Intrepid Intermediates

On the proposed site, intermediates will get the sense that the neighborhoods are happening places. Each neighborhood is a complete bookstore, with access to every book in the catalog. But there will be much more to do than buy books. Discussion groups, book-of-the-week clubs, investment clubs, health-care forums, and special events will take place in every neighborhood. Authors will be encouraged to make scheduled and sneak appearances in groups discussing their books or areas of expertise. And they will, because it's in their best interest to get to know their readers.

The people in Aviva's Parents group need more than books. By making her neighborhood part of a network of parenting sites, Aviva intends to reach out to people other than Justbooks.com customers. Our proposal includes allowing hosts like Aviva to set their own neighborhood policies on link exchanges and content syndication with outside sites. Corporate-level control will be minimal, giving Aviva the freedom she needs to connect with parents.

Claudia's sports enthusiasts are very event-driven. They are interested in tennis during Wimbledon and soccer during the World Cup. They really enjoy reading about their sports heroes, and many buy reference books explaining the rules of different sports. Claudia wanted to offer starter packs – book combinations that appeal to intermediate sports fans. She wanted to sell them practically at cost to celebrate people's entry into her neighborhood and at the same time get them interested in more books. She also had ideas for some special gifts to include in the box each time the customers placed an order. She'd like to get her customers autographed copies of books whenever possible. A sports fan herself, she would make use of her network of sports contacts to arrange book signings as often as possible. She would also like to help people auction their sports memorabilia on the site.

In our proposal, a section of the site shows intermediates how to write a good book review. Readers who belong to a neighborhood can send their reviews to the host for comments. The host acts as a writing coach and helps them polish their work. Every week, the host of a section will publish the most thoughtful, passionate submissions on the neighborhood home page, often choosing reviews with opposing points of view on the same book. These point-counterpoint customer reviews are extremely popular.

Perhaps a host's most important responsibility is to adjust the pace of the activities and discussions in her neighborhood. She does so by choosing her featured reviews carefully and occasionally moderating the group discussions. If people feel overwhelmed, they will be unable to keep up. If they feel the site doesn't change, they will go someplace else. The hosts must constantly ask people how the site fits into their schedules and how comfortable they are with the discussions. A site can sustain itself through polite disagreements and the occasional flare-up, but if conflicts result in mass confusion, the community will quickly burn itself out.

Intermediate Results

Justbooks' executives took our challenge and approved the first phase of the site re-org, which included the 15 sections with features for beginners and intermediates. It wasn't particularly expensive to implement, but it took some attitude adjustment. The rest of the employees thought they would end up competing to keep their jobs. But the CEO asked everyone to go along with the experiment. They would decide as a company what to do after the first set of results were in.

Six months later, no one wanted to work in what was now the old part of the site. That was because it wasn't getting any traffic. Everyone – management and employees – voted to throw out the original content-based approach and expand the customer categories. That meant realigning the company behind the hosts and their customer groups. It meant asking the designers and IT people to get out of the driver's seat. Because everyone could see that the new sections were on fire, the transition went more smoothly than even the CEO had anticipated. The largest re-org in the company's history took place almost voluntarily, as employees aligned themselves with the neighborhoods that interested them. They even repainted and redecorated their physical offices to reflect the character of the customer neighborhoods.

The hosts wanted to encourage spontaneous book giving. They brainstormed and implemented a book-zapping system. Customers could "zap" a book to someone on a predefined list with a simple click of the mouse. Soon, customers were zapping books to people they'd never met in person, as thanks for pointing them to a good book or a good site, as stimuli to continue a particular discussion, or as bolsters to the sides of a debate. Zapping started small but caught on in a big way, and books lost their stigma as the gift of last resort.

Now that the intermediates were buzzing like bees and zapping like Zorro, a group of neighborhood hosts got together with their most enthusiastic customers to discuss what they could do for experts. During a two-day Phase 2 kickoff meeting, they generated hundreds of ideas, ranked them, and began implementing the winners even before they got back to their desks.

A Home for Experts

Remember Justbooks' affiliate program? The one other stores copied? Justbooks' employees came up with something much more sticky. Anyone in a customer group can start and maintain a web page right on the site. So, for example, the group member who's an antiques expert can publish her own opinions and reviews at Justbooks.com. Her page describes her interests and her qualifications for recommending books. She can even do a little permission marketing by creating an e-mail newsletter for others interested in antiques and collecting. Best of all, the company would pay these in-house experts five percent of all the revenues they generated.

In essence, the company provided the traffic *and* a referral fee for each sale. The expert customers piled in. In each neighborhood, experts tried to attract the most traffic to their own bookstores inside the site. Individual reviewers began to have their own followings. The internal-bookstore idea soon turned into a huge popularity contest, while the external affiliates continued to drive new visitors to the site.

When a customer came up with a great idea, the hosts ran with it. They gave popular internal bookstores their own subdomains (putting a name like "sofiacoppola" where the "www" usually goes) within the site. Anyone who draws at least 100 visitors per week to her page for three consecutive months, or at least ten book sales in a three-month period, would receive a Justbooks T-shirt. Ten or more book sales per month garnered the customer a box of personal business cards with the Justbooks logo and toll-free number, the customer's phone number (if desired), and the customer's personal web address. Anyone could call the Justbooks' toll-free number and ask for a particular customer's list of recommended books.

At first, the system engineers objected to the idea, saying the use of subdomains would play havoc with their system. They recommended putting the names at the end (as in www.Justbooks.com/sofiacoppola). But the hosts were united. "WE WANT THE CUSTOMER'S NAME TO COME BEFORE OUR NAME, BECAUSE AT JUSTBOOKS, THE CUSTOMER ALWAYS COMES FIRST!" they shouted.

Undoubtedly, some customers would take unfair advantage of this offer. An expert with a subdomain might send mass e-mail messages to her friends, telling them to visit her page. That was okay with everyone at Justbooks. T-shirt owners would literally become walking billboards for the site. If a customer was interested enough to stick with a personal bookstore for three months to get the T-shirt, he or she would be welcome to it.

The personal bookstore competition quickly heated up, and Justbooks' CEO knew exactly what to do: He poured gasoline on the fire.

He asked the hosts to give away cars – *yes, cars!* – to the people who sold the most books in each neighborhood every quarter. After that announcement, the engineers had to scramble to keep the computer system from breaking down. The hosts began listing the 30 most popular internal home pages in a column on each neighborhood home page. Soon, the internal affiliate program was the hottest thing in e-tailing.

Fisher began to put the photo and a short write-up of an outstanding customer contributor on his neighborhood home page every day. Soon, all the hosts had followed suit, giving customers their 15 minutes of fame. Customers vying for this honor have become even more involved in the discussions and more helpful to newcomers. The experts chosen each day are usually so excited that they send e-mail to everyone they know telling them to visit the site.

The Customer-Led Bookstore and More

After building the neighborhoods, the hosts worked to make each one action-oriented, not content-oriented. A customer can be in a rush one day and in the mood to explore another day. Why shouldn't the system give her the ability to say she needs help quickly or that she's in a mood to explore? What do kids want to do when they come to their neighborhood? Each host made a list of actions and possible "moods" for her customers. For example, parents might want to learn about a specific health condition (and perhaps buy a book on the topic), join a discussion, find a book, ask a question, buy a gift, write a book recommendation, see if their friends are online, and so on. Most of the actions were fairly easy to automate, but they had to be intuitive. A person visiting from an office in Paris or a cybercafé in Bombay must be able to use them easily. The people-action-content framework now serves Justbooks very well.

On her first visits to Justbooks.com, a customer might want to bookmark several different neighborhoods. A person who is a single parent, for example, may also be an avid golfer. Because this person will play all three of those roles when she comes to the site, she starts by bookmarking the Parents, Singles, and the Sports neighborhoods. As soon as she would like to keep track of all three neighborhoods, she can create her own home page at Justbooks.com simply by adding various neighborhoods to the checklist in her profile. Every time she visits the site, the system builds her a custom-made bookstore that reflects her interests and contains many people she can relate to. Over time, as her profile develops, the customer continues to refine her choices. Eventually, she naturally progresses to a one-to-one relationship with both the company and her friends.

As a company, Justbooks jumped wholeheartedly into the customer-led approach to business. Beginners start at the home page and settle into one or two neighborhoods. Intermediates meet, share their views, and zap books to each other. And experts stay busy making money by defending their expert status on more than 3,000 topics! Whereas the original site was hermetically sealed, each neighborhood now points to many other sites of interest. It's no surprise that traffic has gone up, not down, since the site turned the reins of control over to the neighborhood hosts – and their customers.

The neighborhoods are starting to take on very different characteristics – they're now more like community centers than specialized bookstores. People visit Justbooks.com not for what they can see or buy, but for what they can learn and share. A teenager and a corporate lawyer encounter very different environments at Justbooks.com, but each now calls the site home.

Obviously, Justbooks.com is not a good name for a customer-led company. The people who visit the site are interested in much more than books. Justbooks has asked its customers what else they want – and how *they* would rename the company. Soon, thanks to foresighted executives, enthusiastic employees, and helpful customers, the company will emerge as a customer-led enterprise, ready to go where no bookstore has gone before.

What happened to the strategy consultants? We futurized our way out of a job. It's time for us to move on to our next client.

OLD MISSION STATEMENT | Be the authoritative source for books online.

NEW MISSION STATEMENT | Be the place to explore the world of ideas and the magic of books online.

Software
Company

CHAPTER 16

IN THIS CHAPTER, we watch a fictional company that thought it was in the business of selling software pull back from the brink of disaster by getting out of the retail channel and into services. Many software companies face this choice: Should they deliver software electronically, or should they deliver the software *experience* electronically? In this case, the key was a high-level decision that brought new thinking into the company and unleashed a flood of exciting new possibilities.

The Channel Kings

In the late 1980s, Joe Gill and Joe Walbaum had a bright idea to start a company that sold software to help people edit their digital images. Since the number one program was for professionals, their program would target consumers. And on the strength of that insight, the two Joes built Allpix into a model company.

The two Joes were well suited to run Allpix. Joe W was the brilliant programmer and product manager. Joe G was the channel marketing expert. Through his efforts, the company quickly achieved a powerhouse position with distributors and retailers. The company went public on the strength of its single image-editing product.

Joe G then asked for more products to strengthen the brand and to increase shelf presence. There was no real need for that many different products, but more products gave their brand more shelf space, leaving less room for competitors. Joe W went shopping and acquired drawing programs, page layout programs, clip art, photo libraries, and other simple products for consumers, all packaged in their signature blue-and-gold boxes. Joe G began the industry's biggest spiff program – rewarding sales associates and distributors who moved their products through the channel. They were known in the industry as "the Hawaiian shirt guys," because they gave Hawaiian shirts to any sales associate who'd met his or her monthly quota. In addition, they gave away trips to Hawaii, laptop computers, cash – anything to get the sales floor moving those blue-and-gold boxes. Soon, they found themselves in the affiliate-label business – taking other companies' products into distribution and keeping a large percentage of the profit.

By the mid-1990s, Allpix had 1,800 employees and 35 products in the channel. Their flagship product – the image-editing software – became even more consumer oriented. It had become a suite of products, all aimed at home publishing projects. They redesigned all their packaging in Hawaiian shirt prints, and that increased sales even more.

Sliding Sideways

And so the company grew. The two Joes managed to convince Clyde Wainwright to become the chairman of their board. Clyde was a wealthy ex-venture capitalist, a gruff businessman with an MBA from the School of Hard Knocks. In the last few years, he had taken several Internet companies public. The Joes convinced him to help them move Allpix online.

They tried several things. They worked with online software vendors, giving them spiffs and helping them develop upselling software – special programs that match their products with customers' online purchases. Joe W, who had been working for years on a special technology to let people exchange electronic greeting cards, invitations, and photos online, tried to get the browser manufacturers to include this technology with their browsers. In the end, they turned him down because they didn't see enough acceptance by the public to make it worth their while.

A year passed. They bought a few small Internet companies – those they could afford. They opened their own commerce site to sell their software, but the company was already going in too many directions. Sales of their main products had peaked and were on the way down. To cut costs, they laid off 250 people. Then three of their best engineers left to join Internet start-ups.

An E-Mutiny

At the next board meeting, Clyde and the other board members fired Allpix's two avuncular founders in the first ten minutes. The Joes were stunned. They had guided this company for 12 years! Clyde had been behind them the whole time, and now he was throwing them out on the street! How could he do that? As it turned out, Clyde had both the votes and the will to do what he needed to save the company.

Clyde had been spending a lot of time posing as a quality-assurance engineer on the Allpix intranet. He discovered that many employees had started a secret mailing list where people in the company were having their own private conversation all day long without speaking to each other directly. An entire parallel subculture had grown up around this mailing list, with people taking on identities different from those they had in the company corridors.

Clyde was surprised to find the entire company talking behind management's back. They said the Joes didn't get it, that the channel was disappearing, that buying more companies wasn't going to tack ".com" on the end of their name or raise their stock price. It seemed to them the company was spiraling out of control, and they wondered when the next round of layoffs would put them on the street. In this environment, the people were quite bold about speaking out. It wasn't just complaining. They were also trying to help each other, and doing a remarkably good job.

Everyone liked the Joes. They were the parents of the company family. Much of the company's culture – perhaps too much – was centered around them. But the Joes hadn't been able to get their arms around this Internet thing. Everyone admitted it was time for the Joes to step aside. Joe G was a channel guy. Joe W was a product guy. Clyde said it was time to bring in a service guy.

Two Months of Planning

With the board's blessing, Clyde brought in Jackie Foster and made her CEO. Jackie came from Kodak's consumer division, where she had been similarly frustrated by her company's inability to take advantage of the changes she'd seen in many of its markets. She and Clyde already had a plan, but they would need eight weeks to work with the other managers on a completely new strategy for the company.

During these two months, Jackie was everywhere. She rolled out an Internet boot camp and encouraged everyone to surf at least half an hour a day, every day. She started her own internal web site and put it on the company intranet. She worked on weekends to fill it with information people might want to know about her and to exchange ideas for changing the company. She sent out company-wide e-mail messages encouraging people to see new web sites and learn what their customers were doing online. On Fridays she posted something new on her site. On Tuesdays, she held her office door open so anyone could drop by to discuss anything at all. She even advertised her Tuesday office hours on the company's existing web site, so anyone could come in and chat with her.

Clyde and Jackie brought the "elders" of the company's underground mailing list together for an off-site, facilitated meeting. They wanted to start building a more fluid management structure, where employees in charge of a customer group could put together a plan, get it approved, and execute it. The elders were enthusiastic. They immediately volunteered to build their own intranet around various customer subgroups.

On the day of the big presentation, Clyde rented an auditorium for the event. All of the company's 1,500 employees came to this meeting, enticed by Jackie's promise of an appearance by a special mystery guest.

Killing the Cash Cow

Clyde welcomed everyone and wasted no time in introducing Jackie. She thanked them for coming. Then she unveiled her plan. She said the first order of business was to kill the company's cash cow as soon as possible. Allpix would soon be pulling out of the channel. The company's flagship product would be allowed to sell down, and the support group would cover the product until customers stopped needing support. That caused more than a little concern among the employees.

Jackie announced that she planned to rededicate the entire company to serving one market: families. The new model was to help families work with their digital images, both online and in physical forms. Rather than trying to imitate what most people do with photographic film (make prints, put them into albums), she started by asking what people would want if they could have a professional production company working for them.

Jackie created several scenarios that outlined possible opportunities that could be pursued from the next incarnation of their web site – Allpix.com. She told stories of several families she'd interviewed, talked about where the customers were headed, and unveiled her three-phase plan. The first phase was to get people to upload their photos onto the server. The second phase was to get them printing and ordering products from their photo collection. The third phase was to become an advertising-based portal for families.

There was an awkward silence. What did the company know about creating an Internet portal? What *was* an Internet portal? Jackie envsioned families from all over the world gathering, meeting each other, doing projects together, sharing photos, keeping journals, setting up student exchange programs, and other activities. But, she said, Phase 3 was a year or two away. First, they had to execute Phases 1 and 2. They had to become a true service company.

Today, she said, customers must scan in their images, edit them, and print them with a color printer. But to reach the broadest possible audience, the company would have to cater to people who didn't own – or want to own – scanners and color printers. They would have to take their core technology and turn it into a service. And they would have to turn their corporate culture from one that ships products to one that serves customers every day. There was another awkward silence. Jackie used the opportunity to bring down the lights and start her multimedia presentation.

A Family Focus

Jackie used a vacation scenario to make her pitch to the assembled employees. She told a story of a family that takes a vacation and has a great time. They come home with photos, postcards, ticket stubs, restaurant menus, journal notes, and other memorabilia. Now, imagine that they send everything off to the Allpix processing center. The company develops their film, scans all their photos and assets, and uploads it to their own private pages on the Allpix site. Now the family can see everything online. Allpix provides special trip templates that show their itinerary, complete with interactive maps, sound files, and other entertaining ways of commemorating and annotating their journey. Special software helps them notify their friends about their web site and, if they want, to have it listed in the community directory.

Jackie described how Allpix.com will offer an array of printing services to commemorate the trip in hard copy. The company can make prints and send them to everyone on a mailing list, without the customer having to address them individually. They can make greeting cards, collages, spiral-bound books, or hardbound albums commemorating their trip. Allpix can combine 15 photos and captions into a collage or place them over a poster-sized map of the territory they covered.

Jackie said there are already thousands of excellent photographs of vacation places on the Web. So if you visited a place and didn't take photos, you can link to those sites from your trip site and still show visitors how beautiful it is. If you took a group vacation, people in your group could exchange photos with each other. If someone got a good shot of Machu Picchu, that person can share the image with the rest of the group.

Jackie pointed out the potential for online communities to form around trips, locations, and extended families and friends. The value of the service increases exponentially if customers keep coming back to compare notes, give advice, and get recommendations. Travel enthusiasts – individuals and families alike – would have greater loyalty if the company helped them plan new experiences as well as commemorate old ones.

That was just one scenario. Allpix.com would offer web-based templates for many different kinds of projects. Customers can build family trees and combine photos with family history. They can make interactive albums, cards, booklets, flip books, comic books, cookbooks, and other projects. To celebrate weddings, they can include guest books, special telegrams, family stories, roasts, toasts, and so on. Every event in people's lives would have different templates for commemorating it.

Allpix.com will offer many kinds of printing options, from proof sheets for easy offline reference to archival prints, posters, and even brochures. They can offer cards, frames, bound books, videos, and other output services. They can offer pages where visitors can order calendars, T-shirts, mugs, plates, party favors, and other souvenirs – all incorporating their own photographs and text. These things are an easy sell, because people already have their photos online. If they need a gift quickly, they can come to the site and create one.

Jackie's presentation got everyone excited. They wanted to see more.

Phase 1: Getting Market Share

Jackie said that in an Internet category, being number one is great, number two is good, number three is okay, and there isn't a number four. Jackie didn't want to leave any room for a start-up to take her family customers away. She told her assembled audience what it would take to convert the average family of four to digital photography today: lots of scanners.

Not everyone has a scanner, she said. But everyone has a box filled with negatives and prints. Her goal was to digitize every negative and every slide every family owns. Jackie had purchased a fleet of new, highly automated scanners that produce high-quality scans of negatives at reasonable prices. She was going to set up their scanner operation in Spokane, Washington, where the cost of doing business was low. Then Jackie said she was going to make families an offer they couldn't refuse.

Jackie's VP of marketing had worked with Allpix's ad agency on the storyboard for their new advertising campaign. The goal was to entice families to send their entire box of prints, negatives, and memorabilia for scanning. This campaign would tell everyone about the new Allpix.com service. But Allpix.com wasn't going to offer to scan every negative for free. Instead, the company was going to *pay* people for every negative they sent in!

That sent some whispers through the crowd. How were they going to do that? On a new customer's first order, Allpix.com will pay the customer one penny (in credit, not cash) for every image on every negative she sends in. So if someone sends in 100 sets, she would get $36 in credit toward services. Since most people want their photographs scanned along with their negatives, Jackie's team set up a price structure by which the average first-time order came to $40 after the credit.

For a nominal fee, the company will return the photos and send the customer a printed booklet with all her photos as thumbnails. Each photo has its own ID number, so people without computers can simply call a toll-free number and order what they want. Customers can also pay for a set of CD-ROMs with all their scans on them.

Basic membership which includes the storage of 1,000 photos, is always free, but additional features cost extra. With a new account, everyone receives frequent-buyer dollars just for signing up. That gives people the incentive to order as much printing and other products as possible, and it encourages people to spend time on the site working with and organizing their photos.

Jackie explained that the site/service combination is viral – the more people come to the site, the more they can do, and the more value it is to everyone. A traveler planning a trip to a city should be able to come to the site, type in a city name, see a listing of trips people have taken to that city – and contact those people to learn about their experience.

Online, she explained, families aren't looking for tools – they're looking for the fastest, easiest, and most enjoyable ways to share their experiences. Sorting through a few thousand pictures is tedious. Figuring out what to do with overexposed negatives is also tedious. At the company's web site, there's no button to help customers correct red-eye in photos. The system automatically corrects every photo that comes in. The more technological advances that can be completely hidden, the better. Jackie said this would be the next big challenge for their software group – making all of this advanced functionality happen on the server with minimal customer intervention.

Jackie explained that all this scanning in Phase 1 won't make the company much money. The company may even lose money in the first year. But this offer, combined with a commitment to giving people the best printed products for their money, will give them market share in the New World. If people tell their friends to sign up for the service, and if people trust the company to handle their precious photographs, they will succeed in getting millions of new customers in the first year alone.

Phase 2: Paper and Pixels

Jackie said that in Phase 2, Allpix.com will become the number one place for families to do more with their digital photographs than they ever thought possible. First, Jackie wanted to help people learn to take digital photos and upload them directly onto the site. She planned to set up an online digital photography workshop, staffed mostly by enthusiastic volunteers and featuring the work of well-known photographers. The site would be organized around different kinds of families: those with young children, those with teens, and those with older children.

During Phase 2, Allpix will continue to expand its catalog of printing services. This is when the company will be able to capitalize on its scanner investment and the marketing efforts of Phase 1. She expected the company to turn a profit within 18 months. That, she said, was the company's mission. But she was also looking ahead, to the time when Phase 2 would run out of steam.

After the company's initial offer captures its first million customers, Jackie wanted to launch a secret weapon that would extend the brand even further. The idea came from Cathy, a customer who had walked into her office one Tuesday to talk about web strategy. She liked the idea so much, she offered Cathy a job. Together, they planned to build something that would put the Allpix.com name onto every computer in the country.

Jackie explained that every computer has a background image, called wallpaper, which is often blue or gray. Using a new, automated service called Allpaper, families will be able to create wallpaper images and screensavers using their own photos. Each time they turn on their computer, they see not a monochromatic desktop but one of their family members or pets. Periodically, the image fades and a new one appears. If they prefer, the images can show up in a resizeable window or as a screensaver. She showed a video demo of her Allpaper concept, which made use of the technology Joe Walbaum had developed last year to share documents.

How do customers get this feature? Simple. They designate which of the photos they've stored on the Allpix.com server they want to see. They can choose the sequence, size, and duration of display as they build their own Allpaper album. Or they can ask the program to select images at random. This way, they can be reminded of a special event or trip whenever they are at their computers. A click on the Allpaper icon takes them to the site to see more of those memories.

The program can even play short videos or sound recordings. Since no one wants to watch an entire home video anyway, Allpix.com will help people convert and edit their material into short film clips. The family dog can wander across the screen and do something entertaining. A video loop showing a river full of fish can flow in the background as a fisherman works on his computer. A grandchild can come onscreen and say something new every day. Allpaper packages these video clips and images as presents for others.

Jackie said that once people have albums, they'd be able to link to other Allpaper albums and see their friends' photos and videos during the day as well. They can also meet new friends in the online activity center and trade albums. They can set up random links, so that a constant stream of new people floats by their screen as they work or play online. They can even make albums of poetry, performances, web sites, or anything else that can show up in a browser window.

Someone in the audience asked whether this wasn't just push-media all over again. Jackie explained that push technology – sending web sites and information automatically – had been tried before, and people hadn't gone for it. But now that many consumers were getting high-bandwidth connections, push-media would just be another option offered by many web sites. Some sites will display as you click, others will constantly update the information you've asked for. Besides, she said, the Allpaper concept was personal. It is meant to give people a personal experience once a day. People will want to see themselves and their families and meet others through photographs. It would be fun and meaningful, not anonymous and frivolous. If their pilot project for Allpaper is a success, a community would form that will later become their portal.

Phase 3: The Photo Portal

Jackie said the company would have to follow customers as they become acclimated to the Internet. In just a few years, she said, there would be less demand for photographic prints. As everyone becomes more accustomed to digital technology, customers will find it easier to display and enjoy their photos on a screen, rather than on paper. Customers may still want T-shirts, mugs, and framed photos, but printed booklets and albums would gradually disappear.

In Phase 3, the company would dedicate itself to building a personal portal, where people can get the most out of their images, sounds, and videos. It would be similar to a web directory, but people would contribute photos and narratives, rather than web pages. The portal would connect families around the world. It would be a place for families, by families. And Allpaper was part of the transition that would help them build it.

Jackie didn't have a set of plans for building the portal, only that she thought it would be a viable business once the Allpix site was full of people working on their photo albums. In time, they would be able to charge for advertising and extra services. For now, she said, Allpix would focus on building a profitable business by digitizing people's photos and sending them printed products. She was convinced that Allpaper would lead them to Phase 3 if they let their customers help them plan it.

Clyde said he thought Allpaper would give them a degree of customer loyalty many software giants would envy. Allpix would be able to set up their portal on millions of desktops, as long as they let the customer stay in charge of the relationship. He said there would be no more cash cows. As a service company, Allpix would have to focus on customers relentlessly and give them an exciting personal experience every day.

Looking Forward

Jackie knew she was going to need a big finish. She brought her special mystery guest onstage. After eight weeks away, the two Joes returned, smiling and wearing their trademark Hawaiian shirts. The crowd gave them a standing ovation. The Joes told the entire company they were behind Jackie and her new plan. The board had added another seat that the Joes would share. Freed from day-to-day pressure, the Joes could be a big help in getting corporate partners to understand the company's new goals. They also said they would make themselves available to help the employees during the transition. And they would be in the Internet lab every Wednesday to show people the latest progress on Allpaper.

Jackie startled people by saying there would be no re-org. People would have to do that themselves. She wanted people to create an internal market for new positions and maintain that market mechanism. She said it was everyone's job to make his or her job obsolete within six months to two years, then find another job inside the company.

Well? What did they think? Jackie had the house lights turned up and spent the next hour answering questions. The reaction of the company's employees surprised her. They loved it. They could hardly contain themselves. They all had ideas for services they could offer to get families excited about digital photography. They were entering a completely different world, but they trusted Jackie to lead them forward. They gave her a thunderous round of applause as the post-meeting reception began onstage.

OLD MISSION STATEMENT | Providing consumer-level productivity tools.

NEW MISSION STATEMENT | Helping people enjoy and share their memories.

Bank Intranet

CHAPTER 17

JOE CUTLER WAS WELL AWARE OF THE DANGERS involved in building a corporate intranet for a bank with 28,000 employees. As the IT manager for fictional Big Bank Incorporated, he was determined to make the intranet a customer-driven resource. He had read case studies of companies that built big, fancy intranets with sophisticated knowledge management systems. Almost all of the systems failed miserably, because they didn't do what people wanted. He knew that over 60 percent of all features put into custom systems were never used. Another 20 percent were used only rarely, and 15 percent were used occasionally. In reality, companies made good use of just five percent of the features built into most custom-built systems.

Joe knew that people don't use a system they don't trust. So he built airtight applications – programs – for the human resources people, for the loan officers, and for executives. It was all part of the company's digital nervous system – a concept he'd learned from Bill Gates. He had over 20,000 desktops to manage and made sure that everyone had the same version of the software. He set up a 24-hour help desk, staffed by well trained operators to help troubleshoot any problem. Joe had a small army of programmers and a nonstop parade of expert consultants, all working together to make this digital nervous system a lifeline for everyone in the bank.

The Digital Nervous System

Rob, one of Big Bank's loan officers, makes good use of the digital nervous system. When a client comes in with a loan application, Rob has easy access to credit history, property information, current rates, – everything he needs to give the client an immediate answer. In most cases, he can tell clients exactly which pieces of information they still need to provide and what the terms would be. The time from meeting a client to closing a loan has dropped from 42 days to 11, and most of that time is used by the title office, which is still processing applications on paper. Rob's loan volume has doubled in six months. For internal customers like Rob, the system really works.

As part of Big Bank's digital nervous system, Joe implemented a state-of-the-art knowledge management system – an intranet that helps anyone find information easily. If everyone took ten minutes a day to record information (customers, contacts, deal terms, research, risk assessments, strategies, tips, etc.) into the system, everyone would be able to use and share the collected knowledge.

Unfortunately, Joe's ambitious intranet doesn't work for everyone. As much as he's tried, Joe can't motivate people to put meaningful information into the system. Take Elsa, for example. Elsa works at Big Bank's headquarters in New York. She's working on restructuring a loan package for an international company based in Minnesota. The company is merging with a European conglomerate. Big Bank has offices in a few European cities, but Elsa doesn't know anyone overseas. She needs corporate data, economic data, sector performance, and currency forecasts from seven countries. Joe's knowledge management system hasn't been much help. Even if all that information were in the system, Elsa couldn't deal with most of it. She needs advice, not data.

Maggie is a new vice president who's just moved from headquarters to the San Francisco office. She's in the middle of a huge restructuring effort and is putting in 60 hours a week. She needs to learn as much about the employees as possible. She needs information about other offices in northern California, who handles which accounts, competitive information, and other business intelligence. She also needs to find an apartment, buy some furniture, lease a car, set up child care for her daughter, find a doctor, and handle many other moving details. Joe's knowledge management system hasn't been much help to Maggie, either.

Joe could install new features to make the intranet more useful to knowledge workers like Elsa and Maggie, but they had trouble describing to him exactly what they wanted it to do. Joe got frustrated. "If you can't spec it, I can't build it," he would say. There were so many other critical systems on his priority list that he had decided to wait until there was a clear mission for the intranet.

Why do Joe's systems serve Rob so efficiently and Elsa and Maggie so poorly? Does Joe just need more resources to expand his digital nervous system? No. Joe could spend $850 million on his digital nervous system, and most of it would go to waste.

What Joe hasn't figured out is that tools can help automate action, but they can't automate *ideas, knowledge,* or *personal power in an organization.* Systems that optimize processes often make those processes much more efficient. But systems that try to connect people, places, or things usually fail. If the employees are motivated to get personal results when they use the system, they'll make the system work; if they don't see an immediate payback, they'll make sure it fails.

A Human Solution

Joe wants everyone to use one big structured repository, but there's no way to get the structure right because everyone has a different view of the banking world. Joe's knowledge management system and your computer desktop are examples of hierarchical structures. In a hierarchical structure, there is only one path to any particular object. It's easy to lose a loan calculation, for example, because you can't remember whether it is in the folder with all the spreadsheets, or the folder with the contracts, or the folder for that particular client. It should be in all three.

The World Wide Web, on the other hand, is an example of a relational structure. It has no beginning and no end, no top or bottom, no preferred frame of reference. A single link can shorten the path from any object to any other. New pages arrive and work their way into the web of links. Old pages disappear, leaving links that point nowhere. It's messy and unstructured. Just like our brains. Just like The Brain.

In this context, a Brain is a connected set of Thoughts (I'll capitalize both words in this chapter to distinguish them from our human brains). A Thought can contain a word, a paragraph, a list, a document, a link to another document, an image, a sound file, a database, a phone number or address, a software program, a set of links to web sites, and so on. A Thought can contain another Thought, or even a link to another Brain.

Think of The Brain as a person-wide web – a loose collection of information and links.

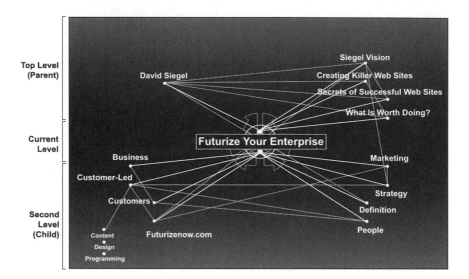

The Brain works the way your brain does – by association. It stores Thoughts relationally, not hierarchically. The Thoughts above the center line are called parent Thoughts. The Thoughts below the center are known as children of the parents. This is just a way of displaying the links below and the links above a certain item. The links can be circular, so that there is no particular top Thought. Or the links can be set up as a tree structure – a strict hierarchy, whose topmost Thought is paradoxically known as the root of the tree.

Sheila has been a marketing manager at Big Bank's San Francisco office for two years. Sheila keeps lists of everything. She has lists of restaurants, office supply stores, travel agencies, suppliers, contractors (writers, illustrators, designers, ad agencies, printers, etc.), clients, holidays, trade shows, doctors, lawyers – everything she needs to keep her job and her personal life organized.

Sheila's been helping Maggie get settled in San Francisco. When Maggie asked for a babysitter recommendation, Sheila offered to print out her list of sitters. That was when Maggie showed her The Brain. It took about two hours to get all of Sheila's lists into The Brain. Sheila was so excited about her Brain, she started creating more lists immediately and linking them all together. Maggie told Sheila, "You don't have to plan everything out. Just start putting stuff in. You can rearrange it as you go. That's the beauty of The Brain." For Sheila, the best part was that she didn't have to ask Joe for anything. She just went to Thebrain.com, logged on, and did everything herself.

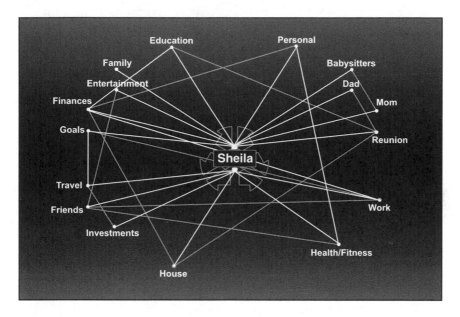

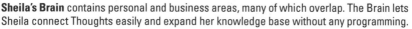

Sheila's Brain contains personal and business areas, many of which overlap. The Brain lets Sheila connect Thoughts easily and expand her knowledge base without any programming.

That same day, Sheila stayed late and built another Brain, this one for her team. She created Thoughts for different people, documents, tasks, resources, clients, links to web pages, and so on. The next morning, all her teammates received an e-mail explaining how to go to The Brain's web site, log on, and start exploring. By the end of the second day, six of Sheila's colleagues had created their own Brains and linked them into the team Brain. Now they had a team-wide web.

The next night, Sheila and Maggie built a Brain for the entire San Francisco office. They spent most of Friday afternoon using Sheila's digital camera to take people's pictures and creating starter Brains for anyone who didn't have one yet. In two weeks, the whole thing had grown organically into hundreds of linked Brains and thousands of Thoughts. The Brain is a secure environment – each person decides which parts of her Brain she wants to share with others. Anyone with a web connection and a password can run a keyword search to find a suitable entry point and begin exploring the parts of people's Brains they want everyone to see.

Since all the Brains were stored on a central server outside the office, anyone could do from home or on the road what she did from her desk. The Brain was the system people had been wanting Joe to give them for over two years, and they had built it themselves in two weeks. Now they had an office-wide web.

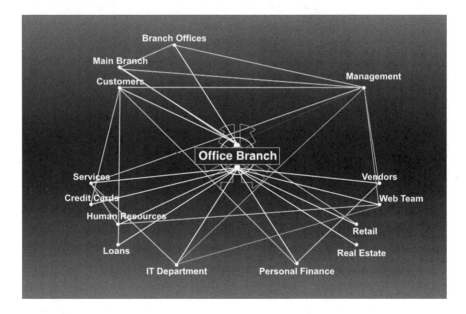

The San Francisco Brain is just a network of personal Brains. Everyone can designate a Thought to be shared or private. The web of shared Thoughts becomes the office Brain.

There was one more step to go. The programmers in Joe's department started using The Brain to write specifications for new systems. They scrapped their old bug-tracking system and built a bug Brain in just a few days. They used it to create a living documentation system, which was always up to date. They gave customers access to the system and stopped printing paper manuals.

Sheila was astonished to hear people bragging about how many visitors they'd had to their Brains. People were actually excited about sharing what they knew.

The marketing people used The Brain to develop proposals. Within a month, they had all but forgotten PowerPoint. Now, to make a presentation, a marketing manager simply fired up a web browser, pointed it to Thebrain.com, logged on, and started an interactive dialogue with their audience. The facilities people soon installed computers with web connections in every conference room. This stopped the laptop-roulette game in which there are four conference rooms and four laptop computers, but no one can ever find the laptops.

> **THE BRAIN**
>
> Everything you see in this chapter can be set up easily with a tool for designing web pages, but The Brain is better at managing information, making changes easily, and searching.
>
> The Brain comes from a company called Natrificial Software Technologies in the Los Angeles area. It's an unstructured, associative way of looking at people, places, and things that's more compatible with the way we store and find information. Learn more at Thebrain.com.

Joe wasn't very happy about The Brain. It was "off campus" and a possible "security risk." He used to be popular. People used to need him. He used to write proposals for more extensions to his digital nervous system, saying how many more resources (people) he needed to make it state-of-the-art. He was going to tell the president how many hours people were wasting on this Brain "toy". He had his PowerPoint presentation all ready.

Then one Monday he was shown a knowledge management Brain some people in the private banking group were already using to share information about clients. Any banker could field a phone call from any client. Simply by linking Brains the bankers could share all their knowledge instantly. This was something Joe had budgeted six months for, yet a few of his people had put it together over the weekend.

The word got out. Sheila started getting e-mail messages from people in other offices asking about The Brain. With Maggie's help, she designed a series of Brain workshops and took them to all the bank's offices. It was so successful that the people at headquarters asked her to come show them how to use it for presentations. A few months later, Big Bank had a company-wide web.

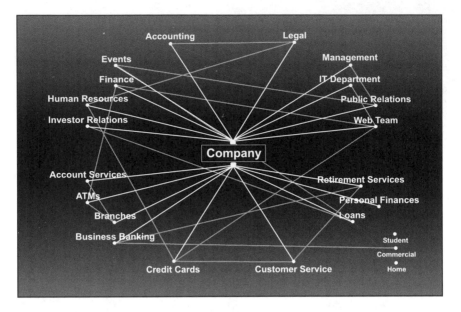

The Big Bank Brain connects all the offices into one large, organic system. Just by building individual Brains and connecting them, the entire company builds a knowledge management system the way bees build a hive.

Gray Matters

Why does The Brain sound so familiar? Because it's just like the Web. The truth is, you can build a sophisticated intranet with a simple web-authoring tool. Each web page can hold images, text, links, lists, and other content. To build their own information network, people need the ability to link from their information to anyone else's information. If companies would just give everyone some space on the company server, a half-day authoring lesson, and some search capabilities, they'd be able to do just about everything I've talked about in this chapter. The Web was built with primitive tools, yet the degree of participation and self-expression in a linked environment is astonishing.

The Brain is messy and unstructured. Like communication. Like business. Like life. You can work your way in from a particular starting point or circle around to the other side. Two Brains can merge into one big Brain, then split into several smaller ones. The structure is dynamic. You don't have to change the framework with each new perspective. You just add that view to the system and start using it.

Big Bank can also let outsiders into its Brain. The Brain can link up customers, partners, and suppliers into certain parts of its company-wide web, forming an ecosystem of information. This isn't about transactions – for that, you need other systems. This is about people, places, and things. This amorphous extranet can be an excellent tool for those outside the company to connect with people inside. It's a phone list, a document management system, events calendar, and message system all in one. It's another way to widen the bottleneck between employees and customers.

At Big Bank, the Brain has led to a huge boost in productivity. The new system is relative, not absolute, and that makes people like Sheila feel more like owners than users. They take pride in maintaining their Brains. Many employees are now known as experts in certain fields, and their Brains have become popular destinations for others inside the company. By creating their own little area of expertise and watching how many colleagues come to feed there, their status in the company goes up, not down. Employees are more valuable because of what they share, rather than what they know. New projects start their own Brains immediately. The unstructured support layer becomes a growth medium for new activity.

Maggie's re-org went smoothly. Sheila became the intranet facilitator, helping people across the company add their own functionality to the company-wide Brain. Joe got a job at Lotus, working for the former CIO of Essex Steel. More than one analyst changed Big Bank's rating from a "hold" to a "buy" after the bank's management team made their quarterly question-and-answer session using The Brain.

OLD MISSION STATEMENT | Our intranet gives people what they need to be more productive.

NEW MISSION STATEMENT | Knowledge management by the people, for the people.

Drug Manufacturer

CHAPTER 18

IN OTHER CHAPTERS, I have emphasized a depth-first approach to satisfying customers online – choose one or two groups and engage them completely before moving on. In this final chapter of Part 3, I will take a larger company and a broader approach. This is the story of how a Fortune 500 company can dedicate itself to its e-customers across the board. Because this chapter would be too long if I made a complete case for each customer group, I will focus on the general strategy the company should take and the goals it should set for five of its many customer groups.

The Business of Drugs

Mondo Drugs is a multibillion-dollar (fictitious) drug company whose web site is designed to look like a theme park. In creating the 10,000-page web site, Mondo's information technology department has enjoyed a happy collaboration with Mondo's marketing department. Much to their surprise, few people visit the site, and those who do, don't stay long. What could be wrong?

Like a teenage girl trying to look sophisticated, Mondo.com has all the bells and whistles the department could think up. It took more than a dozen contractors to create this patchwork of scrolling headlines and rotating logos. The home page features an animation of Mondo's corporate headquarters in a scene that changes with the seasons. Today, it's snowing on the virtual headquarters.

Many sections use JavaScript roll-overs – images that light up when a visitor rolls his mouse over a category name. Visitors can navigate a section on hair loss with a Java-based virtual TV remote-control. The

Java programs cause visitors' computers to crash 40 percent of the time, but since it works fine on the internal computers at Mondo, no one does anything about it.

The main areas of the site are Products, News, Publications, "Science in Action," About the Company, Jobs, and an electronic version of the company's newsletter. As is typical with such sites, a database team manages the content, which means it takes about ten days to correct a spelling error.

After all the time and money put into this site, the deepest experience visitors can have is determining whether they're good candidates for a particular drug. Rather than being a service to the customer, Mondo Drugs' site insults visitors' intelligence by telling them jet lag is the body's way of asking for a sleeping pill. Visitors recognize immediately they'll have to go elsewhere for unbiased health advice.

Fixing the Web Site to Death

Some people on the web team read a book on making the site more accessible to different customer groups. On the home page, a new banner says: "Who are you? Follow these links to see how Mondo products can improve your quality of life!" The choices: health professionals, students, parents, men, women, and seniors. When a visitor clicks on a group, she sees a list of predetermined links into other areas of the site that might appeal to these groups. The web team has simply added two more layers to the old site, making it even harder and more time-consuming to find anything.

Here is a company whose web site is deaf. Is there any chance the company is hard of hearing as a whole? This sad state of polishing the polish is where most large corporate web sites are today – each in its own way a reflection of the attitude management takes toward the Web. Mondo Drugs has invested several million dollars in its web site, and management can't say what the goal is or whether they've achieved it.

This is not to say that all large companies have dysfunctional sites. But if you can see anything of your company in Mondo Drugs, you'll be interested to see how to change your site and your company for the better.

The Business of Health

Since its inception, Mondo has been a product company. A quick visit to its online annual report reveals the company's objective: "To grow through continued research, better marketing for existing brands, and reduced costs of manufacture and delivery." That is perhaps the most pernicious statement on the site.

The Internet provides Mondo Drugs with fantastic new business opportunities. But the company can take advantage of that opportunity only by maintaining the health of *patients,* not *brands.* To thrive in the New World, Mondo must get out of the drug business and into the health business.

In Part 1, I said a poor web site is a sure sign it's time to fix the company. In the following sections, we'll be customer-led consultants to Mondo's executive team. To help them fix the company, we'll look at five important customer groups: doctors, patients, pharmacists, the media, and shareholders.

Doctors

Drug companies want to increase their connections within the medical community. But just converting their company newsletters into HTML isn't going to raise doctors' heart rates. The real currency with doctors isn't a jazzed-up web site – it's results. Doctors are concerned about their patients. They're also frustrated by the lack of time they have to give their patients and by the difficulty of following up with every case. It may be tempting in those circumstances for a doctor to give a patient a prescription rather than to spend time educating the person about prevention.

Pharmaceutical companies have no argument with that approach because it means more sales for them. But that attitude of business-first will eventually undermine their relationship with doctors and even people's health. Let's look at two of Mondo's product categories to see how the company's focus on selling products may be dangerous to the company's own viability.

Antibiotics. Antibiotics are very profitable for Mondo Drugs. They account for more than $1 billion per year in sales. Yet researchers at the Centers for Disease Control and Prevention (CDC) estimate that some

50 million of the 150 million outpatient prescriptions for antibiotics every year are unneeded. In the mid-1990s, nearly 90 percent of children diagnosed with ear infections received antibiotics, and more than 4 million prescriptions were written every year for common colds. Yet both colds and ear infections are usually caused by viruses and do not respond to antibiotics. That heavy and often unnecessary use of antibiotics in treating both humans and livestock has created the environment for the evolution of highly resistant bacteria. Those newly created "super bugs" are beginning to pose serious health risks.

Type II diabetes. According to the CDC, about 95 percent of people with diabetes have Type II diabetes (what used to be called adult-onset diabetes). All the research of the past ten years concludes that this disease is a direct result of being overweight. In study after study, reducing one's weight reverses the progress of the disease. Mondo manufactures several drug therapies that treat the symptoms of this type of diabetes.

More than 30 percent of Americans are clinically obese. Rather than seeing that as a national health problem, Mondo sees it as a market opportunity. The more people who are overweight, the bigger the market for its products. In many cases, the company's mission statement – "promote existing brands" – is in direct conflict with the doctors' mission.

Other conditions for which Mondo prefers to treat symptoms rather than patients include osteoporosis, heartburn, colon cancer, and heart disease. While many of Mondo's products – including antibiotics – save lives, Mondo must take a different view of its relationship with doctors to survive. Rather than waiting for doctors to come to the company, the company should go to the doctors.

If Mondo were to think about the Web as a vehicle for long-term customer loyalty, the company could host an unbiased discussion to help concerned patients understand the health issues surrounding their treatment choices. Mondo could extend its laboratory to include millions of patients and doctors around the world willing to contribute to discussions on degenerative diseases and how to prevent them. By taking part in this discussion, Mondo will learn more about doctors' concerns and how to address them.

Mondo can work with web sites like Drkoop.com to get their Drug Checker into the office of every practicing physician in the country. The company can help develop electronic patient charts that warn doctors of prescription conflicts even before they are written! Mondo doesn't know when a patient has a bad experience with one of its products. Mondo doesn't know when or why patients seek alternative therapies. The company can ask its lawyers to help give patients a mechanism for telling the company when they've experienced problems.

Mondo could focus more resources on developing better diagnostic tests to help doctors determine whether a patient has a viral or bacterial infection. Mondo could spearhead efforts to monitor the use of antibiotics worldwide and develop profitable services for patient monitoring and doctor – patient communication. Mondo could lead research into alternative therapies that represent not competition, but opportunity.

In short, the company can start helping doctors listen to patients. Initiatives like these will make Mondo a trusted brand in 2010, rather than an arms manufacturer in a conventional war that can't be won.

Patients

First things first: Mondo should get rid of the bells and whistles on its web site and spend that money instead on customer ambassadors to various online patient communities. Wherever patients hang out online, the ambassadors should be there, and they should be listening carefully. Their first assignment should be to understand patients who are sharing their stories and helping each other online. "Ask your doctor about acid reflux" isn't going to work anymore. Patients will ask their search engines about acid reflux, and in a few minutes they'll know more than their doctors do.

Mondo should assign ambassadors for specific diseases (horizontal), for demographic groups (horizontal), and for groups of interest (vertical). An ambassador might spend time in an online community devoted to a particular illness – for example, the community around Msonly.com, an online journal committed to patient advocacy for those with multiple sclerosis. The ambassador would quickly learn that many patients don't trust drug companies. She would also learn that individuals respond to their health problems in various ways. Some are interested in helping each other (as Stanford University's Dr David Spiegel has shown, the effectiveness of cancer therapy increases tremendously when patients and doctors support each other emotionally). Others are more interested in sharing information anonymously. Without understanding those preferences, Mondo is operating in a customer vacuum.

The demographic ambassadors will spend time in horizontal online communities – seniors, women, and smokers, for example – to understand and become more sensitive to how they as a group perceive health messages and think about their future health needs.

The ambassadors should get online and meet people belonging to specific online interest groups, like Diabetes.com and the Colon Cancer Alliance (Ccalliance.org). The company needs to learn much more about patients, so it can engage them in a constructive dialog on new approaches. Mondo's ambassadors might learn that two people with the same illness approach their condition in completely different ways, based on their belief systems. The placebo effect, for example, varies based on people's beliefs and attitudes toward doctors, illness, and health. A doctor's demeanor can influence the effects of a particular drug as much or more than the drug itself. Mondo's ambassadors observe these online communities to better understand people's belief systems and how they affect perceptions of certain drug therapies. That understanding should lead Mondo to work with doctors and focus groups to discover new drug therapies designed to accommodate different people's beliefs. If Mondo doesn't turn patients into partners, someone else will, and Mondo's sales will drop as listening companies seize new markets.

Online giving should be part of the company culture. Remember the give/get diagram from Chapter 10? In the spirit of the Web, Mondo should become a better corporate citizen online. The company gives away millions in research dollars and drugs, but it can also provide online services that are not specifically drug-related.

In 1996, Apple Computer set an outstanding example of just such vision and compassion. Apple employees worked with very sick children, most of whom had cancer, to build a site called Convomania.com. The site was a place where it was "okay not to be okay." Imagine kids in hospitals around the world, plugged into machines and IVs, turning on a computer not to play video games but to find children like themselves!

It was truly a visionary gift to the children. They could talk seriously about their illnesses and treatments, compare notes on doctors, play games together, write stories, and have fun with each other. The site was up for two years. Thousands of kids used it. Thousands of friendships sprouted. Then Apple cofounder Steve Jobs came back to run the company. In an effort to improve earnings, he killed the site. He should have given it to a company like Mondo Drugs.

Opportunities abound for Mondo Drugs to give to the online community. For example, dozens of web sites are dedicated to organ transplants. Several of these organizations have databases, but they aren't centralized and they aren't on the Web. Mondo gives millions of dollars to charitable organizations each year. Wouldn't this be an opportunity for a large company like Mondo to give back to the patient community and build goodwill among e-customers?

Pharmacists

Most pharmacists now use computers to keep track of their customers' prescriptions, inventory, and orders, but they don't have access to the Internet at work. The average pharmacist doesn't pay much attention to Mondo. She reads her journals, goes to an occasional conference, and tries to keep up on the latest news in health care. Mondo's salespeople usually sell to major drugstore chains or to distributors who serve the smaller businesses. Short of sending junk mail and conference invitations, Mondo hasn't reached out effectively to pharmacists.

We ask Mondo's executives to take three hours out of their day and surf the Web looking for pharmacists. Their assignment is to bookmark all the places they find pharmacists congregating online.

What did they find? Yahoo! listed only a few good sites for pharmacists. But with more persistent digging, the executives turned up hundreds of sites around the world with pharmacy-related discussions going on. Thousands of pharmacists were logging on from home, trying to learn the answers to specific questions. In a very decentralized way, they were collecting information about how products were being used in real-world situations: Does this feeding tube need to be cleaned with saline? Is this medicine okay for people with epilepsy? Do these two drugs pose a conflict doctors don't know about? The executives learned that pharmacists are truly concerned about drug side effects and adverse reactions from drug combinations.

Mondo could help pharmacists build their own community, a place where they can freely exchange information, express opinions, complain, get advice, use Dr Koop's Drug Checker and other tools, look for jobs, and learn about the latest research. This forum would be the pharmacists' home on the Web – built by and for pharmacists.

Mondo could also offer to help pharmacists get access to the Web at work. Once pharmacists have Internet access from their desks, Mondo could appoint company ambassadors to the pharmacists' online community center. It's more effective to work with them on their site because they are more comfortable in their territory.

Why should Mondo help pharmacists at all? Many of the company's patents are expiring. Patients have more choices. Pharmacists are the people who look at patients and ask, "Would you like Mondo's version of this drug or the generic version? You'll save a lot of money if you go with the generic." How will they phrase that question when Mondo is their partner online?

The Media

All companies understand the benefits of getting good media coverage and the problems caused by unfavorable coverage. In the age of the e-customer, news – good, bad, or wrong – travels very quickly. Mondo needs to set the pace. Mondo archives its press releases on its web site and provides some contact names and numbers there if a reporter wants more information. The company pays its public relations firms to do many things the web site can do better and more cheaply.

Reporters want access to information, and they usually want it quickly. It's surprising more companies don't have extensive online media kits with images in multiple formats, ready for placement in newsletters, papers, magazines, web sites, and other publications. Mondo can make all its research papers and public documents available in one place. It can put up biographies of company researchers and give reporters access to them by e-mail or a search engine that locates people by research specialty. The company should have an online concierge for this part of the site – someone who can respond to new requests immediately.

If a particular reporter covers science and medicine as an ongoing assignment, Mondo can invite her to a discussion with its scientists and managers. The company could set up several electronic mailing lists that facilitate discussion of specific health-related issues. Anyone inside or outside the company, including the press, could join in. Reporters could search the mailing list archives for discussions on topics they are investigating. They could also broadcast a request for information on any topic, expecting that several people would see the request and a few would be able to respond quickly. If Mondo becomes known for answering reporters' questions faster than any other company, reporters will turn their attention to Mondo when Mondo needs that attention most.

Shareholders

Most companies have standard ways of dealing with shareholders. They send annual reports and other items on request. Soon, more than 15 million people in the United States will be trading stock from their own online accounts. While no board of directors wants to have to answer questions sent in by thousands of individual investors, it's also dangerous to ignore them. Disgruntled investors will talk about the company on other sites, and off-site flames could erupt into a fire the board will have to work hard to extinguish.

Under no circumstances should Mondo host a general discussion of the company and its stock on Mondo.com. Any moderation of a discussion Mondo hosts could lead to charges of stock manipulation or fraud. Instead, the company should find active investment sites and host information desks there. Online ambassadors can answer visitors' questions and clear up or prevent misunderstandings. Ambassadors should not participate in the forums unless they can do so legally. But they can watch for signs of rumors and problems. They can act quickly, building a reputation of responsiveness for investors. An unbiased, consistent, and responsive outreach program will build friendships and create enthusiastic investors who will tell their friends how solid the company is.

As expensive paper annual reports diminish in importance, online annual reports will become important tools. Online annual reports are difficult to navigate, search, and decipher. Mondo should work with information architects and engineers to create a searchable database on its site that educates investors and responds to questions with relevant information. Timelines and charts should be data-driven so they always include the latest information. The frequently asked questions (FAQ) page should be more than just a list of questions and answers. It should be an information guide that can point people to other resources. By making a serious one-time investment in a comprehensive online report, rather than an annual publishing exercise, Mondo can save money and communicate better with investors at the same time.

Institutional and mutual fund shareholders require a more serious approach. Mondo uses presentations and conference calls to communicate with research analysts. An extranet site would allow the analysts to search for information on their own. The company should provide each analyst with a tailored set of data and preformatted documents that they feed automatically into the analysts' systems. Once this link is set up, the analyst always has complete, up-to-date financial information without ever having to ask again.

Institutional and mutual fund shareholders are important constituents. If they have concerns, the company wants to hear from them first – before they tell everyone else. The company can use the Web to hold conference calls, make presentations, and inform investors of upcoming events.

Synergy

I haven't covered all of Mondo's important customer groups. I've left out buyers, hospitals, distributors, veterinarians, students, health plans, the research community, government, and others. I've also left out Mondo's employees. Each group needs the same amount of inquiry, response, and partnership as the doctor, patient, pharmacist, the media, and shareholder groups I've begun to cover here.

Mondo must become proactive rather than reactive online. The effort must begin with the company. If the company waits until everyone else does these things and then copies the competition, all the core values, all the built-to-last management philosophies that made Mondo into the multinational giant it is today, will work to tear the company down to its last share of stock.

If Mondo does find a way to address all its customer groups, something amazing will happen: synergy. By listening to its customers, Mondo would learn how to create new products and provide new services before its competitors do. By creating a corporate culture that focuses on customers, Mondo can arrive at the next business proposition with those customers leading the way. If Mondo can do *all* these things – if it can adopt a corporate lifestyle that encourages employees to take a long term view of the Web rather than looking for quick fixes – the company will remain healthy and profitable for years to come.

The Truth Company

Does the Internet force a drug company like Mondo to rethink its mission statement? Yes. That's the point of this book. Mondo makes money when people come back to doctors – not when they stay away. By thinking about whole patients and the lives they lead, the company will find new business propositions that don't have inherent conflicts.

Many industries are starting to realize that they must address sustainability, and drug companies are no exception. By putting patient's long-term needs over short-term opportunities, Mondo can see how best to help doctors, pharmacists, and other customers.

Although this chapter is about a drug company, it's not really about drugs, diseases, or even patients. It's about why a big company like Mondo should care. It's about what the chairman of the board sees when she looks in the mirror in the morning. It's less about telling the truth and more about understanding why telling the truth is so important.

Companies that seek to improve the quality of their customers' lives – even if their products aren't perfect – will thrive online. Companies that try to keep customers in the dark will remain blinded by their own propaganda. Companies that cultivate those values will prosper in the twenty-first century.

OLD MISSION STATEMENT | Your trusted source of relief.

NEW MISSION STATEMENT | Your partner in health and healing.

PART 4

Predictions

I feel awake ... wide awake. I don't remember ever feelin' this awake. Everything looks different.

– Thelma, *Thelma and Louise*

Introduction

This part of the book is food for thought – future food. In Parts 1 and 2, I concentrated on what companies can do today to respond to the Customer-Led Revolution. In Part 3, I showed how companies can change in the near future to implement these principles. Now, in this final part, I present a natural extension of the Customer-Led Revolution and the technological changes that will take place by 2010. In each chapter, I will focus on the future of an e-customer – a future that should arrive by 2010, as most of the world goes online. While this part of the book seems unrelated, and it doesn't give you any answers, it provides an important map of where your customers are going.

Although our lives could all change this dramatically – there are no technological leaps of faith here – psychological and political barriers will prevent everything from happening all at once. I'm taking you into the realm of the plausible. I'm betting they'll all become relevant in your lifetime. Consider it a trail of breadcrumbs to follow as your customers race off into the future.

Some of the material here is technical. With the exception of Chapter 24, my goal is to shield you from most of the details and focus on the changes in society and our everyday lives as we accelerate toward global connectivity. The changes I describe in this section will happen quickly, beginning some time around 2003. By 2007, most of the pieces will be in place. By 2010, the world will be a completely different place.

I want you to think about your response to these changes and prepare accordingly. I'll start with a fairly simple case – a job seeker – and things will pick up from there. Set your watch for 2010 and come along to see the results of the Customer-Led Revolution.

The Job Seeker

CHAPTER 19

IN THIS CHAPTER WE EASE OUR WAY into the year 2010 by following Brad, a senior research scientist at a large biotechnology firm. Brad is ready to move on to a company where he can be more of a key player, and he's prepared to move anywhere in the country for the right opportunity.

Before we see how Brad pursues his next opportunity, let's go back to the start of his career and see how he found his first job. Two decades ago, Brad went to work for a fictional company called Big Biotech Inc. (BBI). Here's how the process worked then.

The Paper Chase

July 1990. The research manager at BBI, needs another programmer in a hurry. She's been through the process many times before and knows it may take months to fill the position. Sighing, she begins to fill out the four-page job request form.

The job request goes to the division vice president for approval and then moves on to human resources. A clerical worker in HR types the information into a database. A professional copywriter writes the ad, and a buyer places it in different labor-market publications. Two to three weeks after the initial job request, the ad appears in Brad's local paper.

Brad, who's just gotten out of graduate school, has worked with a designer friend to create a nice-looking résumé. They chose a traditional, easy-to-read type style, worked on the layout, and followed the insider's rule for résumé page counts (one page for the résumé, one additional page for each Nobel Prize). Because he's sending his résumé to so many different kinds of companies, Brad's stated objective is fairly generic.

Brad chooses nice-looking paper and envelopes and has the local print shop run out 100 copies on a high-resolution printer. He then spends the entire weekend writing cover letters, printing mailing labels, and licking envelope flaps. The next day, Brad takes the stack of envelopes to the post office and dutifully writes out a check for the postage. One of the letters is addressed to BBI, in response to job #4476, which he's written on the envelope as well as the cover letter. He drops the letters in the mailbox and goes home to wait.

Ten days later, BBI's human resource department puts some 2,000 résumés, including Brad's, into a pouch and sends them to Guam. In Guam, a data-entry company scans the résumés and then edits them, translating the information to the proper format for BBI's database. Per BBI's instructions, all multipage résumés that don't list Nobel Prizes go into the trash. BBI has provided the data-entry company with a standardized form containing a number of fields: last name, first name, address, area of expertise (chosen from a predefined list), job title history, skills, and so on.

Because the information must be in a standard format so that applicants can be matched to job requisitions, many of the résumés require extensive editing. The data-entry company has more than 200 clients in the United States, and each client has its own set of standards. The clients' keywords are similar but not identical, so the company has to be careful not to mix them up.

When all the résumés have been edited and entered in BBI's format, the company in Guam makes a computer tape of the résumé information, sends it by courier to BBI's HR department, and then archives the paper résumés in case the biotech company calls with any questions.

At BBI, the HR staff mounts the tapes and puts the records into the database. Six weeks after getting the research director's job request, the HR department matches job seekers to the job and sends any candidates to the department administrator by intra-office mail.

When the administrator calls the applicants to verify they're still in the job market, he discovers that a tenth of the phone numbers were transcribed incorrectly by the data-entry company (the administrator is supposed to fax those back to Guam for correction, but that rarely happens). A full 50 percent of the applicants have already taken jobs elsewhere. The administrator screens the remaining candidates and hands the résumés of those who make the cut to the hiring manager. It's then a matter of scheduling interviews, identifying the most suitable candidate, and following up with an offer. Because all large companies are this slow at hiring employees, Brad is still in the market for a job. At least six weeks have passed by the time Brad meets with the research manager, who eventually gives him his first job.

The Electron Chase

April 2000. After ten years at BBI, Brad is ready for a new challenge. He knows the Web has changed the way people apply for jobs, and he is excited to use the power of the Internet to find his dream job as a research manager.

In 2000, the human resources field is much more technologically sophisticated. There's no need for the résumé designer or the data-entry company in Guam. Company copywriters still write copy, but now the ads appear on the company's web site as well as in the Help Wanted section of the newspaper. To apply for a particular job, Brad fills out an online form. Employers still have to deal with a few paper résumés every week, but 90 percent of the job applications now come in through the Web.

In an electronic version of the company mail room, traffic handlers tag the e-résumé with keywords that help match each résumé to possible jobs within the company. In companies with more advanced computer systems, résumés are routed via e-mail; others must print out the résumés and send them by intra-office mail. Using the power of the World Wide Web, the company has cut the time to interview a new prospect from six weeks to three.

Brad finds himself going from one company web site to the next, checking the job postings and filling out application forms. Every company has a different form. Brad fills out forms for the top ten companies he's interested in. Now he's ready to submit his résumé to the online career centers.

In the year 2000, online career centers are booming. Hundreds of career sites are on the Web, and each promises to expose a job seeker like Brad to thousands of employers (including, possibly, his current one). He can respond to a specific job posting or submit his résumé to the career center's database, which employers periodically mine for prospects.

During Brad's job search, his résumé is duplicated more than 400 times by the online career centers he signed on with. Several biotech companies interview him, and he's eventually offered a management position at Huge Biotech, Inc., that pays quite a bit more than he makes at BBI. He accepts the job but soon discovers that the online centers that spread his résumé so effectively have a drawback he didn't foresee: He's still getting calls from companies who think he's still in the job market. He sends e-mail messages to all the centers asking that his résumé be removed, but the calls keep coming.

The Universal Résumé

September 2010. Brad is now a senior scientist at HBI, determined to be the research director at a biotech company. This time his job search is a dramatically different experience.

The key to Brad's newfound control over the job search process is a software standard called the Universal Résumé. It sits on a server, available for free to anyone who wants to use it. The Universal Résumé consists of a series of modules for identity, education, experience, awards, goals, and other relevant personal data. It's actually more like a big software program than a document. No one needs more than five percent of the available fields, as many modules are used only by specific job seekers in specific countries.

Brad can narrow his search to specific kinds of jobs or employers. He can easily tailor his résumé to a start-up or to a larger company by filling out the appropriate modules. With the help of an online wizard, Brad takes only a few minutes to complete his own Universal Résumé.

Brad could drop off his Universal Résumé at different career centers or send it electronically to companies himself, but in 2010, most of the

AN ONLINE STANDARD FOR RESUMES

In 1999, a committee of technical people and human resource managers volunteered to work with a company called Structured Methods (Structuredmethods.com) to develop a standard markup language for online résumés. They defined the Human Resource Management Markup Language (HRMML), which I expand in this chapter to the concept of Universal Résumé. As we'll see in the following chapters, descriptors like the Universal Résumé are based on the Extensible Markup Language, XML.

career centers are gone. Instead, Brad simply puts his Universal Résumé on his personal web site and waits for companies to come to him.

Now that Brad has decided to leave HBI, he checks Number 4 in the job availability box and goes to bed. By the next morning, dozens of companies' software agents scanning the Web have already noticed his résumé.

In 2010, the VP of research at Giant Biotech, Inc., simply answers a few questions at a search engine, and all the résumés of available people who meet her criteria show up on her screen. She can have Brad on the phone a minute after she decides she needs a new research director. And she can program her Internet software agents to alert her when highly desirable people change their status to "willing to be taken to lunch."

Brad gets a call the next day. No posting of job descriptions. No HR department. No employment databases to manage. The Web has become the database, kept up-to-date by the applicants themselves. Companies don't wait for applicants to knock on their doors. And when the research VP looks at Brad's Universal Résumé, she knows she's looking at the current version and that the information is accurate – no more wrong numbers or out-of-the-market applicants.

If Brad accepts a job offer with Giant Biotech, he'll change his availability field back to zero. Immediately, bots and programs can tell he's off the job market. If Brad is on a short list for a job at another company, a bot will remove him from that list within an hour. The average time it takes to hire a new person is now eight working days. But Brad isn't through using the Web to win his dream job yet.

JOB AVAILABILITY

One of the fields in The Universal Résumé reflects the intensity of Brad's job search. Volunteers in the HRMML community have now agreed on seven levels of availability:

0 Not available, and not looking.

1 Not looking, but would like to keep tabs on the job market.

2 Willing to be taken to lunch.

3 Willing to take a recruiter's call.

4 Available to interview immediately.

5 Will consider contract work.

6 Looking for temporary work, contract work, or any available position.

The Universal Interview

In 2010, a new kind of career center – I'll call it Universal Recruiting – provides job seekers like Brad the opportunity to add a digital video introduction to their Universal Résumés. The Universal Recruiting office in Brad's city coaches him and then records a series of live segments: a short introduction that summarizes Brad's goals, a longer introduction that summarizes his schooling and work history, and a segment of his responses to a series of general interview questions. Brad adds his own questions to the interview as well. In the online interview, he is candid in discussing his professional needs and wants, his past successes, and his past weaknesses and how he's addressed them. He also attaches the profile results of his Myers-Briggs personality test. All these become part of his Universal Résumé.

The staff at Universal Recruiting works for Brad. He's willing to pay for their help because he knows that by providing a video interview for employers, he'll be considered for more jobs and more competitive salary packages. The people at Universal Recruiting know that, too, and may allow Brad to defer some of his payment until he gets his new job.

Companies now publish Universal Job Requests on their web sites, so Brad can ask his electronic agent to search for specific jobs online. When he clicks on a job description, he also finds a list of interview questions. He can type in his answers and submit them, along with a pointer to his Universal Résumé, or he can answer the questions on digital video and put it on his personal web site with the other interview videos. The ready access and the quantity and quality of the information Brad has provided make it easy for a hiring manager to determine whether he's worth considering seriously.

Two can play these video games. Companies want to attract not only the best people but also those who would mesh best with the company. If a hiring manager has put a digital video about her business unit and her staff on the company's web site, prospective employees can evaluate the company and the manager they'd be working for to see if they would be a good fit.

Adding video to the hiring process also provides companies with access to people who would be hard to bring in for a personal interview. And the employers and job candidates can make their respective videos at their own convenience and use them again and again. The Universal

Interview not only saves the employer and the job seeker time and money, it gives them both more choices – a win for everyone.

Brad's Universal Résumé has two levels of privacy, and he could set up more if he saw the need. The top level is public – doesn't reveal Brad's name or personal information. If a company expresses interest in the work experience and knowledge outlined in the top level, Brad can screen the company and, if he's interested, provide access to the second level. Codes can be designated for specific visitors and uses, and Brad can cancel them anytime he chooses. Eventually, Brad will trust the Universal Recruiting bots to give permission to employers that meet his criteria.

Universal Change

Brad's Universal Résumé is ready to go. Managers can search for appropriate job candidates, narrow their search lists, request further information from Brad, watch and exchange video interviews online, even e-mail Brad's references – all within 24 hours. With the help of some inexpensive software agents, the Universal Résumé and Universal Recruiting have reduced the time and cost of filling a job opening to around three working days and under $400.

Brad's Universal Résumé is a living document. It resides on his personal web site and is easy to update according to his availability. He can remake his video interviews and his references as often as he likes, but once every five years should be fine. Brad is happy to invest in his Universal Résumé because he knows how well it represents him on the Web. It gives him the responsibility – and the power – to market himself.

The Homemaker

CHAPTER 20

IN THE LAST CHAPTER, I MENTIONED that Brad keeps his résumé on his personal web site. In 2010, everyone has a personal web site. A personal site is no longer a luxury but a necessity – a right, not a privilege. In this chapter and the three that follow, we'll see how integral the Internet is in an average family's life. We'll follow Mike, an aerospace consultant, and his wife, Laura, who works full-time. Mike works part-time from his Seattle home and takes care of the couple's two children: Chloe, age seven, and Spencer, age 17.

The Personal Web Site

Like most people's personal web sites, Mike's site is full of documents stored at different levels of privacy (and security). Some of the documents are very simple, like Mike's Universal ID, which contains his name, street address, birth date, and whom to contact in an emergency. Mike's Universal ID is actually a module in his online résumé. It's also part of his Universal Driver's License, his Universal Passport, his Universal Birth Certificate, and other documents he stores on his site. All these documents are part of the Universal Personal Site, a standard way of storing personal information.

Mike's Universal Personal Site holds every document he owns. It's a complete filing and tracking system that helps him manage everything in his life. The Universal Personal Site has seven major sections, each of which has six levels of password protection. In his personal section, for example, Mike has emergency contact information, descriptions of his various hobbies and interests, contact lists, photographs, his schedule, his copy of Laura's and his marriage license, an inventory of everything he owns, and much more. His professional section has his résumé, his client list, references, a list of awards and achievements, contracts, notes, spreadsheets, and a marketing web site that tells clients about his services.

Mike's Universal Personal Site contains thousands of documents. It is infinitely expandable and extremely secure. And it's connected to thousands of other people's Universal Personal Sites as well.

	PERSONAL	PROFESSIONAL	FINANCIAL	MEDICAL	GOVERNMENT	HAVES	WANTS
Public	Identities					Used car for sale	Mercedes 500 SL
Emergency	Name Contact info Buddies	Lawyer Buddies	Accountant	Doctors Insurance Conditions Blood Type Allergies Buddies	Police Lawyer		
Acquaintance/ Colleagues	Marital status Schedule	Employment status/position Business card Résumé References		Allergy researcher	Birth certificate Driver's license Passport	Timeshare for lakeside condo Piano lessons on weekends	Carpool for work Sponsors for fundraiser
Friends/ Family	Education records	Partnerships	Credit Information Financial records	Medical conditions Genetic/DNA Information Prescriptions	Social Security records	Heirlooms Extra travel tickets	Babysitter Space for private party
Spouse	Personal will		Bank account Tax records Investments				
Self	Journal		Money management		Legal record	Gifts	

The Universal Personal Site has seven major categories and six levels of security. A document stored on the site may have elements on any of the levels.

Mike's personal section contains a set of online directories listing his friends, relatives, colleagues, and members of the various organizations and recreational groups he belongs to. Each name is actually a link to that person's Universal ID. Similarly, Mike's Universal ID is linked to his name in their directories. If Mike moves to a new house or changes his phone number, all he has to do is change the information on his

Universal ID. His new address and phone number update instantly. All of Mike's work, insurance, medical, and other documents also update immediately.

Mike's personal section also contains everything he once carried in his wallet: his driver's license, cash, insurance cards, credit cards, phone cards, membership cards, and so on. All his keys – from his house key to his locker key at the gym – are also on his site. To ride the metro, use a public phone, buy groceries, rent a car, pay a bridge toll, buy a ticket to a concert, or pay for dinner – in any country in the world – Mike simply enters his Universal ID and then his password on a keypad. The clearing-house authorizes the transfer of money to the recipient.

Mike's password system gives him control over others' access to his site. If he wants to share something on his site, he simply gives the person a special password that gives her the access he wants her to have.

Keypads connected to the Internet are everywhere, even at home. To get into his house, Mike walks up to the door and enters his Universal ID and his password, and the door opens.

How did this happen? In 2003, a group of volunteers under the auspices of the World Wide Web Consortium (w3c) proposed a universal identifier system to facilitate electronic transactions of all kinds. In 2005, most major governments adopted the system, which has four essential elements:

The Universal ID. Today, everyone has a unique identifier – similar to a passport number. A person's bank and credit accounts, identities, history, criminal record, and reputation all link back to that unique number.

A unique web address. Each citizen is entitled to enough secure server space on the Internet to create a personal web site. Everyone gets a web address with her ID number. The unique web address then links to an individual's personal web site, so now her Universal ID is associated with her Universal Personal Site.

A set of passwords allows each person to control everything on her personal web site, even from a computer at the local library. Sophisticated password management software makes it easy.

A clearinghouse makes sure that all electronic transactions are legitimate. To use the system – for example, to buy something online – a customer simply enters her Universal ID and types in her password. The clearinghouse ensures that the recipient never sees her password – only the money.

With these four elements, digital cash becomes a reality. Anyone can send money to anyone else, purchase from a web site or a vending machine, ride a bus or a train, rent a car, pay a taxi driver, pay for parking or a telephone call, pay taxes, tolls, and fines, pay bills, invest in stocks, sign electronic contracts, and conduct transactions in almost any country – securely.

As with the Social Security numbers of the twentieth century, citizens of most countries now receive a Universal ID and a web address on the day they are born and keep that number for life. By moving from checks, cash, tokens, and debit/credit cards to electronic money and passwords, governments around the world have cut their expenses by 20 percent. International security is much more efficient and effective. As we'll see, people can also manage identities that help them keep their information as private as they like.

The Packet

Like most people, Mike is time-constrained and would rather not have to enter his ID number and a password just to open the door to his car or house. He prefers something much more convenient: a packet.

In 2010, packets are sold in department stores, convenience stores, and even from vending machines. A packet is a programmable, digitally encoded record of a person's Universal ID, which simply provides the address of the public level of his personal site.

The actual packet is about the size of a grain of rice. It can be incorporated into jewelry, sewn into clothing, or even pressed into vitamin pills. Mike and his son, Spencer, have their ID numbers encoded in their watches (most watch manufacturers offer this feature). His wife has dozens of them – mostly in her bracelets and earrings. Their daughter, Chloe, wears hers on a necklace. A surprising number of people prefer to either swallow a packet daily or have a packet implanted under their skin.

Using a packet is more convenient than entering numbers on a keypad. Most commercial places and vehicles are equipped with packet detectors *and* keypads. The detectors in Mike's car and house sense his packet as soon as he comes into range. If he likes, he can also add his password to his packet so that he doesn't have to enter it every time. When he walks up to his car, the door opens automatically. He gets in, starts the engine by voice command, and drives away. If he prefers, he can encode his password on a separate packet and carry both. It's his choice. He can have as many packets and configurations as he likes.

Like many people, Mike prefers the convenience of putting his ID and his password on the packet programmed into his watch. He knows, however, that if someone steals his watch, he has to get online to cancel that password very quickly. He has set up a number of overriding security passwords just for those situations.

Mike's kids both have packets, but their passwords aren't encoded on them. They each have two passwords: one for normal use, and another to signal that they are in trouble. They know their passwords by heart and don't give them to anyone, not even each other. They can make calls from a public phone or take the bus or a taxi simply by using their packets and passwords.

BIOMETRICS

In 2010, the Universal ID and password system is sufficient proof of identity for most situations. For special situations, like international airline travel and buying a handgun, companies and governments require a biometric match.

Voice recognition is an inexpensive way to control access to household appliances, cars, security systems, phones, and other conveniences. Voice recognition isn't universal. It can't identify everyone, but it can identify people who have been previously authorized.

Photographs are a convenient but not very secure method of biometric matching. A document with a photograph is relatively easy to forge. Some countries still use photo IDs, but most are now out of circulation.

Digital fingerprints are still used as identity verifiers in many government offices. The U.S. government invested heavily in them during the 1990s and early 2000s because it had a huge database of fingerprints it could digitize.

Iris scanning is now the most effective way to identify people. Each eye has a unique iris pattern. Clearinghouses with iris databases receive a scan and match it against their data set, returning a positive or negative result. Iris scans are becoming more useful as the iris databases grow.

Although Mike chooses to use his primary identity most of the time, he can make and use as many alternative identities as he likes. He can have one identity for public events, another for buying online, another for giving to charities, and another for access to his safe-deposit box. Using multiple identities is just another way Mike manages his information.

Today, Mike picks up Chloe from school. At home they get out the peanut butter and jelly to make a quick snack. Chloe is excited. It's Friday, and Mike has promised her they will look online for her first bicycle. Little do they know, their search will lead them just a few blocks away to the home of a ten-year-old girl and her mother.

SMART CARTS

How does a grocery store work in 2010? The shopping carts are all "smart." As the shopper puts an item into the cart, a detector in the cart reads the shopper's packet. A small display shows the running total. It knows the shopper's cash and credit limits.

Because she uses the same identity for shopping as she does for controlling her refrigerator, the cart can tell her what is in her refrigerator and reminds her that she is low on certain items. As she leaves the store, there are no check-out lanes. She smiles at the guard and leaves. As she walks out the door, her account is charged and the items belong to her.

Selling

Last weekend, Molly and her daughter, Erin, were cleaning out their garage. They found a lot of things they didn't need anymore: golf clubs, a small trampoline, a bike that's now too small for Erin, and an old computer. Because Erin is eager to buy a new pair of hockey skates, Molly said she would put those old items up for sale. But she doesn't plan to have a garage sale or take everything to a flea market. And she won't be using an online auction site or classified ads. Those are all gone. Instead, she accesses her personal web site and makes a few small changes.

Each item Molly owns came with an online universal descriptor, which was automatically transferred to the "haves" section of her personal site. A universal descriptor is an electronic description of an item using industry-standard terms. Everything Molly owns has a descriptor: eyeglasses, toasters, chairs, jewelry, clothing, and so on. Almost all of them reside on the "family" level of the "haves" section of her personal site.

Now that Molly wants to sell Erin's old bike, she must update its universal descriptor to reflect its current condition. A program on the bicycle-industry web site asks her a series of questions. In a few minutes, she updates the bike's condition. Next, she indicates the bike's market status, on a scale of zero to six. Just by changing the market status from zero to four, Molly puts the bike up for sale on the public "haves" part of her site. It's that simple.

Molly does the same thing with each item she wants to sell. What does she do next? Nothing. She waits. She tells Erin someone will see the items for sale and send them offers. When they've sold all the items, she is sure Erin will have enough money for a new pair of skates.

MARKET STATUS

Items in the "haves" section of a personal site have one of six possible market status values:

0 Not for sale.

1 Will trade or consider offers under special circumstances.

2 Price is firm. First person who comes and pays for it takes it.

3 Price is firm. Willing to ship item.

4 Make an offer.

5 Must sell immediately.

6 Highest offer by a certain date takes it.

Buying

Chloe wolfs down her snack and is soon ready to look for her new bike. Mike believes in children managing their own money, so Chloe plays a very active part in the process. She has set aside some money for a bike, but she doesn't know how much bikes really cost. Mike takes this opportunity to explain to Chloe how it all works so that she can make the best decision. He explains that the method of searching depends on how soon she needs to have the item, her willingness to consider substitutes, and her flexibility on price. He shows her three scenarios, based on when she needs to have her bike.

Must have now. If Chloe really wants to be riding her new bike with her friends tomorrow afternoon, she will need to find a bike somewhere near Seattle. Mike surfs over to a search engine and lets Chloe fill out a search form, which uses the universal request descriptor for a child's bike. Mike explains that request descriptors don't describe a single item.

They describe a *range* of items that might satisfy her needs. Chloe can indicate what kind of bikes might suit her, what price range, and what condition is acceptable. Once Chloe answers those questions, the search engine finds almost all bikes in the world that meet her criteria but shows her only those within a one-hour drive of their home.

At the top of the list is Erin's old bike, which is sitting in Molly's garage just a few blocks away. Chloe is excited, but Mike points out that the bike has been through a few accidents. The paint is scratched pretty badly, and the frame is already starting to rust.

Second on the list is a brand new bike that is quite a bit more expensive than Erin's. It's at a local bike shop. Today, retail inventory-control systems use universal descriptors to describe every item stores have in stock. These systems now tie directly into the stores' web pages, keeping the online inventory up-to-date. Mike tells Chloe that if they go to the store first thing in the morning, the bike will be waiting for her.

Willing to wait a few days. Chloe is eager to get her bike right away, but the new bike at the store is more than she wants to spend. Mike explains that if she's patient, they can probably get a better deal. If Chloe is willing to wait, she can expand her search to include the entire country. She might find a store or an online catalog willing to give her a good deal on a great bike and ship it to her. Or she might find someone in Oregon with a bike in better shape than Erin's for the same price.

Search engines are able to update prices and availability of products they know about, but they don't find new items that come on the market immediately. If a new bike store opens or someone changes the market status of her bike to a number higher than zero, it may take a day or so before the search engines notice.

Since Chloe is willing to wait a few days, she doesn't have to use a search engine to find her bike. She can take that same request descriptor and simply leave it on the "wants" section of her site. Then she can send her electronic agents – her bots – online in search of a bike. It can take a bot a few days to traverse the entire Web, but Mike uses bots that go to the top 20 search engines first. Then they prowl the Web looking for bike sites and other places likely to turn up deals. They work for Chloe while she sleeps, so that when she wakes up in the morning she has a comprehensive list ranked according to her criteria.

Willing to wait a few weeks or more. If Chloe is willing to wait even longer, she and her father can maximize the quality of bike she gets and minimize the price. They could surf the old-fashioned auction sites, but there aren't many left. The only auction site where Chloe might find a bike would be one that auctions distressed merchandise. Using her "wants" page, however, Chloe can participate in a reverse auction.

A reverse auction lets a seller offer an unlimited number of items for bid by a certain date. As more people bid, the price goes *down*. At the end of the auction, all buyers pay the lowest price the manufacturer is willing to give for volume discounts, and the manufacturer then builds and ships the products on demand. Chloe can get in on a buying group by visiting reverse-auction sites, or she can indicate on her universal request descriptor that she's interested in participating in a buying program. Then the offers will come to her.

Chloe's bots will keep looking for a bike that matches her criteria until she tells them to stop. When she sees an acceptable offer, she accepts it, and the deal is done. If she's willing to wait to join a buying group, Chloe is likely to get the lowest price on a new bike.

Chloe decides she'd rather save her money than buy a new bike. She decides Erin's bike will be just fine, even if it's scratched. She sends e-mail to Molly asking if she can see the bike the next morning.

The "wants" and "haves" sections of people's personal sites now account for half of all items bought and sold online. Chloe and Mike's search for a bike took a few minutes because thousands of people volunteered to create universal descriptors for everything from air purifiers and airplanes to zoom lenses and zithers. As we'll see in the next chapter, Mike and his wife, Laura, are about to use universal descriptors in a very big way.

COMMODITIES

Reverse auctions for commodities are commonplace in 2010. If Mike wants to bake a loaf of bread in his oven, his oven makes a request for 90 minutes of electricity. In general, utilities now operate on a pure supply-and-demand basis – Mike pays more for electricity during the afternoons when electricity demand is highest.

For most people, automatic reverse auctions happen several times a day. Mike's car uses the Internet to conduct a reverse auction whenever the tank is low on gas. It simply transmits its requirements to the supply network and then directs Mike to the gas station in the area offering the best price.

The Breadwinner

MIKE'S WIFE, LAURA, IS A SENIOR PARTNER at one of Seattle's largest environmental design firms. Mike has his hands full taking care of the couple's children and running his consulting business, so Laura handles the family's finances and investments. When Mike and Laura decided to buy a vacation home in the Southwest, Laura took on the responsibility of finding the right property and arranging the financing. In this chapter, we follow her as she goes shopping for her family's dream vacation home. But first, we have to learn a bit about Laura's everyday tools.

The Balance Sheet

In 2010, every personal possession and asset on an individual's web site has an up-to-date universal descriptor. Laura's and Mike's assets include their Seattle home, two cars (one electric), a sailboat, and a number of investments. Everything they own has an equity component and a liability component, both of which are updated continuously on the financial pages at the deepest (and most secure) levels of each of their personal sites.

Because almost all money is electronic, they don't actually keep their money anywhere. Their personal web sites have all their records securely backed up, including digital signatures on all the contracts. In a sense they are their own bank. Laura's bots help her manage the positive balance in their account by prowling the market for overnight loans and other investment opportunities.

Laura and Mike's balance sheet is always up-to-date. Every item they own has a current-value field in its universal descriptor. There are various ways of determining current value, based on several factors, and the

CHAPTER 21 THE BREADWINNER 249

valuation method is always included. As long as the information Laura and Mike provide is correct and verifiable, their balance sheet is valid.

Laura and Mike don't put their financial information at the public level of their personal web sites or tell marketers how much they have. Their bots do all the work anonymously, looking for good investment opportunities and reporting on what they find. Only if Laura decides to make an investment does she reveal her identity.

The Income Statement

The entire U.S. economy now operates on a cash basis. All transactions happen instantaneously via online clearinghouses that validate the electronic transfer of money. For complicated transactions, buyers and sellers use automated escrow services. And for those who wish to manage their own money, a large consumer-to-consumer loan market makes banks and government agencies unnecessary. This so-called consumer bond market works quite effectively, as people's financial reputations are easy to verify through clearinghouses. People with better credit ratings are able to borrow more at lower interest rates. Companies now pay interest on every day their credit is extended. Miraculously, all the companies that previously claimed they couldn't possibly pay any sooner than 45 days now manage to pay on the day the goods change hands.

Because all financial transactions happen in real time, Laura's and Mike's taxes are always filed. Though people still make quarterly assessments and make their tax decisions on an annual basis, the April 15 income tax deadline and all its work-arounds are largely a thing of the past.

Because their income statements and balance sheets are always current, Laura and Mike have a standing Universal Credit Application ready to go on their respective web sites. They can send their bots out to shop for a new loan, replace existing loans, or consolidate them. They may choose a set of institutions and ask for bids or send their bots to gather information anonymously, create a report, and make a decision.

Money lending is a completely customer-led industry. Just as institutions receive better rates for borrowing large amounts, customers can form online groups and get the same leverage. Because people often make loans to each other, banks now manage 40 percent less in assets than they did three years ago. The government has stopped tracking the consumer savings rate because the difference between saving and investing no longer exists.

Laura's bots have searched the Web and brought back a number of loan options to consider. Now that she can get a loan simply by approving one of her many online choices, Laura is ready to look for her family's vacation home.

For Sale by Owner

Mike and Laura have vacationed in New Mexico and Arizona many times, so they know the area fairly well. They would like to find a place near Taos, Santa Fe, Sedona, or Flagstaff. Laura could use a traditional real estate agent, but there aren't many left. Instead, she asks local people and search bots to help her filter the properties on the market.

In 2000, Americans paid real estate agents $42 billion to help them sell some 6 million homes annually. Today, buying a house is much less complicated. Rather than using real estate agents, people deal directly with each other online. The previously standard commission is negotiable and influenced by market forces, not controlled by industry lobbying groups.

What broke the stranglehold real estate agents had on the market? A group of homeowners got together and defined the universal descriptors for houses, apartments, condominiums, lofts, and other dwellings. Now, the Web's search engines and people's personal sites are the best sources of houses for sale. Every house has its own online universal descriptor. To put a house on the market, the owner simply checks the box labeled "for sale" in the Universal House Descriptor and waits for the offers to come in.

A homeowner actively looking to sell usually vacates the house and has it repaired and cleaned. The seller then hires an independent contractor to write a condition report and take photos of the property. Most homeowners also provide computer-generated plans and the web addresses of all required disclosure documents.

Sellers can complement the photos with online computer models that allow potential buyers to visualize the home under different lighting and with various furnishings – all computer-generated. Buyers can even place some of their own furniture and artwork into the scenarios to see how they would fit. In most cases, computer models are transferred with the Universal Title Deed to the property.

Most sellers invite comments from neighbors and post e-mail addresses of neighbors willing to answer questions. Various agencies rate neighborhoods and even specific addresses for safety, air quality, child friendliness, access to public transportation and amenities, and other factors important to home buyers. Detailed online photographic maps give online visitors the ability to tour a neighborhood.

As for property values, several companies scan the market every 24 hours and offer instant appraisals. Some charge a fee, others are sponsored by lending institutions. Many people subscribe to an inexpensive real-time appraisal service that automatically updates their property value every time a home in their area is sold or when they change a field in their home's universal descriptor.

With all this information online, Laura can conduct her search for a vacation home in the Southwest during her lunch break. She simply answers some standard questions and selects the search command. Laura asks to see all listings in and around Taos, Santa Fe, Sedona, and Flagstaff that are four-bedroom, single-story homes under 15 years old; need only minor repairs; have good views, a pool, and large backyard; and are within six blocks of a city park. Seconds later, she sees a list sorted according to price, location, or any other factor she chooses.

Laura has found four promising homes for sale in Santa Fe. She remembers that Spencer, her son, wants to see the properties she's considering. He's apprehensive about being stuck in a boring town every summer. Laura quickly sends him the web addresses of the four houses and heads off for a meeting.

Three days later, Laura and Mike decide on a Spanish-style house that has Spencer's blessing. They used the online computer model and looked at the posted photographs, so they feel they have a pretty good idea of what each room looks like and the view and light from the windows. The structural engineer Laura hired online found a problem with the foundation, but he took good photos of the condition and got three competitive repair estimates from local contractors within 24 hours.

Through a message board, Laura was able to contact four couples who had toured the house recently. She asked them a number of questions and liked what she heard. They all appreciated the home's design but thought it would end up being sold for more than they could afford. When Laura contacted people in the neighborhood, she learned an environmental designer she'd met at a conference lives nearby. She called him, and he said the neighborhood would be perfect for her family.

Even though Laura and her family haven't set foot in the Santa Fe house, she feels confident enough about the choice to bid for it at the auction tomorrow morning.

The Teenager

CHAPTER 22

MIKE AND LAURA'S 17-YEAR-OLD SON, Spencer, is a well-rounded young man, not nearly as into computers as his father is. He loves being outdoors, and he loves taking photographs. As we're about to see, being a teenager in 2010 is quite different from growing up in his parents' day.

Spencer's Watch

Spencer never needs to set or adjust his watch. With a network of more than 200 low-earth-orbit satellites circling the globe, one is always overhead, providing a continuous high-bandwidth connection to the Internet. With that satellite connection, Spencer's watch adjusts automatically to the correct time and to any change in time zone. Each transaction is so small it costs practically nothing. Spencer's watch also serves as his phone, his global positioning device, and his packet (he never carries a wallet or cash).

Spencer's watch is also a communication appliance (CA) with full access to the Internet. The only real differences among CAs are battery power, weight, and display size. You can buy CAs in department stores, magazine shops (not many of those left), and even from vending machines. They have replaced pay phones. Some companies even mass-mail them as promotional items (ads take up part of the screen). They all have the same computing power and communication speed, and they are all programmed to hold a packet, or a number of packets for all an individual's identities.

In 2010, communication appliances and computers do the same thing: They both give Spencer access to the Internet, his personal web site, the Web, and thousands of powerful computers running online software. He has a single account that lets him buy online time, computing time, storage, and security. In 2010, one communication appliance is about as good as any other. They are as common as televisions. In most cases, they *are* televisions. They all respond well to voice commands once the user has logged on. Communications appliances for public use are readily accessible. They're built into the backs of airline seats, for example, and into kiosks in train stations, airports, and hotel lobbies. Most hotel rooms are equipped with CAs, as are most government buildings. All public phones are communication appliances.

Spencer usually wears his watch every day, but in his rush to catch the ferry to Orcas Island this morning with his friends, he forgot it. Luckily, he didn't forget his new digital camera.

Spencer's Camera

Spencer's camera is a professional model. It features high-resolution video, 3-D image capture, text recognition (it can read a document out loud in 74 languages), stereo sound, remote control, and recognition of a dozen photo-programming languages.

Actually, in 2010, even the cheapest cameras have those features. What separates a professional camera like Spencer's from a less expensive one is his fancy retractable zoom lens. These days, there's enough capacity on a single memory card for a camera to store 800 high-resolution photos. But that would be silly. Memory cards are just a digital replication of film, and who needs film?

Cameras don't have film anymore. They have antennas. They also ring occasionally. And now, as Spencer and his buddies sit on a bluff overlooking Rosario Strait and watch for killer whales, Spencer's camera rings. His mother has just sent him the web addresses of the four homes in Santa Fe she wants him to see. Because Spencer's camera is really just a communication appliance that happens to have a retractable zoom lens, he and his friends can view those homes as they eat their sandwiches (yes, people still eat sandwiches). They all look at the four houses. Then Spencer sends his mom a voice message saying which one they prefer.

Spencer's camera has a high-resolution color screen and a stabilizer built in, but otherwise it functions as his phone, a voice-controlled computer, personal assistant, and even as a flashlight. It takes a few seconds to transfer a complete high-resolution photo to his server and an instant to send a low-resolution image. Whether Spencer's in Angkor Wat with his family or canoeing with his buddies, his camera is always in touch with his personal web site.

Spencer stores all his photos – all 56,000 of them – on his web site. Each one is in the Universal Photo format. A Universal Photo records an image and everything about it: the camera settings, the light readings, the global positioning data (where the camera was on Earth, to within ten centimeters), date and time (down to the second), the photographer, personal notes, and searchable keywords.

Through his camera, Spencer can view every photo he's ever taken. Because he's online, he can view every photo almost *anyone* has ever taken. He organizes his favorites in albums – his own indexes to all the photos on the Web and on his site. It's Spencer's way of saving his search terms and settings. Spencer's personal web site also has several galleries where visitors to his site can see examples of his work.

Spencer's camera is also a video camera with its own web address. Spencer can give anyone a password that lets the person see what Spencer's camera sees. Until he was 14, his mother insisted that he set his camera so she could see whatever his camera saw. She used to check in on him occasionally, to see that he was okay.

Then one day, Spencer – tired of being checked on – threw his camera into Elliott Bay and watched the ensuing rescue scene from a safe distance. Since then, he's had to buy his own cameras, but his mother doesn't say anything about what he does with them.

Cameras are so cheap, many people install them permanently and leave them online. All good surfing beaches and ski resorts have on-site cams so that surfers and skiers can check the conditions even from their cars as they drive to the beach or the slopes. Rock climbers tune into the cameras on their favorite routes to watch the action. Anglers install cams near trout streams, either to see whether the fish are biting or just to watch on a corner of their computer screen as they work at their desks.

Combine a six-pack of cameras with motion-detection software available online, and they become burglar alarms. Put them in your vacation home, and keep an eye on the place while you're not there. Put one near a robin's nest, and watch the eggs hatch. Family resorts have them all over the place, while resorts for singles have none. Most schools have them installed permanently in classrooms, for the safety of their teachers. If you want to see how your child is doing at kindergarten or ballet class, you just turn on your CA and scan the various cameras on-site.

Kids know where the cameras are and where they aren't. They use them more effectively on their parents than their parents do on them.

DEMOCRACY

Spencer and his father, Mike, are members of a nonprofit human rights organization that raises funds to buy more than 300 satellite-linked digital cameras each month for pro-democracy groups in countries with repressive regimes. With satellite-linked digital cameras, people in democracy movements around the world can send video signals straight to an Internet server, where volunteers archive and distribute them to the media and organizations like Amnesty International. There is no film or videotape for the local government to confiscate, no immediate record of what the camera or its owner has done.

Worldwide, people like Mike and Spencer have helped prevent 400,000 politically motivated murders since 2006. More important, the digital cams have been instrumental in the overthrow of at least 18 governments that used fear and repression to control their citizens. With the help of digital cameras, a government abusing its citizens' basic civil rights has a much harder time hiding that abuse. Observers both inside and outside the country are no longer dependent on local news sources. Informed citizens are the foundation of democracy. Thousands of digital cameras are often more powerful than thousands of guns.

Audio on Demand

Spencer and his friends listen to music constantly. A set of headphones turns any communication appliance into a portable music studio. Digital recordings are all stored on servers using the Universal Song Descriptor. If Spencer wants to listen to the latest Roksana album (you wouldn't know them, but you might like them) or a digitization of an early Fred Astaire record, he simply finds it online and plays it through his CA. No one has tapes, CDs, or even music memory cards. The fanciest stereo you can get is just a CA with a set of really great speakers. Music is no longer a product – it's a service.

No one wants a CD that holds 100 albums or 1,000 albums. With every song ever recorded online, why carry music? Spencer pays for each second of each song he listens to – according to a sliding royalty scale that charges less as a song ages. And he doesn't pay much. Listening to the same amount of music in 2010 would cost one-third as much as that same music did in 2000. Most people these days consider that a convenience.

As with photos, Spencer constructs his own play lists. He can program an agent to be his private disk jockey, and the agent will search for his specific requests or genres of music and play them for him all day. Some DJ agents stir ads into the mix, reducing the royalties. Other agents bring in news, sports, and music – all charged by the second. Spencer can choose exactly what he wants to listen to and exactly how many ads he's willing to put up with. If he wants his audio to be free, he has to put up with a lot of ads and answer questions about his purchasing habits. Some of the agents are similar to the personality-driven radio stations teens listened to in the not-too-distant past, but most people prefer to separate their music from their talk.

Video on Demand

Spencer tells his friends he must catch the five o'clock ferry back to Seattle because he has a movie date with his girlfriend, Kara. Spencer contacts Kara through his camera and tells her he can't guarantee he'll be back in time to catch a theater showing. They decide to skip the theater and watch a video at Spencer's house instead. That's cool with him. But Spencer has no plans to drop by a video store on his way home.

In 2000, there was a video-rental store on every neighborhood corner. People picked up a movie on videotape, watched it, dutifully rewound it, and returned it the next day – all for a small fee. Spencer remembers going to the video store with his parents when he was little, but he finds it hard to believe that grownups went to all that trouble to see a movie at home.

And no wonder. Spencer has become accustomed to asynchronous television and motion picture programming. Spencer and his friends can tune in to a game show, watch the latest news, or watch a movie. The home theater at Spencer's house consists of a communication appliance, a large screen on the wall, a sophisticated set of digital speakers, and a comfortable couch. Spencer can start and stop the show any time he likes. As with music, Spencer can choose to see movies with targeted ads, pay full price to watch them ad-free, or any combination. The ten price categories range from second-run movies and new independent releases all the way to the vast digital bone pile – the realm of cultural archeologists and film students.

Films are priced to search (by the minute) and to view (prepay for the entire movie). Thanks to the Universal Movie Descriptor and the efforts of thousands of volunteer film fans, most movies are now searchable by title, director, scene, character, actor, dialogue, location, prop, special effect, sound, and body part.

When Kara arrives at Spencer's house that evening, she says hello to Laura (working on her house-auction strategy) and Mike (putting training wheels on Chloe's new bicycle). She's changed her mind about going to a theater to see a movie. On her way over, she noticed that the latest *Nanogirl* adventure movie is opening tonight. Would Spencer like to go?

Even though thousands of movies are available online, *Nanogirl III* isn't. Just as ten years ago, Laura and Mike were willing to pay eight dollars apiece to watch the latest James Cameron film in a movie theater, Spencer and Kara are willing to shell out ten dollars each to see *Nanogirl III* in the same venue. In the next chapter, we'll find out why.

The Moviegoer

CHAPTER 23

BEFORE THEY GO TO THE LATE SHOWING OF THE MOVIE, Spencer and Kara decide to have dinner at a nice restaurant. Spencer turns on his camera and asks his electronic agent to see if any of their favorite restaurants have a table for two. As luck would have it, another couple has just canceled their 7:00 P.M. reservation at Miko's – a small neighborhood restaurant with a fantastic fish selection.

In 2010, every good restaurant has a web site that lets people fill out their own Universal Reservation and features a real-time queue of waiting parties. When a table becomes free, the server comes to the front, announces the guest's name, and shows the party to its table. No one ever needs to call for a reservation or an estimate of when there will be an opening – people can see for themselves or ask their agents to alert them as necessary. Because all restaurants use the same reservation format, Spencer could ask his agent to find the first available table at any of the restaurants on his preferred list.

All restaurants share the same queuing software, reducing the staff necessary to run a restaurant by one or more people. Miko's keeps a record of every meal served to every customer – no names or identities, just aggregate statistics – and the software uses that database to give customers the most accurate information possible on when their tables will be ready.

The Movie

After their dinner, Kara and Spencer walk to the movie theater to see the third film in the exciting *Nanogirl* series. In 2000, there were just over 10,000 first-run movie screens in the United States. In 2010, there are still just over 10,000 screens doing about the same amount of business. Not much has changed at theaters, except that the movie "prints" they show are now digital files downloaded via the Internet.

Why are movie theaters still going strong? Is it because the projection and sound systems in theaters are technically superior to the systems at home? No. They both use the same technology. Is it because the social aspects of moviegoing are so much more fun? No. Most people would actually prefer to watch first-run films in their home theaters than to drive, park, stand in line, get a bad seat, and not be able to pause the movie if they would like to take a break. Yet in 2010 the only new releases movie fans can watch on their CAs are independent films that failed to work their way into the traditional movie distribution system. Why? Because the Old World movie distribution system is still the most profitable way to bring a new film to market.

In contrast to listening to music, watching a new movie is typically a one-time experience. Because a consumer listens to a piece of music over and over, the price of playing a single song must be extremely low to encourage repeat listening and discourage pirating. But in 2010, studios can't afford to treat first-run films like videos or music. To maximize profits, they must build momentum over the first few weeks and sell the product over several months.

Because movie stars like to be paid well, and because on-location shooting is still very expensive, the cost of making first-run films remains very high. When a movie debuts, most people are only willing to pay full price once. Spencer, Kara, and eight of their friends would pay a total of $100 to see a first-run movie at a theater. The studio would receive $50. If they could access the same movie from home, how can the studio get its $50?

Unfortunately, no practical pricing model exists for studios to deliver first-run movies on demand. If they charge too little, the studios leave too much money on the table. If they charge too much, the film won't build momentum over the critical first two weeks. For a one-time event, people are expected to gather in groups to watch – they are willing to pay the higher price of an event. Studios still maximize their profits by distributing first-run films to theaters, even when they pay exhibitors 50 percent of the ticket purchase price just for the service of counting and charging each person who sees the film.

Fortunately, the price of making independent films has come down dramatically. Even as Hollywood continues to employ armies of people and pays megabucks to megastars who can draw audiences, independent filmmakers are telling compelling stories with minuscule budgets. The total market for independent first-run films, which are at the top of the video pricing schedule, is now almost as big as the market for first-run Hollywood products. While Hollywood continues to turn out 50 to 100 high-budget films per year, independent filmmakers now produce more than 600.

A Nanogirl Auction

Kara grew up with Nanogirl as her hero. She is an avid collector of Nanogirl memorabilia. Because every piece she owns has a universal descriptor, her entire collection is online. She chooses to show it on the public level of her site, and several Nanogirl sites show her collection by setting links from their sites to hers. When she trades or sells a piece, the sites that show her collection online automatically update.

Because Kara is a Nanogirl insider, she managed to get three of the debut posters for the new film. One she is keeping for her collection, another she gave to a friend, and the third she will sell online. Because the studio only printed 2,000 posters, Kara will do best to auction her prize online.

The best way for Kara to auction the poster is to set its market status to six ("Highest offer by a certain date takes it") and name the starting price and ending date for her auction. She could promote her auction, but smart auctioneers don't. They want to make their auctions seem private and exclusive. Kara knows that the people willing to pay the most for her poster will find her, and quickly. Their bots are always on the lookout for new additions to their collections.

Kara has something of value that is in very limited supply. Unlike auctions for common items, this is a seller's market. She rebuffs the usual offers that buyers send privately to try to convince her *not* to auction the poster. She tells them they'll have to bid along with everyone else. Because she lives in a cash economy, Kara has already put her poster into escrow. When the auction closes, the money goes straight into her account.

1 Products of limited supply can be auctioned to the seller's benefit. Products like homes and collectibles are the best candidates for auctions. The rarer the item, the more advantage the seller has and the better his margins are likely to be (assuming, of course, the item is desirable to more than one person).

2 Perceived scarcity leads to impulse buying. The actual supply is rarely as important as what the buyer perceives the supply to be. In 2000, perceived scarcity made television auctions of jewelry and other "hard to find" and "collectible" items work.

3 Products of low value can be auctioned. Any money you get for a low-value item is better than nothing. That's why used items, distressed merchandise, and closeout goods sell so well online. A seller can get good volume, but the margins are often slim to nonexistent.

4 Products of infinite supply cannot be auctioned to the seller's benefit. Mass-market products – new books, new cars, and first-run movies – are always worth most when they debut. After they have been in the market for some time, however, their prices usually fall with the demand. No one will pay a higher price tomorrow than today for something that is readily available.

5 Customer demand can be auctioned. If Spencer is looking for two hours of entertainment, he can give his bots some instructions and send them off to bargain on his behalf. Customers can get together to run reverse auctions – pooling their demand and letting suppliers bid for their business. Reverse auctions are brutally efficient at bringing prices *down*; the more people bid, the lower the price. At the end, all participants pay the lowest price of any acceptable bid.

Products of infinite supply are well suited to reverse auctions only if the buyers know exactly what they are getting ahead of time. Products that have a given set of understood features (cameras, cars, items you would find in a department store) and commodities are best suited to reverse auctions. In these cases, both buyers and sellers benefit.

6 Standard online descriptors create a buyer's market. Online, perceived scarcity in a market of 1 billion people is almost impossible. With universal descriptors, bots and search engines can find all equivalent items listed on the entire Web in a matter of seconds. In 2010, only truly rare items can be sold at an advantage to the seller. The online auction sites that killed the newspaper classifieds in the early part of the decade all merged and then changed their business models when people started using their personal web sites to auction items for free.

7 Siegel's Rule of Online Pricing: No one ever asks too much for anything. People only pay too much.

Online Events

Monday, Kara is back at school. As a reporter for her school's intranet, she reports on teen happenings around the world. That means she usually has one online event to cover every school day and several on weekends.

Kara keeps her schoolmates informed of upcoming online bonfires. Bonfires are programs by kids, for kids – something like online raves. The kids prepare exciting stunts – from skydiving to robot wars to synchronized roller ballet. Kara has become really good at watching several events at once. She loves meeting kids from other countries and "partying" with them online. Then, after the bonfire, Kara posts her review on the school intranet.

The difference between online events and television is unclear at best. Most online events are commercial-free, but the most popular ones have sponsors and ads. Talk shows are extremely popular. An audience of 2 million viewers can participate by registering to ask questions and talking in groups among themselves.

Viewers rarely watch an event passively. They often watch and listen to others commenting on the event at the same time. If several cameras are covering an event, viewers can choose the one they want to watch. In the events Kara reports on, teens volunteer to play the role of online host – choosing the camera angles and presenting commentary over the event. A popular event might have a dozen hosts from which the viewers can choose. At a bonfire, it's normal to hear people making remarks about – talking on top of – the show. That's why the remote control for Kara's CA has two volume controls.

Kara's favorite TV shows are those with alternative hosts. As long as the alternative hosts add their own commentary to the product, they can sell ads and benefit from the protection of satire laws. The comedy couple Forrest and Waverley is famous for their commentaries on beauty pageants. They do so much research on the contestants – bringing in past boyfriends, girlfriends, and family members, showing photos they've gathered, and telling true stories from the girls' pasts – that their shows' ratings are much higher than the pageants themselves. This puts the pageant promoters in a dilemma: Because of Forrest and Waverly, the pagents are in demand; but – again because of the two comics – no one wants to be a contestant or judge.

One of Spencer's favorite shows is *Science in Motion*. Two former science teachers travel the world and conduct a daily outdoor science class that more than 20 million kids tune into. The cost of this kind of programming is minuscule compared to traditional TV programming.

Kara's future as a commentator looks bright as well. She seems to be going places, even though she works from her bedroom: Her experience and great reporting style have landed her a national correspondent's role for MTV.

The Frequent Flier

CHAPTER 24

IN 2010, UNIVERSAL DESCRIPTORS have changed almost every industry, taking power away from individual vendors of information technology and putting it into the hands of the people who use that technology. It's all because of a new philosophy in information technology – a philosophy behind a document description language called XML. In this chapter, we follow a frequent flier as another industry benefits from the conversion to public data standards.

Felix

Felix is the CNO of Essex Steel Products in Columbus, Ohio. He reports directly to Nicole, who was recently promoted from CNO to CEO. Felix flies often, because he likes to meet the teams his company works with and participate personally in their processes. He usually buys his own tickets online, but he doesn't use a special travel site. He uses a search engine or his own software agent.

Every seat on every airline flight has its own e-ticket, waiting to be filled in by a buyer. All the tickets for all the seats on all the flights scheduled for the next nine months are just sitting on the Web as inventory. They aren't in any special databases. Now Felix goes to a search engine to compare travel dates, times, prices, seat locations, airline reliability, and so on. Because airlines use the Universal Air Travel Ticket Descriptor – commonly known as the Universal E-Ticket – he can now compare seats and prices directly.

To buy a ticket at the best price, Felix sends his software agent to find all the seats on all flights he would be willing to take. Then he directs his agent to negotiate the best price, usually with the airlines' software agents. The process usually takes a few seconds. When he arrives at the airport and checks his luggage, he takes the packet he uses for traveling (he always travels using his primary ID) and types in his password. This confirms his seat on the plane. At the gate, a friendly customer representative welcomes him on board. There is no confusion, no counting empty seats, and no check-in lines. Universal descriptors haven't been able to keep the weather from delaying flights, but they have made the traveler's experience much less stressful than it was ten years ago.

Remember the server-based software Miko's restaurant used to hold reservations in Chapter 23? With only a few modifications, that same software is also an airline seat reservation system. Thousands of programmers worldwide are now making other contributions to society because the definition of an airline ticket – which was previously specific to each company and each system.

Behind the Schemes

To understand how such a flexible and cost-effective system works, we need to learn a bit about the technology behind the Universal E-Ticket. Let's compare the way it's done today with the way it was done back in 2000. I'll use as an example Felix's favorite airline, Airbran – which is famous for serving fresh, hot muffins on every flight.

In 2000, the Airbran IT group came up with its e-ticket concept – a set of descriptors that lived in the Airbran corporate database. This set of descriptors was a schema – a set of fields, names, and relationships that define the data in the database. When a traveler purchased a ticket, a copy of the old e-ticket form was filled out, and a unique record number identified that transaction. The Airbran database people were paid very well to run the system they designed. Because they were never required to share this information with any other company, their e-ticket schema was proprietary. Airbran considered it a competitive advantage.

In those days, each airline had its own e-ticket format. Airbran's IT group defined fields using its own terminology (like SURNAME or TICKET-NUMBER). Other airlines used their own terminology (like NAME or NUMTIC) for their corresponding fields. Some e-ticket schemas used 16 fields, others used 22, and still others used 37. Since these were internal conventions designed around different systems, no one really cared about the differences. Each airline needed a dozen programmers or more to build and maintain its system.

An e-ticket was an apple on one system and an orange on another. To trade information, airlines would have had the impossible task of devising translators from one format to another – from apples to oranges. When two airlines merged, their respective IT departments often took months or years to get in sync. Now that universal descriptors have replaced all the different schemas, it takes seconds.

The XML Revolution

In the real world, people don't use the "Universal" names I've given these documents. People use a special language, called XML, for defining universal descriptors. By itself, XML was just a formal way to make HTML – the initial language for describing documents online – more flexible and more appropriate for many different kinds of documents. But the power of XML was in its philosophy, not its syntax.

The philosophy of XML is that every document – whether it

A SHORT HISTORY OF XML

In 1979, a man named Charles Goldfarb, building on the ideas of several other early pioneers (some as far back as 1945), invented a language for writing universal descriptors for different kinds of documents. He called it SGML – Standard Generalized Markup Language. It was very powerful and very complicated. In 1992, some physicists and students took a very small subset of SGML and called it HTML, HyperText Markup Language. They used it to build the first web sites. HTML wasn't very powerful, but it was simple enough that people could figure it out fairly intuitively. It was so primitive that the browser companies kept adding new features without waiting for the W3C – the standards body behind HTML and the Web – to issue new standards.

Then, in 1996, a small group of people adapted SGML for the Web in a more efficient way. They called it XML – Extensible Markup Language. It became a public standard in 1998. Since then, people have formed working groups and committees to help standardize the descriptions of goods and services across the globe. That spark – the philosophy of XML – lit the fire of cooperation that created the world of 2010 I've described here. I'll leave you to discover the rest of the fascinating history of XML, including my own small contributions, at Futurizenow.com.

describes an e-ticket, a stethoscope, or even an apartment building – should be standardized and in the public domain. Today, all loan applications use the same descriptors. To find the best loan for a remodel, a homeowner fills out one application, puts it on the "wants" section of his personal site, and lets lenders compete for his business.

In XML terms, a universal descriptor is called a document type descriptor (DTD). Think of a DTD as a form ready to be filled in. Every item or service worth comparing or sharing should have its own DTD. Every certificate, purchase order, invoice, license, catalog item, blueprint, construction permit, web site, letter, book, play, and newspaper now has its own universal descriptor.

THE ANATOMY OF A DOCUMENT

A document has three parts. The first part is the document descriptor – a way to specify what fields the form has, what they are called, and how they relate to each other. The second part is a document instance – a filled-out form containing specific information in its fields. And the third part is a document expression – a presentation of the document that makes the information available to people.

A document descriptor (DTD) is a blank form ready to be filled in. A menu, for example, has a structure that includes fields for information about the restaurant, the language it is written in, the major sections, and the description of an item (including ingredients, price, substitutions, availability, etc.). Even though there are millions of menus in the world, there is only one menu document type descriptor (DTD) – the Universal Menu.

A document instance is a filled-in DTD. Once you fill in the menu fields – once you've entered all the menu items and prices – you've created a document instance: today's menu. The document instance is a data set *and* the DTD that describes the relationships among its items. You can't see or hear a document until you ask for an expression.

A document expression is a consumable version of a document instance. Once you have a document instance, you can experience it in many ways. You see a different expression of today's menu when you print the menu on a laser printer, when you print it on a flyer to give to your take-out customers, and when you have it printed in color to give to your diners. You see an electronic expression when you locate it on the Web and display it in your browser window. You could be looking at an out-of-date version online, or you could be looking at an expression that was just made – rendered – when you requested it.

If you prefer to read an Arabic or Japanese version, that would simply be another expression of the same information. When you call the restaurant's automated voice menu, you hear an audio expression. When you navigate the web site from the small display on your palm-sized communication appliance, that expression has been specially rendered for that view. And when you publish the information on another web site that keeps all the menus for your city up-to-date at all times, you are setting up a syndication link between your document and the expression(s) on that site.

When companies began to use universal descriptors, the Internet search engines became much more accurate. An online search for a concert ticket is as easy as a search for an airplane ticket because the layout of seats in a stadium and airplane can be described using the same approach. The software for building and maintaining the two ticketing systems is almost identical.

By displaying everything on the Web, companies no longer need complicated databases to answer queries or deliver web pages. Instead, companies use content management systems to maintain the accuracy of their online information. Once the information is on the Web, the public search engines do all the work.

Because most inventory and scheduling systems in 2010 publish their content on the Internet, Felix can go to a search engine and find a gear box for his vintage 1998 VW Beetle, a plumber who can be at his house in under one hour, a used spinnaker for his sailboat, or a few kilograms of Plutonium[239]. The search results won't be based on keywords found on web sites – they'll be exact matches, tuned to Felix's specifications.

A printed piece of paper is simply an artifact – an expression of a document instance that lives somewhere else. Business is now much more efficient than it was in 2000 because *there are no copies of documents* – there are only multiple expressions of documents. Every document instance, whether it is a driver's license, today's *London Times*, or a receipt for a certain bicycle, has a unique web address. It never has to go anywhere. Different people may access it in different ways from different locations, but no one moves it. Other documents that refer to it rely on its being there. There is really no need for more than a single list of sports scores, stock prices, or weather data – everyone who uses these data can simply link to their original sources.

Large-Scale Cooperation

The challenge of XML wasn't technical. It was political. In spite of the odds against its success, XML caught on, and with it came the responsibility of maintaining public standards. Felix knows this all too well. As Nicole's handpicked successor, he spends a lot of time on volunteer committees, helping define the next generation of descriptors for the steel industry. Volunteers and industry associations continue to adopt new features, subdivide descriptors that become too complicated, and keep the standards simple enough for most people to understand. Felix's Universal E-Ticket is the product of many groups getting together – airlines from around the world, concerned travelers, travel agents, corporate travel buyers, airport security officials, governments, and others.

All XML committees have agreed to update their DTDs every two to five years, balancing innovation with stability. Some DTDs need updating even more often. For example, as tax laws change, interested parties now incorporate those changes into standard tax documents and approve them, producing regular, stable releases that all tax software can use.

In the last ten years, thousands of public interest groups formed and worked out their own standards, often with the help of industry groups and a few nonprofits set up to coordinate the effort. XML is an international standard. Individuals from countries and governments around the world cooperate to build linguistic and cultural flexibility into the DTDs.

Today, anyone can create XML-based software knowing she won't have to pay royalties for a proprietary file format. While proprietary formats made some companies rich in the past, companies now reap rewards for what they do with information – not for how they structure it.

XML was only the beginning of a broad movement toward public data standards. XML addressed the structure, but many other aspects of documents still needed to be defined. Today, committees of volunteers continue to work on public standards for presentation, data types, syntax (language), ontology (meaning and structure), internationalization, privacy, security, business rules, and other issues. Without this kind of cooperation, the Web would still be a mess, the way it was in 2000.

In a buyer's market, buyers have the power to set standards. Once companies realized XML was more beneficial to customers – and they didn't have much choice in the matter – they adopted it. Companies like Essex Steel that embraced XML and helped lead the way enjoyed a significant advantage: They could finally concentrate on their businesses instead of their computer systems.

The Student

CHAPTER 25

MIKE AND LAURA'S SON, SPENCER, hopes to get into a good college next year. In this chapter, we'll follow Spencer and see how schools approach the admissions process in 2010.

Spencer's Application

Spencer is interested in applying to six colleges. In September, when the Universal College Application for the next year comes out, he goes to the Universal App site and answers a number of questions – what kind of school he wants, what fields he's interested in, and so on. By prescreening people, the site helps avoid mismatches.

Because so many schools now participate, the Universal App contains more questions than any single school wants answered. For example, a school with an emphasis on humanities has a few questions that differ from a school whose focus is marine biology. And there's always the ubiquitous "Why are you applying to *our* place of learning?" which the applicant must answer specifically for each school. After Spencer chooses his schools, the Universal app site constructs an application for Spencer, which he then puts on his site. If he wishes, he can add a school and receive the appropriate extra questions.

When Spencer is happy with his application, he submits it by sending a special password to each institution to which he's applying. Each school gets a code that gives its admissions people access to relevant answers. The application stays on Spencer's site, and the schools' various systems know where to find it.

Customer-Led Admissions

In 2010, many schools only have one person in admissions. Even Boston University, which during the baby boomlet received over 30,000 applications per year, has only two people in admissions. How did the schools accomplish this feat? Can administrators trust this important job to the high-school applicants themselves?

As a matter of fact, they can – if they let the applicants mature for about four years first. At St John's college, a nondenominational school with two campuses (Maryland and New Mexico), the students are a big part of the admissions process. Each spring, 1,000 eager young people apply to fill the 130 seats in the incoming class. Because in 2002 St John's was the first to implement this system, I'll describe its process.

The admissions person at St John's is Randall Tweed (a fictional character). Randall took his job very seriously, reading hundreds of applications and making difficult decisions that he knew would affect the lives of thousands of people. In 2000, after reading a book on how powerful the Internet could be in the admissions process, Randall decided that for next year's application process, he would invite the students to participate. The first year, he tried it with a few seniors he knew he could trust. Within two

---

THE COMMON APPLICATION

In 2000, there were over 3,500 colleges and universities in the United States. Each school had at least one and as many as a dozen people working in admissions. Although state schools often admit most of their applicants, a small private school typically receives about five applications for every student it admits. Larger schools, like Stanford, receive ten or more.

The Universal College Application was actually invented in the late 1970s, not by colleges and universities, but by the National Association of Secondary School Principals. These administrators were tired of seeing their students miss so much school because they had to fill out a different application for each college and university. So they took matters into their own hands and defined the Common Application (also called the Common App – see it at Commonapp.org).

Every year, representatives meet to define the essay questions and other aspects of the application. In 2000, you could download the Common App from a web site, print it, fill it out, photocopy it, and mail it to any of the 200 colleges that accepted it.

The Common App didn't take off until 2003, when it became an XML document fully endorsed by more than 3,000 schools and changed its name to the Universal College Application.

years, the concept had caught on so strongly that the entire senior class was eager to participate. By 2004, the students at St John's voted overwhelmingly to convert to this process of student-led admissions, now known as replacement admissions.

The concept itself is simple: *Each departing senior is responsible for his or her replacement.* The difficulty is in the execution. A lot is at stake in the admissions process. Randall's years of experience and careful choices had probably shaped the school as much as anything the alumni or admissions committee had done. But he decided the students could do the job better, and he was right.

Randall was convinced that if the school does its job properly, the students themselves are best suited to choose the incoming class. He designed an intensive three-week seminar, which all seniors take in the month of January. In the first week, they discuss as a group what values the school holds and what brought them together. They discuss the goals of their admissions program and how to fulfill them using the answers to this year's Universal Application. With Randall's guidance – and the help of a textbook he wrote – the seniors select the criteria and the methods they want to apply to the process. They understand the duty they have to the school, and they respect the fact that they were chosen under similar circumstances.

In the second week, the students practice. They prepare by reading essays of former classes and discussing their answers. Often, applicants answer essays by writing what they think the school wants to hear, so the students discuss how to identify potential "Johnnies." In one exercise, the seniors take their own year's incoming essays and run them through the process (applications never have names on them). How many of today's seniors would have been accepted had they themselves been doing the admissions? The results of the exercise always lead to interesting discussions among the senior class. With two weeks of intensive preparation behind them, they are ready to begin.

Each year's senior class does it slightly differently, but the basic process is as follows. After deciding on the elementary requirements, the class uses a web-based program to filter out all the applicants who don't meet the seniors' numerical criteria. After eliminating half the applicants this way, the seniors divide up the remaining 500 applicants' essays. Each application has six essay questions. Because each senior is responsible for filling his or her seat, and because two people must read each essay, the seniors initially read 46 essays each. Each person then divides the essays into three groups: good candidates, people with potential, and people who are probably better off at another school. From these groups, the students construct a ranked list of all applicants based on their essays.

Because applicants specify their preferences ahead of time, all 2,500 schools using the Universal Application now perform a match at midnight on January 30. In a match, all students and all schools enter their preferences. For six hours, an online program matches applicants to schools while a team of specialists checks the results for accuracy. In the morning, each school receives a list of its incoming class, and each applicant receives an e-mail message saying which school he or she will attend that fall.

To prepare for the match, Randall and the seniors devote the final week to ranking their list of applicants from 1 to 500. The top 100 students are usually fairly easy to spot. But the next 100 students are more difficult. Randall's class spends a day using online evaluation tools, the guidelines the students laid out during the first week of the course, and group discussion to evaluate the remaining students.

Usually, a class agrees to set aside about eight percent of the seats for two categories that might not make it otherwise. The first category is called "show us." The show-us kids look as if they could use a break. They are promising, but they haven't quite managed to get past all the hurdles. Rather than taking ten more "St John's material" kids, the seniors decide they'd like to give ten kids the opportunity and see if they can make something of it.

The second category is called "surprise us." The surprise-us kids don't come close to qualifying under the seniors' chosen standards, but somehow they stand out. A student might not have good grades or fantastic essays, but he might have taken a year off to teach English in Korea. Another might have done a research project on the effects of loud rock music on people with perfect pitch. Although the students in each class can't tell for sure if they were in either of these groups themselves, the debate each year ensures that the show-us kids and surprise-us kids continue to hold a place in each class.

By January 30, the seniors have made their list. Students and admissions people in about 2,500 other schools have done the same. The next morning, each school learns only the names of the students it has admitted.

St John's was Spencer's first choice. On January 31, he tells his parents he is going to be a "Johnnie." Mike and Laura are thrilled. Spencer specifically wanted a school where the students themselves select the incoming class, because he feels it leads to a more responsible, involved, and close-knit student body.

Replacement Admissions

Based on a random distribution, Randall asks each senior to write a personal welcome letter to an accepted applicant and offer to be that person's e-mentor for the next year. Because the seniors remember the value of *their* e-mail mentors, they are happy to volunteer. This clever device also helps weave outgoing students into the fabric of the alumni community, both online and off.

In many small schools, the student body debates and votes every year on whether to use replacement admissions for the incoming class. In large schools, it's impossible to have thousands of students responsible for incoming classes. Many schools now offer the replacement-admissions course as an elective, rather than a requirement, to all students who would like to help. In general, the larger the school, the smaller the percentage of people who are willing to choose their replacements.

As Randall says, participation is a skill to be learned. At St John's, the replacement-admissions course is a way for all students to start practicing that skill. Randall knows this is a profound improvement over the old process. He asks students to fulfill their academic duty in a way helps them understand themselves and that continues to redefine the school.

The Lawyer

CHAPTER 26

SOMETHING VERY INTERESTING HAPPENED to the legal world during the last ten years. People in the legal profession got together and managed to separate the meaning, writing, and presentation of their documents. For the first time, the actual practice of law is separate from the syntax, the jargon, and the artifacts we used to call legally binding documents.

The Anatomy of a Legal Document

It started with a lawyer named Ming Yau (a person I made up). Ming was fortunate enough to be the daughter of a law professor and a professor of English composition. She grew up thinking the legal system was unnecessarily complicated. She knew that much of the actual practice of law was mechanics – the repetitive solving of problems others had already solved. And she knew from experience that most lawyers were terrible writers. She dreamed of trying to make a simpler system.

Ming got her law degree at Stanford, then she went to MIT's Media Lab to work on her PhD in intelligent systems. She and her colleagues worked – mostly by e-mail – with teams of volunteer lawyers to develop a contract-writing system that uses the Universal Contract as its foundation. They broke the system into seven major components: intentions, concepts, meaning, language, parameters, reference items, and presentation.

Intentions are linked to goals. The framers of the U.S. Constitution probably *intended* for women to vote, even if it seemed a bit strange at the time. Intentions are the prime motivators behind a series of events that result in a legally binding document. If you understand the intent of an action or document, you can usually find a way to implement or interpret it.

Concepts are general ideas that people mutually understand. If a large company wants to buy a small company, and the small company wants to be acquired, both companies have the same intent. They also understand that they will have to reach a mutual agreement on the small company's valuation. They may not agree on what the numbers are, but they agree on the concept of valuation. They know the components of a valuation, the different ways of approaching valuation, and they know that a given valuation will be supported by a number of specific documents. Concepts like bankruptcy protection, arbitration, and indemnification are important building blocks of contracts. Two parties realize an intention by agreeing on a number of concepts and then executing them.

Meaning takes place at the sentence and word level. Legalese is full of terms of art, like "quantum meruit" and "holographic," that are completely unknown to the average person. Yet it is important that average people understand the documents they sign, and that lawyers agree on exactly what they mean when they use words like "income" and "verifiable." Ming and her team worked with lawyers from around the world to construct a precise ontology of legal terms – a complete catalog of words, terms, meanings, and relationships. An ontology is a way to structure a particular world (in this case, the world of legal terms) so that everything has its place and there are no circular references. Ming and her team came up with plain English replacements for complicated terms of art. Now they had a set of building blocks they could use to put concepts into sentences.

Language is the connective tissue for concepts, terms, and meaning. It's pretty clear to most people that lawyers are some of the worst writers on earth. They typically never take a writing course (Harvard's Law School *still* lists no writing courses in its catalog), and they have trouble expressing themselves in fewer than 20 pages. Ming wanted to build a standard framework for expressing common legal expressions (clauses, sentences, referrals, inclusions, exceptions, paragraphs, sections, subsections, appendixes, exhibits, documents, and families of documents) that would simplify the language of contracts.

Parameters are the specific business terms that constitute an agreement. Parameters include numbers, dates, specifications, special language, exceptions, timelines, milestones, people involved, approval methodologies, third parties, and other important information for getting the deal done. Modern contracts separate parameters from the concepts and language of the agreement so that nothing is hard to find. In Ming's system, all deal parameters go into specially designed and programmed appendixes that are more like a spreadsheet than a piece of paper.

Reference items are things like facts, statements, timelines, exhibits, tables, schedules, photos, books, and other relevant information a document requires. Ming and her colleagues standardized the names and descriptors of reference and exhibit items so that many documents could refer to one item in a standardized way.

Presentation is the physical display of a document, whether on a screen or as a paper artifact. Because lawyers know nothing about typography, legibility, or layout, their documents were made even harder to read by arcane traditions, requirements, and standards. Ming's team of psychologists, visual scientists, typographers, designers, information architects, and others created visual standards for presentation that applied to different audiences with various viewing tools and specific needs.

The Universal Contract

Ming's goal was to build an online application that lawyers and individuals could use to create signable legal agreements that were easy to understand, easy to interpret, and legally valid. The Universal Contract would take all the repetitive work out of the process and simplify it for everyone.

The team built a database that contained all the parts of a contract most people would need. A document like a nondisclosure form can have up to six major sections and one miscellaneous section at the end. A licensing agreement, on the other hand, can have up to 28 major sections, many of which go into detail on specific international rights.

The Universal Contract is now a large application that sits on a web server. Anyone can use it. It consists of hundreds of documents, from standard nondisclosure forms to obscure mining rights. To use the online application, each party answers a series of questions, starting with intentions and working toward exhibits. The application asks questions about legal jurisdiction, arbitration, limits, warranties, and anything else pertinent. It provides a work sheet for deal parameters and the locations of exhibits. It also asks for information about how the parties want to use and execute the document: Do they want paper contracts or electronic? If they want paper contracts, how would they like them presented? In either case, the final product is a legally binding agreement both parties can sign.

Once an electronic contract is signed, it stays on a central server that acts as a public record or stays on both parties' servers. Electronic agreements can't be changed without both parties' electronic signatures, which involve special passwords. This ensures the document can't be modified and that it was signed as-is on a particular date.

The Universal Contract team put hundreds of common contracts (apartment leases, waivers of liability, state incorporation, and the like) online for easy access. For many standard agreements, the two parties fill out a simple form and apply their digital signatures. When one individual buys a car from another, the exhibit section of the contract points to the Universal Automobile Descriptor that identifies the car. When both parties give their digital signatures, the transfer of the legal title to the car takes place. The system's escrow service even transfers any security deposit from one account to the other upon verification of the signatures.

Anyone can use the Universal Contract server for free. The software advises people to seek a lawyer's advice before entering into any agreement, but the mechanics are now fairly trivial. Ming's group also built an online educational center that guides people through the process of agreeing on terms, building documents, and executing them.

Sharper Tools

The Universal Contract doesn't replace lawyers at all. It simply replaces bad writing, ambiguity, mistakes, and repetitive tasks. For example, if, during negotiation, the parties agree to a global change – a name change or a concept change – that change can be made throughout the document *at the meaning level* rather than the word level. Lawyers are still responsible for stating the parties' intentions, concepts, and means of fulfilling their obligations. They still spend most of their days dealing with facts and advising clients. People who don't use lawyers run the risk of not understanding the legal system and how it works. But now, creating a simple legal document is usually a simple process in itself.

The Universal Contract has changed the way people work with each other. Ming's team realized that lawyers were used to working with language, rather than concepts. When they negotiated contracts, the language, the meaning, the concepts, and the intentions were all mixed together. Using the tools Ming's team provides, two parties first agree on a memorandum of intent (or understanding). Then they agree on terms, exhibits, and methodologies. Then they agree on concepts. They actually negotiate at the conceptual level now, sending draft concept models back and forth, rather than draft contracts. Ming's system helps two parties conduct these discussions online, exchanging concepts, goals, and suggestions until the parties come to a decision on their final intentions.

Only when everyone agrees to the business terms and answers all the questions on presentation, the document itself is rendered in the form of a contract. In fact, you can choose from four different language styles. Using Ming's system, each party can print the contract in a different style of writing and a different layout (paragraph numbering remains consistent). The two parties can continue negotiating at the concept level, rather than the word level. Of course, if lawyers feel the need, they can modify the language of the final contract. Ming and her team are constantly in search of suggestions for how to make the system more effective and require less intervention.

Living Documents

The beauty of Ming's system is that she and her team didn't need anyone's permission to create the Universal Contract. They just did it, and the legal establishment was powerless to stop it. As lawyers adopt the system, they continue to make it better.

The Universal Contract doesn't require lawyers to learn how to write, but it does give their clients more choices. And best of all, it helps keep people out of court by preventing misunderstandings and confusion *before* things get out of hand, rather than after.

Ming received her PhD and took the project to the Attorney General, who helped convince the American Bar Association to give it a permanent home. She got a ten-year grant from the federal government and raised a $12 million endowment from nongovernmental organizations. Her team now hosts the Universal Contract server and rents document-storage space on its server. They also have automated authentication and escrow services and a small consulting group. Hundreds of volunteer lawyers and ten full-time staff members continually revise the documents to reflect changes in law and technology. Anyone can make comments and suggestions on how to improve the system. The team holds major conferences throughout the year, targeting vertical industries like medicine, banking, insurance, and entertainment. For Ming, there is always something new to do – the desire for contracts seems to have no end.

The Patient

CHAPTER 27

IN A HOSPITAL NEAR FLORENCE, ITALY, Sofia lies unconscious in a hospital bed. She is surrounded by her five closest friends. The six women were on a two-week cycling tour of the region. Earlier this morning, Sofia, who had just turned 27, had lost control of her bike on a sharp turn in the road. She crashed into a fence and broke her right arm. When her friends reached her, Sofia was awake but incoherent. Her helmet was in pieces – she had suffered a concussion. Her broken radius was protruding through her skin. The tour guide called an ambulance. Luckily, a large regional hospital was close by.

In the hospital, the doctors confirmed Sofia's concussion. She had lost her short-term memory. She knew her name, but she couldn't answer simple questions. The doctors had to operate on her arm immediately. Since she was conscious, they needed her permission to operate. But she couldn't give them any reliable information.

Fortunately, Sofia had her Universal Patient Chart filled out and ready for emergency access. The doctors went to her personal site and logged in as emergency personnel (Sofia's server asked them for identification). Sofia had done an excellent job of filling out the documents. She had instructions, called directives, in case she ever became incapacitated, in a coma or vegetative state, or dying. She had included religious and blood-product preferences, her transfusion history, instructions for contacting relatives, insurance information, and one thing that the doctors found particularly interesting.

In her emergency directives, one of Sofia's doctors had written a note explaining that she had once had a severe reaction to benzocaine, a common anesthetic used in surgery. The reaction had causes her blood to shut down its ability to deliver oxygen, essentially suffocating her. If the

Italian operating team had given her benzocaine, Sofia would have started to turn blue – a condition called methemoglobinemia. Rather than operating on her arm, the team would have had to diagnose her condition, run emergency blood tests, and find the antidote – which happens to be a dye called methylene blue. Had they been unable to diagnose her condition, she might have died. Fortunately, a routine check of her Universal ID led the hospital staff to her online emergency-medical information. Sofia's surgeon, Dr Francesco Baldi, had read the warning and used an anesthetic that Sofia's doctors indicated was safe. The operation went smoothly, and Sofia's arm was back together.

Dr Baldi comes into the hospital room and asks Sofia's friends how she's doing. He looks at her chart using a communication appliance. All the equipment monitoring her condition sends copies of the information to her server every 15 minutes.

The Universal Patient Chart started in the late 1990s as an offshoot project of the medical informatics community. By 2002, ad-hoc committees of interested people had standardized most of the necessary documents health care workers needed. But the real breakthrough came in 2005, when many governments around the world agreed that all people had a right to keep their patient data on their own servers.

Now, from the day of birth, everything from an individual's birth certificate to her latest flu shot goes onto her personal site under her control. All lab tests, X rays, scans, response measurements, and other data are automatically transmitted to the patient's server. Of course, doctors who have ordered the tests also keep a copy of the results. It's easy to verify data simply by comparing the two sets of records.

As with all Sofia's universal descriptors, the medical chart has six levels of privacy. She controls who gets which passwords. Emergency personnel can learn only what she's decided to tell them ahead of time.

Many people prefer to use a buddy system for giving out information. They list the names and contact information for several people they trust with the password to the deeper levels of their site. The medical personnel must contact one of these people and describe the situation before the friend or relative decides how much information to give them.

The Long-Term Patient

After a week in Florence, Sofia is feeling better. She has her memory back. Her scar is minimal, and her arm, which is now in a cast, will be back to normal in a few months. She tells Dr Baldi that she remembers riding down the hill with her friends and suddenly everything got blurry. Dr Baldi asks Sofia if this has happened before. She said yes, it has. Sometimes it was like double vision, other times blurriness.

Dr Baldi shines a light in front of Sofia's eyes, going from one eye to the other. He then asks to see her patient history. Together, they go to her personal site and Sofia types in her password. They review her various doctor visits, starting from age ten. Dr Baldi asks about her vision prescription, which has changed rapidly in the last few years. She had also seen an occupational therapist about tingling in her hands, and the therapist noted that Sofia probably had some degree of carpal-tunnel syndrome from all the typing she did. Since that was fairly common, Sofia hadn't done much about it. She had also complained of tingling and numbness in her back. In fact, a doctor had ordered an MRI scan of her neck five years ago to see if she had ruptured a disc. She hadn't. On a hunch, Dr Baldi orders another identical scan.

The next day, Dr Baldi and Sofia compare the results of the two MRI scans. Dr Baldi looks serious. He points to a region around her spinal column that is now a bit thicker near the base of her skull. "Has anyone ever talked to you about multiple sclerosis?" he asks. Sofia has heard of it, but she doesn't really know what it is. He asks if she's had any bladder problems. She says no. He asks her to touch her chin to her chest. Does she feel any tingling in her spinal column? Yes, she says, she does. What does that mean? He explains that MS is a thickening or degeneration of the myelin sheath around the spinal cord. It can be diagnosed only by putting together several signs, and the tingling and blurred vision are two important ones. MS is often not detected until a patient is in her thirties. He asks if he can conduct a definitive test, which involves removing a small amount of spinal fluid. With her cycling friends there for support, she agrees.

The next day, Dr Baldi tells Sofia he has found a greater than normal amount of myelin basic protein in her spinal cord. More than likely, she has MS. Through a phone conversation with her doctor in San Francisco and a specialist in Chicago – in which they are all able to look at Sofia's data online – he confirms the diagnosis.

Dr Baldi explains that, while there is still no known cure and no way to reverse the disease, there are now excellent drugs that can stop MS from getting worse. He tells Sofia that early detection is now the greatest weapon in the fight against the disease, and that Sofia's medical records had helped him diagnose it. Without being able to see her previous medical information, he wouldn't have been able to compare the two MRI scans and tell her something was wrong. He wouldn't have asked the questions he had asked, and it would have taken another – possibly worse – accident to tell her she had the disease.

Although it's not welcome news, Sofia is very grateful that she could start a drug program early to prevent any further deterioration. She can live a normal, active life with her disease in check.

The Universal Patient Chart keeps all an individual's data in a standard format. New software is constantly being written to help people understand the chart and spot changes or trends. There are also sites that, for a fee, take the information and give a complete analysis, warning of any diseases or conditions to watch for, indicating the person's rank among others with the same conditions, and giving an early warning for anything that looks irregular. The Universal Patient Chart gives people the freedom to move, change doctors, and get second opinions easily.

In the old days, it was difficult for people to get their medical records, and the recordkeeping standards were so different that people had to go to great lengths to transfer their records to another doctor in a different health care system. While the hospitals and HMOs used this as a selling feature – "We share information with our member providers," their ads proclaimed – people wanted to control their own information and to share them with anyone they wanted. The situation in countries with socialized medicine was even worse. Thanks to the work of patient-advocacy groups and the rising cost of medical infomatics, medical systems that privatize their patient records have found a win-win solution in web-based patient records.

Privacy is a huge issue in health care. With the Universal Patient Chart, patients reveal only what they want to reveal. They entrust certain passwords and instructions to their friends and family, preventing doctors from having to make blind decisions on their behalf.

The Chronic Patient

Dr Baldi is also a patient. Like millions of people around the world, he has suffered from chronic sinusitis all his life. (According to the Centers for Disease Control and Prevention, sinusitis is the most common chronic disease in the U.S., affecting almost 40 percent of the population.) Being a doctor doesn't help – he's constantly exposed to aggressive bacterial life forms. He lives most of his life with sinus pain, pressure, and difficulty breathing, especially at night. As good as doctors are at setting bones and controlling symptoms, most researchers are frustrated by their inability to cure chronic conditions.

Antibiotics have little effect on Dr Baldi anymore. When he takes them, his symptoms go away for a few weeks, but then they come right back. He had an operation to open his sinuses, but that helped for only about six months.

Research on sinusitis, like research on many other health problems, is difficult and expensive to conduct. It requires large amounts of data, which is hard to get because sinusitis is usually paired with other conditions – allergies, colds, stress, reactions to smoke and air pollution, and other environmental factors. Most physicians rely on their own anecdotal evidence – the result of all the patients they've seen and limited communication with colleagues. As with many other chronic conditions, no definitive method for curing sinusitis exists.

Dr Baldi had given up hope. He lived for years taking antihistamines, which he now feels made his condition worse. He tried nasal irrigation, decongestants, sprays, ointments – all to no avail. Then he found out about a project called the Universal Health Infobase. The Infobase is a web site where people can contribute their own health histories. Millions of people have posted their health profiles and described their health situations using standard forms (universal disease descriptors) that make the database a very powerful research tool.

Like about 15 percent of the population, Dr Baldi has allergies. Thanks to the worldwide standardization of allergy skin tests, he was able to link his allergy profile into the Infobase and discover that he had exactly the same profile as 18,000 other people in the database. Of those, he found 4,000 people who also had chronic sinusitis. This group of 4,000 is now working together to learn what works and what doesn't, and more join every day. About 200 of them formed a volunteer committee to systematically explore different approaches. They break into groups and try new ideas for several months. Those people in turn have responsibility for hundreds of group members, who try the approach and report their results.

In the last few years, Dr Baldi's group has made several interesting discoveries. The Infobase allows them to look for any kind of correlation that may point to a common cause. Ninety-four percent live in urban areas where pollution is a factor. Eighty-three percent have fairly high levels of stress in their lives. And they have found their symptoms are the worse during the six months after the allergy season.

Lately, Dr Baldi has been leading a group of people trying a new irrigation mixture involving herbs and salt water, followed by an anti-inflammatory nasal spray. It seems to be working. He's discovered that if he keeps it up, his pain and congestion are much reduced. The site gives him sophisticated analytical tools for understanding the significance of his findings. He can work with his group until they've found something they want to share with the others and then widen the experiment to include more members of the larger group. As more information comes in, they can ask better questions and try new approaches.

In 2010, people around the world are conducting their own health research. Millions of people enter their health information into the Universal Health Infobase to better learn how to treat their conditions. Researchers around the world now use these data to conduct studies they never could have conducted before.

Ten years ago, data sets for studies were small – a few hundred patients. Today, the data sets are enormous – the result of millions of patients keeping track of all kinds of conditions, symptoms, causes, and effects. Now researchers use sophisticated software to help filter out unwanted data and run comparisons on meaningful information. If they find something interesting, they can contact all the members in the group they've been studying – without even knowing their real identities – and follow up or verify their findings.

The average doctor in the United States still receives slightly more than one hour of nutrition instruction during medical school. But the link between diet and health has become much stronger now that people are contributing their data. People with food allergies and other conditions now keep standardized diaries online, allowing everyone to see the results. Many people find it helpful to keep food, exercise, and general wellness diaries, looking for correlations between their diet, their behavior, their environment, and how they feel. Smokers keep cigarette diaries, helping them cut down. Dieters track their eating habits, using software coaches and live online partners, who remind them when they are slipping on their commitments. People who are at risk for degenerative diseases like cancer or alcoholism can track behavior and health data that will help them recognize their conditions early.

The wealth of data in the Infobase allows people to identify trends and contributing factors in seconds that would have been impossible to recognize ten years ago. Today, researchers simply write software that mines this information, looking for any clues that might lead to a new discovery. Epidemiologists have already used the database to make vaccines and other new medicines as they gather even more information on the spread of viruses. Just last year, a 12-year-old girl in France won that country's highest science award for discovering a link between psoriasis (a common skin disease), stress, and climate just by analyzing the data online.

Patient Power

In the last five years, the amount of patient data in searchable public databases has skyrocketed. It now dwarfs all the health data collected in the past hundred years. People who want to protect their privacy simply use a new identity for giving information. To prevent cross-correlation, one person can use separate IDs to describe separate conditions and identify that fact for researchers. People learn so much about themselves when they track their information that a full 15 percent of the U.S. population considers it something of a hobby – like doing genealogy research. The medical community has gone from using anecdotal evidence and word of mouth to advanced power searches on enormous data sets.

Even though Sofia learned she had a serious degenerative disease, she was very thankful to have caught it early. Dr Baldi feels he's on his way to finding a cure for his sinusitis and helping others. Both of these people have benefitted from standardized internet-based records.

As Dr John Spinosa, a pathologist and advocate of patient rights, says, "When it comes to medical information: First, do no harm. Patient records should be outside the system, unconnected to any particular institution. Patients should at least have the ability to reclaim their data from any computer system, and – ideally – they should own it." Today, patients do own their data, and they are healthier for it.

The Reputation Consultant

CHAPTER 28

NIGHT FELL ACROSS SAN FRANCISCO like the body of an investment banker plummeting from a 13th-story window onto Market Street. As the financial district's after-hours denizens took their places, the diners at EosSF.com finished the evening's last plate of Fijian Albacore Tuna Tetaki. The sous-chef at Postrio.com swept the remaining scraps of grilled quail with spinach and soft-egg ravioli into the storm sewer system that flowed into the bay. And the blue glow from a magnesium-encased flat-panel display flickered through the window at number 13 Dashiell Hammett Street. The night watchman at Camptonplace.com knew that light well. It was from the office of Lois Merlot, online reputation consultant.

Lois, in her trademark black stretch-velvet jumpsuit, took a sip of Hakusan.com sake from a shot glass ("borrowed" from Absinthe.com, a favorite Hayes Valley restaurant). She sat at her Knoll.com desk, simultaneously working three browser windows. Her personal digital assistant announced a visitor. She turned her gaze from her communication appliance to the wall in front of her. There she saw an image of a thin man – wearing a baseball cap. I waved at the door-cam. She pressed a button. The sound of the massive front door closing behind me echoed through the elevator shaft as I bounded up the stairs.

Lois's door was open. I walked in as her cat stalked down the stairs. I hung my hat on a giant stuffed penguin and sat down on a Vitra.com chair. As if by magic, Lois appeared from the next room with a bottle of '04 Chappellet.com signature cabernet (an incredible year). She poured a golden pool of Davero.com olive oil onto a Mackenzie-Childs.com plate and cut into a crusty loaf of Gracebaking.com peasant bread. "Deandeluca.com?" I asked. "Nope," she replied, "A gift from a client. Shall we get started?"

Reputations "R" Us

Lois helps people who get into "situations." She does most of her work by e-mail, voice, and video. She is a specialist. She has a network of friends who help her get information on people and companies when the usual routes turn into dead ends. She knows how to explain to clients what their options are and how to, as she puts it, "avoid the avoidable and face the inevitable."

Lois has studied dozens of sites where anyone can say anything about anyone. She brought one up on the screen and typed in my name. She said my personal integrity rating at this site was three out of ten, which she said was actually pretty good, considering all the allegations against me. My profile included a list of past spouses I'd never met, novels I'd never written, and a fair amount of my credit history (some of which was actually true). The site was a digital combination of graffiti, gossip, and *The National Enquirer*.

We found some accurate information: my home address and phone number, the kind of car I drive, how much income tax I paid last year, my unlisted phone number, my alma mater, and a list of my favorite San Francisco restaurants (I wonder how they got that?). Lois told me that much was child's play – anyone with access to a search engine could have learned those things about me back in 2000. There were six photos of me, none of which was recognizable (one was even the wrong sex – I think). I finally understood how celebrities felt when they saw their faces smeared across tabloid covers.

As with most public reputation sites, 99 percent of the content is noise. The other one percent comes from hobbyists – amateur sleuths who enjoy the challenge of digging up dirt on other people. These sites are very popular entertainment destinations, but they aren't taken very seriously. I pulled the cork from the cabernet to let the wine breathe. I asked her who *is* taken seriously.

Lois explained that reputations are only as good as the people who give them. In 2010, almost everyone has multiple identities, and each identity picks up a reputation. But most people come to see her about their primary identity. Since they can't control what others say about them online, they want to know what their options are. Sure, they care about ethical issues, but mostly they care about their lives being ruined.

Lois told me an online reputation has three main components: ratings, referrals, and rebuttals. Each of these has a public and a private component. She offered to illustrate these concepts using the cases

---

ONLINE REPUTATIONS

Public ratings are full of gossip and hearsay. Public ratings sites have rating systems, but few people take them seriously.

Private ratings are issued by agencies, much as the Michelin guide rates restaurants and hotels. Because it's expensive to collect accurate ratings and hard to charge for them, the private ratings sites – like "Who's Who" – are little more than vanity sites.

Within a community – like a trading community or a game-playing community – ratings are more meaningful than they are on the web at large. In a game-playing community, for example, a player builds her rating by beating other players. The longevity of a private rating is as important as the rating itself.

Public referrals are either positive or negative. A positive referral is a fan club site, usually focused on celebrities and high-profile companies. A negative referral is a consumer opinion site dedicated to exposing people and companies. Often started by disgruntled employees or customers, these sites are either biased amateur attempts at retribution or well-run, evenhanded sites organized by groups dedicated to informing the public about a person or group.

Private referrals are issued by investigative agencies who are paid to search and filter the information they can find on people. They answer specific questions about individuals.

They are branded, subscription-based services that try to compile as much accurate information on individuals as possible.

Private referrals can also come from individuals. Within a community, a web of trust gives people the ability to find connections through others who are known to be trustworthy. On the Web, private referral sites aggregate others' opinions. Interested parties can contact the referring party for more information. Private referral sites are by far the most useful in learning about individuals.

Public rebuttals are an exercise in futility. Responding to people's charges, just encourages them to try harder. Political candidates and celebrities are still the only individuals who hire consultants to try to shape public opinion. Companies do better to send ambassadors into online communities to improve their communication with the press and the public.

Private rebuttals usually involve mediation and arbitration. They are handled by neutral agencies or volunteer organizations, like the American Arbitration Association. Individuals can issue private rebuttals by presenting their side of the story to various private sites. They can make themselves available to be contacted through those sites, potentially diffusing a highly charged situation by simply offering to talk about it.

she's worked on in the last few years – changing the names, of course, to protect her clients. I poured the wine. Lois brought up a browser on the wall-projection screen and logged on to her private extranet.

Fifteen years ago, Esmerelda, then 16, babysat a two-year-old girl who suddenly collapsed while in her care. The little girl had a previously unknown heart defect. Despite Esmerelda's quick actions to get help, the girl died. For years after the incident, Esmerelda suffered the questions and rumors around the tragedy as well as attacks on her character. She thought it was all behind her. Now, at age 31, Esmerelda has learned that certain parts of the story have resurfaced on the Internet, and the situation has gotten so out of hand that one of her coworkers recently asked her about her "murder conviction." What should she do?

Lois advised her to deal with the issues as they came up and to tell the truth when asked. She could post a page on her company's intranet that gave the facts in the case and pointed to any online news archives that covered the case. The more open she was, the more the rumors and gossip would be quelled, and the sooner she could get back to her normal life. Lois also recommended an online referral site where Esmeralda could list her name, a brief mention of the incident, and contact information.

Arlene bought an expensive guitar from a well-known store in Los Angeles. When the plastic coating on the guitar started to peel, she took it back. In the process of refinishing the guitar, the repair company scratched it and sealed the scratch in. Arlene tried many times to get the problem corrected. She got no response. When she finally confronted the store's owner, he rudely told her she had waited too long and advised her to take her business elsewhere. What could she do?

Lois laid out several options. Arlene could contact the Better Business Bureau online, whose seal the guitar store displays on its site. Any company displaying this seal has agreed to the bureau's standards of fair business practices. After a certain number of unresolved complaints, the bureau will revoke the store's seal. On the bureau's web site, Bbbonline.org, anyone can find out which companies have had their seal revoked.

Lois told Arlene about other agencies and media companies that tracked consumer satisfaction and used rating schemes to help consumers make choices. Arlene could contact a number of these on her own, or she could pay an agency to distribute her complaint anonymously and track the results.

Tamara wanted to sell her house to a buyer who asked her to finance half of the purchase price. In 2010, this is not an uncommon request. The buyer seemed trustworthy, and the terms were fair, but some ratings sites had said negative things about him. How could Tamara assess her risk?

Lois explained that such situations always carry risk. If Tamara didn't lend him the money, plenty of people would. But if she wanted to carry the loan, she had several options. Ratings sites weren't the place to go. She could learn about his financial history from online credit agencies, where it was easy to get a report if she had his permission. If he refused to give permission, she shouldn't do business with him.

Randy needed to hire a new delivery person. He had several candidates, all of whom had references listed on their Universal Résumés. Randy had hired dozens of delivery people over the years, and their references always checked out. Yet some of those people had turned out to be difficult to manage, and some had stolen from him. How could he check a new applicant's background more thoroughly?

Lois recommended he spend some time at UniversalReferrals.com, a directory of reputations. Sites like UniversalReferrals.com maintained referral records for businesses, government agencies, and nonprofits as well as their individual employees. Randy could type in an applicant's name and get a list of all the people willing to provide information on that person. Personal integrity, job competence, personal financial transactions, personal credit, and personal government records are all potential categories.

If Randy found nothing but positive comments, he probably had a good prospective employee. If he found any negative comments, he could try to contact the sources via e-mail and ask them questions. If those sources were unwilling to be contacted or left untraceable anonymous comments, he should ignore the comments. UniversalReferrals.com even provided a way to filter out such comments. If Randy felt a source was questionable, he should use the site to learn about the sources themselves.

Lois said quality referrals usually happened by phone. Randy should use a referral site primarily to learn if a search turns up any warning signs. If there were, he should follow up by requesting that the referring person call him. The referral source may ask Randy several questions before he or she will be comfortable discussing the past.

Andrew and Sara were going to Vail, Colorado, for a conference and a week of skiing. They have a three-year-old child. They wanted to find a reliable babysitter in Vail, but they didn't have any local contacts.

Lois recommended they visit several online babysitter communities. The best communities ask member parents to babysit other members' children in exchange for babysitting credits. If Andrew and Sara have time, they should join one of these communities, do some babysitting for out-of-town visitors, and accrue credits. The visitors' votes and comments will help establish their ratings.

Lois explained that the babysitting community is a gated community, where webs of trust are very effective. For example, if Andrew and Sara know a couple in Denver who babysat for a couple from Texas who used a particular babysitter in Vail, they would be more likely to trust that babysitter. In a gated community, trust-network software helps sort out the requests and the connections. In general, referrals beyond four links away aren't very different from starting from scratch.

Andrew and Sara were in a rush, so Lois advised them to check out the referral section of a babysitting community. This is a mini version of UniversalReferrals.com. It lets anyone say anything about any babysitter. Andrew and Sara could select babysitters with the most positive comments and follow up on any negative comments that seem out of place.

Tiffany was an avid shopper, and she had more than enough money to indulge her habit. With the amount of information available over the Internet, she was worried her spending could be tracked and she might become the target of thieves. She didn't like the fact that store clerks always got her name and often her address. For certain kinds of purchases – both online and in town – she wanted to establish a separate identity that would conceal who she was and where she lived. How could she stay in control of that identity?

Lois told Tiffany that if she were very careful to maintain her new identity in public settings – use only those packets associated with her shopping identity to make purchases, receive her mail through a forwarding service, and create an alias for her real e-mail address – she will be fairly well insulated from the average person trying to find her than she was without the second identity. Making a new identity is easy – remembering to use it every time you do business with someone is harder.

Lois said cyberspace also helps those looking for their next victim. If someone were to make the connection between her old and new identities, the information could quickly find its way to a public gossip site. Once that happens, anyone who really wanted Tiffany's address will probably be able to find it. She should use bots to search the Web constantly for her actual home address and alert her if they see anything.

Bill started a company with a partner who was an excellent engineer but, unfortunately, a pathological liar. The partner left him in the middle of a huge project and saddled him with so much debt that he had to file Chapter 11. He finally managed to pay off his creditors, but he lost the company. Bill didn't want retribution, only to alert others who might run into this guy.

Lois advised him to go to UniversalReferrals.com and register his complaint. Finding his ex-partner wouldn't be that easy – he had moved to another state, and there are many people in that state with the same name. So he would have to list any attributes he could think of to help identify his ex-partner. He should try to find others to cooperate with – something UniversalReferrals.com helps people do. Perhaps someone might have a photo that others can verify. Perhaps someone could find his address. Working together, they could help prevent someone from being victimized later.

At UniversalReferrals.com, Lois recommended he post his message under another identity, so he could conduct e-mail conversations with others on his terms. He could even call and speak with them using that identity until he knew more about them.

Loring was a budding young architect. He was about to interview for a job with a famous architect, but he was having second thoughts. The office was quite small. The architect had a reputation as a domineering taskmaster. Loring was willing to work hard, but he didn't want to be treated like a human pencil. He could politely query the architect's current employees, but he was really hoping to get some answers before his interview.

UniversalReferrals.com has listings for both companies and their employees. While the architect may have a stellar record as a businessperson and may be highly rated in his personal dealings with friends, his employees may be of an entirely different opinion. Lois suggested that Loring look up the referrals on UniversalReferrals.com's corporate section. The architectural community is relatively small, and some of its members may be reluctant to reveal their identities. But Loring could still read the reports on the architect and send e-mail to referral sources, requesting them to call him. He may have to spend some time on the phone with them before they'll say much, because they may fear he's someone working on the architect's behalf, trying to learn who's saying what about him. Once he wins their confidence, however, he'll be able to ask his questions, get straight answers, and go into the interview with his eyes wide open.

Dani was looking for an assisted living facility for her mother. She was evaluating three places, all of which seemed equivalent on first inspection. She knew what the people who work at the places had to say about their facilities, but she wanted to hear from residents firsthand what the conditions were really like.

Lois and Dani went online together and learned that one facility didn't allow residents to access the Internet. They ruled that place out immediately. The other two facilities did allow Internet access, but Lois and Dani grew suspicious when they couldn't find anything but good comments about the two places online.

Lois fired up her Thirdvoice software (see Chapter 5) and returned to the two sites. One of the rest homes – Orangewood Place (a fictitious name) – had a curious comment overlaid on the site. The comment read "PA/lemon**/Srs." Lois had a hunch that PA was short for PlanetAll.com, a discussion/community site, and that "lemon**" stood for lemonwoodplace. Sure enough, they found a discussion group at Planetall.com called Lemonwoodplace, and the password was Seniors. In the discussion groups there, the group members referred to themselves as "inmates." They had devised all kinds of ways to get around the rules at Orangewood Place, sending each other helpful tips and restricted information. Lois and Dani did some further research and uncovered some unsettling stories of cost-cutting by the Orangewood management. Lois knew how to contact the authorities in such cases. Dani chose the third option.

Monika collects dolls. She wanted to buy a rare porcelain doll from someone who had a bad online reputation. But this doll would complete a series in her collection, making it even more valuable. The price was reasonable, as long as the doll was in the condition the seller claimed. Monika just didn't want to send her money and get a broken doll – or no doll – in return.

Lois suggested a delivery-escrow service. Monika places her payment into escrow and pays the company the appropriate fees. The seller hands over the item for delivery. At the door, Monika is allowed to inspect the doll, and if she decides to keep it, the service authorizes the money to be transferred to the seller. If she doesn't want the doll, the driver calls in the refusal, and Monika gets her money back electronically. Monica loses the delivery fee and the insurance, but not more.

George had a drinking problem. It was starting to affect his performance on the job. Although no one else there had said anything to him, he was afraid someone would. He wanted to get treatment but was reluctant to even make inquiries for fear that someone would learn about his situation and broadcast it over the Internet. He knew that as soon as it was online, his entire office would learn something he didn't want them to know.

Lois explained that he could shield his treatment experience by creating a new identity. As long as no one else at the clinic knew him, his identity would hold up. He could make purchases, eat at restaurants, and go to movies in that neighborhood – all using his new identity. Even if he were to get into a car accident for which a police report had to be filed, he would be held accountable under that identity. A clearinghouse would make sure he paid any fines and penalties he owed. Only if he were to be taken to criminal court would the state have a right to pierce his identity shield. George could use his new identity to help him improve his life.

Futurized

The bottle of cabernet was drained and so was I. Reputation sites were inevitable. Nothing could stop people from airing their opinions online. They didn't need anyone's permission, and they didn't need to be accurate. The credibility of the opinions is linked to the credibility of the site and its contributors. In most cases, truth still prevails.

Lois turned the screen off with a voice command, and the darkness of a San Francisco night came in through the window like a black cat hearing the sound of a can opener. Lois glided to a bookshelf and pulled down a ten-year-old book with a faded green cover. She said there was something about that book she'd always wanted to know: Why did I have to tell everyone about the future? Why didn't I just quit while I was ahead?

I told her I thought standards were too important to leave up to governments and industry associations. I looked forward to a world in which people had greater control over their own destinies – a *relative* world, in which people could add value as individuals rather than within some arbitrary hierarchical structure. I told Lois that over the course of history, clever people had developed several new types of media, but that the Internet was unique because for the first time it let individuals control the *distribution* of information, not just the way it was expressed. I believed we had come to a turning point in human history. It was time to seize the moment, to push for the worldwide adoption of public information standards, to invite people to reclaim their status as human beings rather than cogs in a machine.

Lois looked at me with her piercing gray eyes. She said she was glad it had turned out that way. She said reputation sites bring with them a new social order. They encourage good behavior and reinforce good reputations. They protect people from those who would take advantage of them. Best of all, she said, they make people think twice about doing something they wouldn't want others to know about. I could tell she liked that part by the way she tilted her penguin toward me. I could tell by the hat in my lap that it was time for me to go.

AS THE WEB GETS BIGGER, THE WORLD GETS SMALLER. Between 2000 and 2010, the Customer-Led Revolution will connect almost 2 billion people. The cultural impact will be more significant than any previous changes in the history of mankind. As Andrew Zolli, a cybervisionary, said in 1999, "We are on the first letter of the first word of the first sentence of the book of global interconnectivity."

It is time for the inmates to run the asylum. If I've accomplished anything in this book, I hope it's to convince you that the inmates are capable of running it better, at lower cost, and with more hope for the future to come. In 28 chapters, I have tried to give you all the tools I carry in my little black bag. In this final chapter, I'll try to put the Customer-Led Revolution into perspective by offering seven thoughts – meditations, really – that will guide you through your company's transformation.

Change

In Part 4, I described a very different world, one that is several times more efficient than the world we know today. The driving force behind the Customer-Led Revolution is Metcalfe's Law – named after Bob Metcalfe, one of the fathers of computer networking: *The value of a network increases with the square of the number of users.* If one person has a fax machine, it's not very useful. If 100 people have fax machines, that's still not very useful. But as more people get fax machines, the benefits to everyone go up quickly. Thankfully, fax machines will soon be a thing of the past. But the scenarios in Part 4 were designed to show that once this Internet thing gets going, the big benefits come later.

The pace of change is nonlinear – our economy and productivity will increase faster and faster for the foreseeable future. From 2000 to 2005, we'll finish laying the groundwork for many of the concepts I've talked about. From 2005 to 2010, the rocket takes off on an even steeper exponential curve, wiping out most of the business processes we know today. Time will seem to compress even more. New opportunities will come from unexpected sources. Countries like Finland, Norway, and Iceland – with the world's highest rates of Internet connectivity per capita – could well become strong economic powers. When billions of people are conducting billions of conversations, the scenarios in Part 4 won't just be real, they'll be trivial.

In the face of this change, managers must remember: It is not their job to transform their companies from management-led to customer-led. It is their job to *create the environment and set the examples* that allow the transformation to take place on its own.

Relativity

The 1980s and 1990s were about quality. Today, quality is no longer job one. Today, speed and agility are job one. Today's search engines are primitive, but they are useful. If they stop changing, they'll become tomorrow's encyclopedias.

I've been surfing the Internet roughly an hour a day every day since mid-1994, and I'm still overwhelmed by it. I still wake up every morning feeling behind and about to lose my grip. I still feel there are thousands of sites I haven't seen and that everyone is talking about the latest venture I've never heard of. That's the way it is online. I'm not particularly comfortable with it, but I'm used to it.

No one, no company, is bigger than the ocean of people who are now swimming through digital circuits – shopping for schools, ordering lunch, getting investment advice, buying steel, meeting each other, falling in love, and working side-by-side on different continents. Every day is a new day online. Every day is a chance to make a new discovery or take a different turn. Nothing is set in stone. If you think the plunge is dangerous, wait until you find yourself underwater trying to figure out which way is up.

I use the water analogy because I want to emphasize how different this world is. I believe too many people are looking for terra firma, where they can build the things they know how to build and set up shop online in a way that only use the skills they already have. But many of those skills don't apply online. There really is no dry land. There really is no going back. We must all get used to being uncomfortable. We must all keep swimming or die. It's both terrifying and exciting, and it won't lead to stability. It forces us to swim in groups and learn to take our signals from our neighbors. In the end, I think we'll find we like it better that way, but the transition will be difficult and painful.

As we saw in Part 4, the economy is much more efficient under pure market conditions. People are self-governing. There is no central planning, no authority other than people getting together and making agreements, and no guiding hand on the tiller. Robert Pirsig, author of *Lila*, explained that the Constitution of the United States was founded on two principles: The majority makes the rules, and nothing can stop a minority from becoming a majority. Online, those principles hold at all levels, right down to the individual being the majority in her own market.

Commitment

If you can do 50 percent of what I describe in the first two parts of this book, you're dead. But if you can do 80 percent, you'll make it. Without choosing your customers wisely and sticking to them like glue, all the futurizing and blurring and new-economizing you can do will be for naught.

Many companies are on the 180-year Internet adoption program. They are turning one degree per year. They are comfortable doing that. And they don't know that comfort isn't part of the bargain. If you are comfortable with your online strategy, I can guarantee you it won't work.

I recommend you commit yourself personally to doing business with e-customers. If you can't get your company to make that commitment, there are plenty of start-ups and other companies that will value your attitude. In the customer-led future, attitude will be much more important than skill. You can always learn new skills. But understanding what it takes to make people happy is harder to learn.

I've been to countless meetings in which company presidents or vice presidents tell me that about ten percent of the people in their company get it. They know I get it. They know they get it. What they want to know is how I can help them help the other 90 percent of their people get it.

I don't think they get it. *I* certainly don't get it. I constantly find myself relearning old lessons with new twists. I am always looking for a customer to give me some valuable information I can use to show that I *do* get it. I wake up every day without it, and I have to work hard to get it back by the time I have to give a speech, make a presentation, or meet with a group of people who are all looking for it.

Performance

Before the Truth Economy came along, things were easy. Now we're all more accountable for results than ever before. I'd like to share this with you by looking at the investment industry.

In the really old days, we had stockbrokers. Those people were on commission. They got paid for making trades. When you made money, they made money. When you lost money, they made money. They had plenty of incentive to keep you trading. It was hard to change brokers, so people tended to stick with the brokers they had.

Then came mutual funds. The first mutual funds charged a load – a fee to buy into or take your money out of the fund – in addition to an asset-based management fee. Mutual funds usually take around one percent of your total investment every year, no matter what happens to your account. Thanks to competition and electronic buying and selling of mutual funds, the loads are gone. But the asset-based fee model still prevails.

People aren't too happy with that model anymore. They would rather see their institutions live or die by their investment decisions, not how much money they've managed to raise. In the near future, index funds (funds that give people the chance to invest in large, standardized baskets of stocks) will charge almost nothing to participate. Mutual funds that claim to beat the indexes will have to put their money where their mouths are. If they don't beat the index, why should they make any money at all? Rather than paying a one percent management fee, investors will be more interested in paying zero percent if they don't beat a certain index and 15 percent of every dollar they make over and above the index. Why pay a company one percent just to manage your money if you're not beating the standard indexes?

That brings us to the Performance Economy – a natural outgrowth of the Truth Economy and relativity. People who are interested in safety still keep money in mutual funds or bonds, but most people investing in stocks will measure their performance against the indexes. Every industry – from stocks to real estate to hotels to cosmetics – will face challenges from performance-based competitors.

It's the subject of another book, but I predict that by 2010 many more companies will be paid for results, rather than just distribution. When doctors charge for making us feel better rather than for just spending time with us in the office or the operating room, you'll know the performance economy has already swept through every other business sector.

Humility

Between now and 2010, customers will become ten times more powerful than they are in 2000. Any person who thinks he or she has a special gift for knowing what the market wants is mistaken. All the start-ups that have had spectacular public offerings and think they are on the cutting edge of the Web are balanced very precariously. If they think they know what their customers want, they'll take a wrong turn and find nobody there. If they think it's just a matter of scaling what worked last year, they'll slip behind.

Remember that customers are individuals, and that they gang up on companies to form markets only when it's to their advantage. They get to have it both ways. You must treat them as individuals *and* as groups. Treat them as beginners, intermediates, and experts. Know that whatever you did to migrate them into doing e-business with you won't take them forward.

We shouldn't forget that the New World remains largely uncharted. Medieval maps look horribly distorted today. But when they were made, people thought they were accurate. They used them to navigate successfully and occasionally bumped into unknown continents. In the New

World, as we approach global interconnectivity, we will encounter a new generation of young people who will look at us very strangely when we say words like "electronic document," "long distance," and "e-business."

Balance

Even though this book takes a radical approach to customer advocacy, my goal has not been to trivialize other factors. Strong corporate leaders, role models, vision, insight, and artistry are still important. I don't think anyone wants to tell Jodie Foster how to make her next movie or Paul Simon what to sing. Nor do I mean to say that all companies following the same group of customers should eventually merge. Rather, I hope customer-led companies will recognize creative genius both inside and outside the organization.

I don't mean to denigrate technologists. As an engineer, I think today's technology is fascinating. However, fascinating isn't a compelling reason to push technology on our customers. I don't think anyone wants to have a customer-led web site without a strong team of engineers making sure the system is robust and secure. There are times when you need to do things "right," and times when you need to do things fast. If you get them mixed up, you'll be back in the traps that keep so many companies from achieving their online potential.

My goal has been to balance those factors with a people-centered approach that recognizes the value of individuals. Everyone has heard of Michael Dell and Bill Gates, but thousands of heroes in their companies make them look good every day. And there are thousands of customers still waiting to be listened to. In the next ten years, I hope we can build our systems and corporate structures to better serve people, not the other way around.

Charity

Finally, one of my personal goals is to help speed the Customer-Led Revolution worldwide. *Internet access should be a right of all people,* not a privilege. We should all strive to close the gap between the connectivity haves and have-nots. The vast majority of people still haven't had their first surfing experience. It's our responsibility to see that they get it. I hope that by 2010 we are on our way to a world in which everyone has access to the Internet, whether they live in rural China or in a village in Kenya.

Most countries' telephone systems are still monopolies. People must pay per-minute charges for every telephone call they make. While plenty of service providers are willing to give those people access to the Internet at a flat rate, their phone charges continue to be the limiting factor. No country can succeed online without helping its citizens achieve flat-rate Internet access. I feel it's our duty to help people in other countries get the resources they need to make Internet access affordable. Only when 2 billion people are connected can we say we are ready for the next step in our evolution as a species.

To help balance this inequity, I would like to partner with anyone interested in creating a buddy system, whereby individuals, companies, cities, and countries can partner with others who are behind in the learning curve and offer them a hand up. Please contact me if you would like to contribute to this effort. On second thought – come to Futurizenow.com and join the conversation.

David Siegel
Seattle, 1999

About the Author

David Siegel grew up as the son of an accomplished businessman in Salt Lake City, Utah. In 1982, he received a degree in applied mathematics from the University of Colorado at Boulder. In 1985, he received a master's degrees in digital typography from Stanford University.

He joined Pixar in 1986, its first year of existence. In 1987, David started a business painting Macintosh computers. In 1988, he designed a typeface called Tekton that became one of the best-selling typefaces of the decade. He then designed Graphite, a font that ships with every Hewlett-Packard inkjet printer. In 1991, he wrote his first white paper on the Communication Appliance and how it would change society.

In September of 1994, David saw the Web for the first time. By the summer of 1995, he had won second place in the first Cool Site of the Year Award. His first commercial web site was Klutz.com. He started Studio Verso and produced Hewlett-Packard's first online annual report.

In 1996, with the help of people at Studio Verso, David designed Menuez.com and wrote *Creating Killer Web Sites*, which went on to become Amazon.com's longest-running number one bestselling book. Published by Macmillan in the U.S., the book is in its second edition and has been translated into 13 languages. His second book, *Secrets of Successful Web Sites*, is considered the new-media project manager's bible. It has been translated into five languages.

In 1998, David asked Gino Lee to become president of Studio Verso, which has designed and produced web sites for such clients as Hummer/Winblad Ventures, Marimba, Stanford Research Institute, Net Objects, Office Depot, Rreef Funds, Vantive, and others. Studio Verso is now a wholly-owned subsidiary of KPMG.

As president of Siegel Vision, David spends his time writing books, lecturing (represented by Leighbureau.com), and in limited consulting engagements. He has been a strategic advisor to Computer Sciences Corporation, Bigstep.com, and many start-ups. He is an advisor to the W3C, the standards body of the Internet. He is an advisory boardmember of Ontology.org, a strategic advisor to the American Film Institute, and a senior advisory boardmember of Nasa's Museum Mars Link.

David now spends much of his time as an angel investor, looking for new companies that will prosper in the New World. He helps them find funding and coaches them in executing customer-led strategies that will make them successful. Learn more at Siegelvision.com. (At the time of publication, Mr Siegel was not an investor in any corporation mentioned in the text of this book.)

David lives in Seattle, Washington, with his two cats, Spencer and Miko. You can reach him at david@futurizenow.com. Even better, you can reach other readers of this book at Futurizenow.com.

About this Book

The photographs on the cover came mostly via e-mail from friends and colleagues of the Siegel Vision team. Due to time constraints, some of the photos came from licensed stock-photo discs. The photographs of people inside the book are of representative readers. During May and June, 1999, the Siegel Vision team – with the generous help of the people at San Francisco advertising agency McCann-Erickson/A&L – launched a web site to collect thousands of photos. With the help of several online bookstores and good word-of-mouth, over 14,000 people came to the site. Because the site required people to format their photos, only a few hundred managed to prepare their photos in the proper format. In the end, only 171 met the criteria for placement in the book.

The text type for this book is Adobe Garamond, designed by Robert Slimbach, released in 1989. The type is based on the sixteenth-century designs of Claude Garamond. The italics are based on designs by Robert Granjon, a contemporary of Garamond's. The sans-serif type for this book is Univers, designed by Swiss type designer Adrian Frutiger and released in 1957 by the Deberny & Peignot foundry in Paris. The monospace type used on the cover is Andale Mono, designed by volleyball king Steve Matteson and released in 1997 under the name Monotype.com. The paper is Finch Opaque 60#. The halftones are screened at 133 lines per inch.

The original penguin source image for the part dividers was licensed from Tony Stone Images (TonyStone.com) and was digitally altered for each divider with permission. Jason Chan prepared all photos and drew all illustrations using Adobe Photoshop and Adobe Illustrator. Jacket design by David Siegel. Joe Silva produced the book's mechanicals using a Macintosh G3 computer and Quark Xpress 4.04. The final Quark files were delivered to the publisher on a CD-ROM.